FLORA
MIRABILIS

FLORA

How Plants Have Shaped

MIRABILIS

World Knowledge, Health, Wealth, and Beauty

CATHERINE HERBERT HOWELL
FOREWORD BY DR. PETER H. RAVEN

NATIONAL GEOGRAPHIC

WASHINGTON, D.C.

Pl. XII.

HOW PLANTS SHAPE OUR WORLD

Dr. Peter H. Raven
President, Missouri Botanical Garden

HUMAN BEINGS HAVE EXISTED ON EARTH for perhaps two million years, always living in intimate association with other animals, plants, fungi, and microorganisms. The activities of these other organisms over billions of years led to the development of the environment in which our ancestors evolved; we in turn have depended on them and their properties to support our life here. A great shift in the nature of this relationship took place about 10,500 years ago, when our ancestors first began to cultivate plants as crops, thus assuring themselves a dependable supply of food that could tide them over through unfavorable seasons and allow them, in their growing numbers, to build up the villages, towns, and cities within which most of the properties of our civilization developed.

The period when crops and domestic animals have supplied most of our food spans only about 400 human generations, a short stretch of time but one during which our numbers have grown from several million people to the current level of nearly seven billion. Meanwhile, our domination of Earth has increased to a level that threatens the quality of our own future and that of the other organisms that share this world with us.

Butterflies from Africa and South America visit an Australian lily (above). More realistically, both butterfly and star amaryllis come from Brazil (opposite).

Written language developed in centers of civilization about 5,000 years ago. For the first time people were able to record their thoughts about their past, the meaning of life, and other complex matters, as well as to record the transactions whereby they conducted their daily affairs. The names of plants and their uses began to be written down, with some texts surviving from both classical Greece and Rome. Illustrations appeared in hand-copied manuscripts, often stylized and rewritten so often as to become impossible to recognize and therefore useless, but developing over the years into the beautiful artwork represented so well in this book.

With the introduction of movable type in Europe and the production of multiple copies of individual books, the possibility of comparing the plants of different regions developed. By the late 17th century the encyclopedic tradition had developed, gradually leading to the evolution of the systems of classification that we use today. As illustrated in this book, exploration from Europe reached across Eurasia, to North and South America, and to the Pacific Islands, Australia, and New Zealand. Everywhere, new plants were found to adorn European windowsills and gardens. The excitement that accompanied these introductions led to advances in botanical art. At the same time, the search for spices,

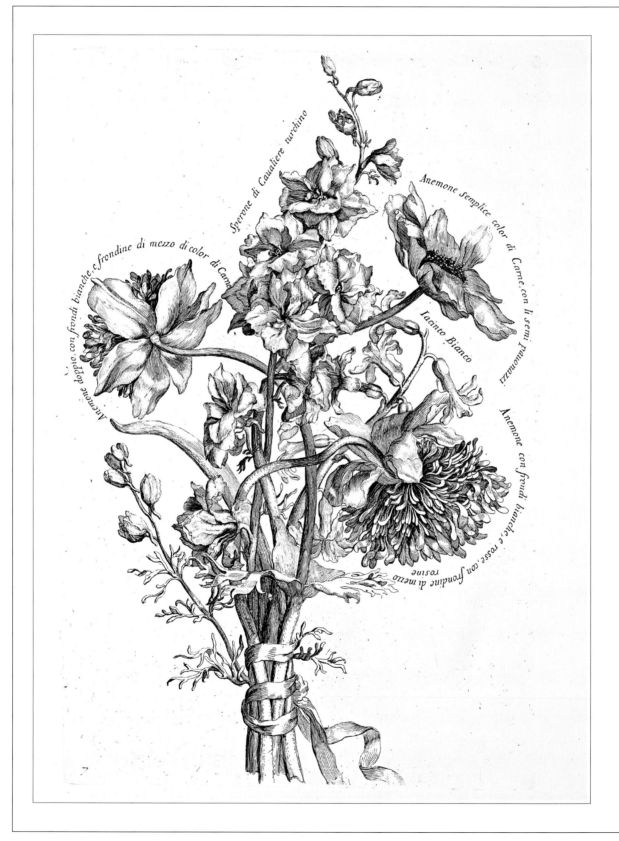

drugs, sugar, and many other plant products fueled the exploration that gradually opened up the whole world to intense human exploitation and further growth.

It is not surprising that plants have always held such interest for us, for we depend on them directly or indirectly for all of our food. Just over a hundred cultivated plants supply more than 90 percent of the calories we consume; and three—maize, rice, and wheat—alone supply more than 60 percent. About 11 percent of Earth's surface is now devoted to cultivated fields, some of them maintained more sustainably than others. Two-thirds of the world's people still use plants directly as their medicine, and even for those of us who obtain medicines from the drugstore, about half of those remedies had a biological source or are still obtained directly from plants. Many medicines remain to be uncovered, and much traditional knowledge remains to be discovered and shared in a world that is losing such knowledge rapidly.

Only recently have we begun to understand the services that plants provide in their role as the backbone of ecosystems, controlling drainage, aiding soil conservation, contributing to the life cycle of pollinating insects, and in many other ways. And there is plants' beauty, which so delightfully enriches our lives and has been prized throughout human history. In view of this long association, it is not surprising that we prize plants in our homes and gardens and enjoy art depicting their very special qualities.

Today we turn increasingly to plants in our search for global sustainability. We seek to live in such a way as not to compromise the needs of those who come after us. Instead, though, we are consuming an estimated

POIRES.

Anemones, hyacinths, and delphiniums entwine in a bouquet (opposite), while pear varieties distinguish themselves (above), both 19th-century illustrations.

125 percent of the world's productivity on a continuing basis, even though an eighth of the world's population, about one billion people, is starving, and more than 100 million are at any time on the verge of death from starvation or associated complications. We must learn more about plants and other organisms, for they can help us create a world in which we do not use more than Earth can provide, in which people everywhere are healthy and well fed, and where future generations have as much opportunity to explore and enjoy the wonders of the planet as we and our ancestors have had. Recognizing that we have outgrown Earth's capacity to support us by living as we do, we are now returning to the nature of which we are a part to find the sources of productivity that will sustain us in the future.

The Missouri Botanical Garden, a venerable institution that has introduced the beauty and interest of plants to the public since it opened its gates in 1859, houses a world-class herbarium and library, the latter greatly enriched by the 1893 gift of Edward Sturtevant's collection of pre-Linnaean works on medical botany, agriculture, and edible and otherwise useful plants, donated with "the strong desire that it would continue to serve a purpose." Like the National Geographic Society, the Missouri Botanical Garden developed deep concern over the environment during the 20th century, as the world's population grew, consumption exploded, and polluting technologies spread widely. We now live in a world that is as clearly our garden as was the Garden of Eden. We are fully responsible for the maintenance of the sustainability and beauty of Earth, our garden—illustrated so richly in the pages of this book—and for its future as well. ∎

INTRODUCTION

PICTURING PLANTS THROUGH HISTORY

Douglas Holland

Library Director, Missouri Botanical Garden

PLANTS HAVE BEEN A DRIVING FORCE OF civilization. Great empires were built and lost on the backs of the quiet plant kingdom. The rich and powerful collected plants to grow in their gardens and greenhouses. Extravagant, expensive, oversize, often hand-colored volumes called florilegia were published to showcase these collections of newly introduced plants streaming in from around the world. As the age of enlightenment and modern science emerged, florilegia faded in favor of more rigorous works attempting to depict all the plants growing in a given region or to categorize all the individual species of a plant family.

An opium poppy flower seems almost to turn away in this portrait by French botanical illustrator Pierre-Joseph Redouté, one of 144 images he chose for an 1803 retrospective volume.

THE FLORA TRADITION

ALTHOUGH THEY REPRESENT VERY DIFFERENT APPROACHES, each could be called a *flora mirabilis*—a wonderful book about flowers. With this volume, we add another to the long and time-honored tradition. *Flora Mirabilis* is the product of a partnership between National Geographic Books and the Missouri Botanical Garden Library, an ideal collection for exploring the history of plants through the fascinating stories of those who have sought them. At the Missouri Botanical Garden Library, we strive to be a repository of all human knowledge concerning plants, including their discovery, their uses, and their distribution. *Flora Mirabilis* draws primarily from the bounty of botanical illustration represented in our collection, providing a visual counterpoint to an engaging narrative leading us through centuries of human fascination with the green growing world.

The basic purpose of botanical illustrations is now, as it has been through history, to assist the viewer—botanist or physician, devoted naturalist or enthusiastic gardener—in identifying a plant. Accurate information is critically important as scientists try to precisely name and describe the world's plant species. Accuracy, or the lack thereof, can have life-and-death significance for an herbalist or physician administering treatment or for an amateur forager tasting mushrooms or weeds.

Botanical illustration often rises above its pragmatic and scientific purposes, however, the beauty of its subject matter and the finesse of its execution allowing works to ascend into the realm of art, as is clearly demonstrated in the pages of this book. The illustrations found in *Flora Mirabilis* range from early stylized woodcuts dating from the 15th century, through the intaglio etchings and engravings of the 16th to the 18th centuries, to the sumptuous color of the lithographs of the 19th and 20th centuries. Photography and digital imaging have made these printing techniques obsolete today, but they have not replaced the hand-drawn botanical illustration. Line art is still the norm in most scientific works depicting plant species. Skilled botanical artists can show more detail with more precision than any photograph, no matter how

Pavot.   *Papaver.*

P. J. Redouté. _ 13.   Langlois.

high the resolution. An artist can highlight particular parts of a plant—tiny hairs on a flower's corolla or the underside of a leaf, for example—parts that might elude the camera's eye but can be seen clearly and revealed by a botanical illustrator.

ART AND SCIENCE

THE EARLIEST WORK DEPICTED IN THIS VOLUME is the *Gart der Gesundheit (Garden of Health),* a compendium of medicinal botany printed in Germany in 1487. While the illustrations in this early botanical encyclopedia may appear flat and stylized to our sensibilities, they still represent a considerable improvement over those that had been available to the medieval world.

Through the medieval period, in the West as well as in the more scientifically productive and enlightened Arab empires, true authority continued to lie in the classical works of Greeks and Romans. Ancient manuscripts, including the illustrations, were painstakingly copied and recopied by hand, which often meant introducing or perpetuating errors. By the late medieval period, abundant corruptions and fanciful interpretations had crept into all existing copies of Dioscorides' *De materia medica,* originally compiled 1,300 years earlier, and many of the illustrations were so corrupted or simplified that the plants were impossible to identify.

The anonymous author of *Gart der Gesundheit* made clear in his foreword that he was abandoning the practice of copying illustrations from the ancients. His plants would be drawn from local living plants

For centuries herbalists relied on information from Dioscorides, a Greek physican (opposite). An Andean fern (above) eased rheumatism and chest colds.

"as they are, with their true colors and form." And yet a good deal of folklore still informed the book's illustrations, as evidenced by the anthropomorphized depictions of mandrake roots with male and female form. Nevertheless, this was the beginning of the age of the printed herbal.

Gart der Gesundheit was followed soon by the vastly improved *Herbarum vivae eicones (Images of Plants from Life)* by Otto Brunfels in 1530 and by the innovative herbal by Leonhard Fuchs, *Primi de historia stirpium (The History of Growing Plants),* in 1545. While the text of Brunfels's work contains many mistakes, mostly the result of his basic lack of understanding of plant geography, the illustrations were, as the title implies, drawn from life. For the first time a botanical artist, Hans Weiditz, depicted plants with great accuracy, showing flowers and root structures with lifelike detail and perspective never seen before in botanical references.

Fuchs followed the same trajectory of detail and precision. He personally oversaw the production of his mighty opus, which weighed in at almost 900 pages, including 511 illustrations. Fuchs considered the illustrations to be of such importance that at the end of his book he included a portrait of its three-member illustration team: Veit Rudolf Speckle, Albrecht Meyer, and Heinrich Füllmaurer.

The portrait of Fuchs's team shows that the earliest botanical illustrations were usually the creation of multiple artisans and not simply the one artist to whom the work is attributed. For Fuchs's book, Meyer created the original drawing from a living plant; Füllmaurer transferred that drawing onto the wooden plank, interpreting the original artwork and adapting it to the medium; then Speckle—one of the finest woodcut artisans in Germany at the time—worked with carving tools to sculpt the image from the block of wood. Botanical illustrations were truly a team effort, which meant that the final image was several removes from the original observation of the plant.

In 1592 a new printing technique revolutionized botanical illustration, as exemplified in Fabius Columna's *Phytobasanos,* which has images printed from etched sheets of copper using an intaglio process. In intaglio the artist, in this case very likely Fabius himself, scratches the image of the plant into a sheet of copper coated with resin or wax. The plate is then submerged in a bath of acid, which bites into the copper wherever incised lines of the image cut through. Ink is rubbed into the lines of the incised illustration; paper is pressed onto the plate; and the image prints. Easier in many ways than carving a woodcut, intaglio results in finer lines and details. The similar technique of engraving also results in clear lines and crisp illustrations, but it is a much more difficult technique, requiring years to master.

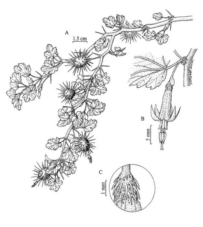

Three artists illustrated Leonhard Fuchs's herbal (opposite). Each performed a separate task, and errors could creep in. More recent artists draw from life (above).

These new technologies for printing illustrations coincided with the huge influx of plants coming from around the world and into the possession of European scholars and amateur botanists as a result of exploration, empire-building, and, soon after, exploding scientific inquiry. In 1665 Robert Hooke shook the scholarly world with his spectacularly illustrated volume *Micrographia.* He opened up an entirely new microscopic world to the public, describing what he viewed through a primitive microscope and including on the pages of his book images of plants and insects, molds and fungi, in giant size and incredible detail. Hooke probably did some of his own drawings and etchings for *Micrographia.* With the relative ease of creating etched copper plates, a naturalist like Hooke could be an artist as well, breaking the protocol of artists working separately from the scientific investigations themselves.

But the talent and skill required to create the amazing images in *Micrographia* should not be underestimated. Hooke was a man of genius, a mathematician, architect, and biologist. He also invented, or at least made major improvements to, the amazing new instrument that allowed him to peer deeply into the microscopic world.

New World Botany

Mark Catesby took the role of artist and naturalist to new heights with his two-volume *The Natural History of Carolina, Florida and the Bahama Islands.* This work was produced over a period of 12 years, between 1731 and 1743. Initially employed by members of the Royal Society of London to explore the southeastern American colonies, Catesby was commissioned to send plant and animal specimens back to his sponsors. As he actively pursued his charge, he also began sketching the plants and animals he observed, ultimately realizing that he might better accomplish his goals of popularizing the diversity and beauty of the American wilderness with art rather than specimens.

In 1726 Catesby returned to England and began to produce his natural history in earnest. Out of financial necessity, he did much of the work himself, and it took him almost 20 years to complete the massive project. About 180 copies of the two-volume work were printed.

Each contained about 220 illustrations, making a total of over 40,000 plates to be printed and colored.

His book—and his artistic style—were a sensation. Folksy but lively, his images depicted plants or animals not in isolation but in their natural settings and in association with fellow creatures, a technique that was completely new for its time. Not so well-known today, Catesby was a major influence on a generation of natural history authors who came after him, including John James Audubon, who created his *Birds of America* almost a century later.

SCIENCE SHAPES ART

SCIENTIFIC ADVANCES AS WELL AS ARTISTIC INNOVATIONS shaped botanical literature. Carolus Linnaeus's development of a classification system based on the number of flower parts made it more important to include detailed

The size of James Bateman's opus on orchids—40 plates, each two feet tall—prompted cartoonist George Cruikshank to satirize it as a "Librarian's Nightmare."

views of flowers: petals, anthers, stigmata, and other reproductive plant parts. *Systema naturae,* published in 1735, and *Species plantarum,* published in 1753, directly inspired many of the most important botanical works of the next century, including one of the most spectacular, Robert Thornton's *New Illustration of the Sexual System of Carolus von Linnaeus.*

The first two parts of Thornton's 1807 book cite many of Linnaeus's theories on plant classification alongside poetry to him and the plants that he specially studied; they are not well known. The third part, titled *The Temple of Flora,* contains 30 sumptuous hand-engraved and hand-colored plant portraits—and this is the part that makes this work stand out in the history of botanical literature. It often took several years, even decades, to produce these lengthy and magnificent books. Thornton took more than eight years to produce his masterwork, along the way issuing it in parts to his patient subscribers. It is arguably one of the most spectacular botanical works ever produced, highly sought by collectors ever since. Sadly, wartime economics and a change in the public's taste kept Thornton from ever recovering his exorbitant production costs. He went on to publish several more modest books and earned a living as a physician, but he died almost penniless.

Pierre-Joseph Redouté represents the apogee of baroque botanical illustration as inspired by Linnaean classification. In one of his major works, *Les Liliacées (The Lilies),* published in eight folio volumes, he portrays all the members of the lily family, at least as he interpreted it at that time. For his subjects he used the plants collected by Joséphine Bonaparte and growing in her garden at Malmaison.

In the exquisite prints, produced from stipple- and roulette-engraved copper plates, we see not only the plant in its entirety, but every plate contains details of flowers and flower parts necessary for accurate scientific classification, making *Les Liliacées* an example of both the florilegium—an expensive and lavish publication depicting the private collection of a wealthy patron—and a valuable scientific work attempting accurate plant classification and description.

Bateman's Orchidaceae of Mexico and Guatemala *introduced a kaleidoscope of floral shapes and colors, such as this oncidium orchid, to the world.*

PRINTING ADVANCES

IN 1798 THE NEW PRINTING TECHNOLOGY OF LITHOGraphy was discovered, destined to reshape botanical illustration during the 19th century. Unlike relief or intaglio printing, which rely on either raised or recessed surfaces to hold the ink, lithography works because of

the simple fact that oil and water do not mix. Artwork is drawn with a grease pencil or grease-based ink onto a finely grained block of limestone, then permanently fixed with nitric acid. The entire work is dampened. The image drawn in grease resists the water, while the stone attracts and absorbs it. When an oil- or grease-based ink is rolled on the stone, it adheres to the artwork but is repelled by the moistened surface of the stone. The image transfers onto paper when run through the press.

Lithography proved faster and cheaper than previous technologies and also allowed the artist an unprecedented ability to achieve tonality and shading in the works. With chromolithography and more brightly colored synthetic pigments invented in the second half of the 19th century came an explosion of colorful, cheaply produced botanical artwork that could be supplied to the eagerly awaiting Victorian scientists—and to art and plant afficionados, to decorate their homes.

One of the most striking examples of early lithography as applied to botany was Robert Bateman's *Orchidaceae of Mexico and Guatemala,* printed between 1837 and 1843. Original paintings, done primarily by Sarah Drake and Augusta Withers, were beautifully interpreted onto the lithographic stone by Maxime Gauci. The 40 images are stunning by their sheer size: They measure almost two and a half feet tall. Combined with the text, the resulting tome weighs in at over 35 pounds, one of the largest botanical books ever printed. The scale of the book inspired caricaturist George Cruikshank to draw up a comical vignette titled "Librarian's Nightmare," showing the poor librarian in Lilliputian scale, grappling with a gigantic copy of Bateman's volume.

One of the greatest lithographic botanical artists of the 19th century was Walter Fitch. Fitch began helping to illustrate *Curtis's Botanical Magazine* in 1834, soon becoming the sole draftsman of this venerable and important publication and continuing that work until 1877. *Curtis's Botanical Magazine* was a highly popular magazine published in close association with the Royal Botanic Gardens at Kew and a virtual clearinghouse of information about the vast array of plants streaming in from the far-flung outposts of the British Empire. Sometime around 1845, Fitch started making his own lithographic plates, becoming both artist and artisan and in effect removing the middleman, who might misinterpret his work.

FLORA OF TODAY AND TOMORROW

THE END OF THE 19TH AND ALL OF THE 20th century witnessed an explosion of new printing and art reproduction technologies available for botanical illustration. Numerous types of photographic processes emerged, and subsequently digital graphics became the standard in scientific publications. Even the newest technologies have yet to supplant the need for hand-drawn botanical artwork, however. Though the great ages of the woodcut, extravagant florilegia printed from engraved copper plates, and gigantic lithographic works have come to an end, descendants of these noble genres still thrive.

Charles, the Prince of Wales, recently released the *Highgrove Florilegium,* for example, assembling a team of talented botanical artists to create watercolors of plants growing in his gardens at Highgrove. The result is a two-volume set containing more than 120 illustration plates produced from the watercolors. The project took more than six years to complete. The plan for this

Langorously graceful, the Sikkim larch (Larix griffithii) *grows only in the Himalaya. It bears the name of William Griffith, a British doctor and explorer who first recorded it for science in the mid-1800s.*

work, unlike the floreligia of old, is for all the profits generated from its princely price to go to charity.

Another innovative take on the tradition is the florilegium under way thanks to the Brooklyn Botanic Garden Florilegium Society. This ongoing project was established in 2000 to engage the talents of dozens of botanical artists to document the 250,000 living specimens at the Brooklyn Botanic Garden. Accomplished artists are invited each year to portray a specific range of the garden's collections. The art is featured in a public exhibition and then permanently archived in the library. At the same time, each plant subject depicted is pressed, dried, and stored in perpetuity in the garden's herbarium. It is, as the Brooklyn Botanic Garden puts it, a "perfect marriage of art and science."

Flora Mirabilis likewise portrays this long marriage of art and science and offers a glimpse into the treasures housed in the library at the Missouri Botanical Garden that few of our visitors have the opportunity to view. It uses time lines, narrative, and historic illustrations to tell the long and fascinating story of how the love of and quest for the botanical riches of our planet weave through all of human history. Botanical exploration and discovery, innovation and commerce based on the products of the plant world—these have unfailingly been driving forces of civilization for millennia. The story told in these pages leaves no doubt that our human history is inexorably connected to the world of plants.

The Missouri Botanical Garden is proud to be part of this project with National Geographic, and equally proud to be an ongoing participant in the history of the human relationship to plants. We know that you will enjoy your journey through *Flora Mirabilis,* part of our continuing mission to "discover and share knowledge about plants and their environment, in order to preserve and enrich life." ∎

W. Fitch del et lith.   Vincent Brooks Imp.

LARIX GRIFFITHII, H.f. & T.

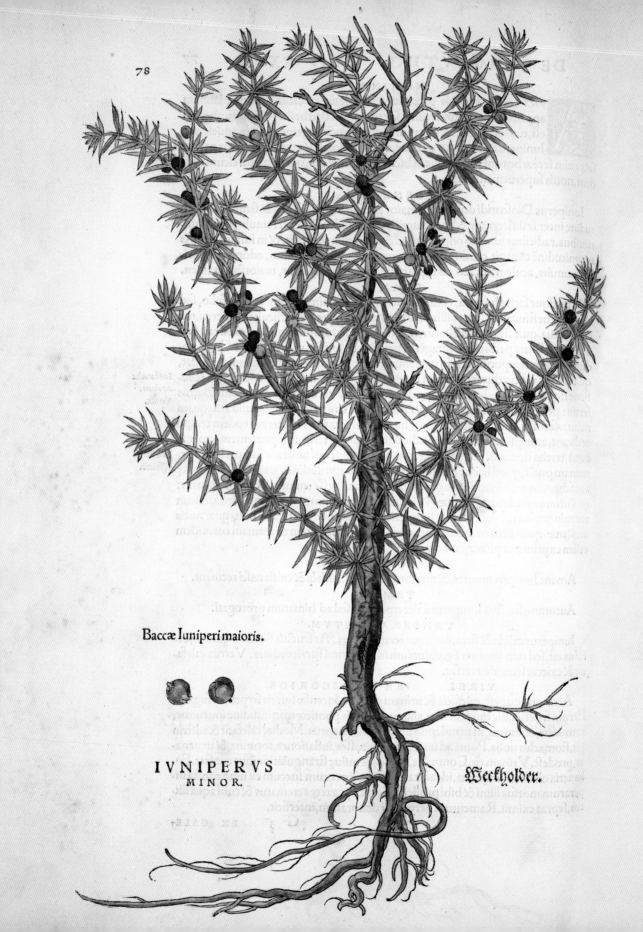

Baccæ Iuniperi maioris.

IVNIPERVS
MINOR.

Weckholder.

ORIGINS

Prehistory–1450

Plants and humans: It is impossible to exaggerate the importance of their interactions through history. The links date back further than our origins, extending to the very air we breathe. Direct interactions with plants followed those of our primate ancestors—as sources of food, shelter, and simple tools. In time we would rely on them for fuel, medicines, clothing, and ceremony and as a means to record and communicate our thoughts and actions. The archaeological record helps order these associations, but the clues are often sparse and fragmentary: a charred grain here, a smear of pollen there, a few fibers of cloth. The origins of our emotional links to plants are more elusive—individual inspiration and aesthetic pleasure leave no traces unless captured in an enduring form. We sense the esteem bestowed on plant life in ancient times, for example, through biblical metaphor, especially the myriad exultations in the Song of Solomon. Once established, aesthetic regard became inextricably tied to practical and economic worth. Plants give life, sustain life, and enable human achievement and cultural florescence. As objects of value, they have been the center of conflict and competition and the impetus for long journeys across land and sea. ∽

Shown in an early hand-colored woodcut, juniper (Juniperus communis), *one of the few cold-climate herbs, has long been used for medicinal as well as culinary purposes by many cultures.* Preceding pages: *The blue Nile lily* (Nymphaea caerulea), *associated with the Egyptian god Ra, symbolized birth, purity, life, and beauty.*

	KNOWLEDGE & SCIENCE	POWER & WEALTH	HEALTH & MEDICINALS
AFRICA & MIDDLE EAST	**1550 B.C.** Egypt's Eber Papyrus lists some 800 medicinal plants. **A.D. 793** Chinese prisoners in Samarqand, Uzbekistan, teach Persians how to make paper from various plant fibers. **12th century** Knowledge of papermaking travels with Islam west through North Africa and then up into Europe via Spain.	**ca 1450 B.C.** Egypt's Queen Hatshepsut orders myrrh trees transplanted from Punt in the Horn of Africa. **A.D. 627** Seizing a Persian castle, Byzantine soldiers discover sugar and carry it back to Constantinople.	**ca 2100 B.C.** The oldest known medical text, a Sumerian tablet, records several plants used for healing. **A.D. 1025** Persian physician Ibn Sina (Avicenna) completes his monumental *Al Qanun fi al Tibb—The Canon of Medicine*.
ASIA & OCEANIA	**ca 500 B.C.** *The Sushruta Samhita*, a medical text naming 700 plants, is published in India. **by A.D. 105** Paper, made of mulberry fibers in China, is traditionally dated to this year, but it may have been invented as many as two centuries earlier. **1178** China's *Chu Lu (The Orange Record)* identifies more than 20 varieties of orange.	**2737 B.C.** Traditional date of discovery of tea by the mythical Chinese emperor Shen Nong. **A.D. 1206** Mongol conquest of China brings prices down, making tea a common drink.	**ca 3000 B.C.** *Ben Cao Jing*, said to be written by the mythical Chinese emperor Shen Nong, is the oldest known list of medicinal herbs. **by 771 B.C.** *Wu Shi Er Bing Fang (Prescriptions for 52 Diseases)*, oldest known Chinese herbal, is published. *An alchemist's oven and distilling flask*
EUROPE	**ca 320 B.C.** Greek philosopher Theophrastus writes two classics of botany, *Historia plantarum (History of Plants)* and *De causis plantarum (On the Causes of Plants)*. **ca A.D. 55-65** Pedanius Dioscorides, surgeon to Nero's army, travels through southern Europe and northern Africa, documenting medicinal plants. **512** The oldest known version of Dioscorides' *De materia medica (Regarding Medical Matters)* is created as an illuminated manuscript.	 **first century B.C.** Roman miller-bakers, grinding wheat and baking loaves, become the world's first food industry.	**400 B.C.** Hippocrates names many healing plants, including barley, garlic, hellebore, southernwood, and madder, in *De diaeta in morbis acutis (On Regimen in Acute Diseases)*. **ca 100 B.C.** Crateuas, a Greek, is reported to have created an herbal with colored illustrations; no copies survive. **ca 160** Galen, physician to Roman emperors, records his methods of harvesting and preparing medicinal herbs.
THE AMERICAS			

*"If we could see the miracle of a single flower clearly,
our whole life would change."*

— BUDDHA (SIDDHARTHA GAUTAMA), FIFTH CENTURY B.C.

SUSTENANCE & FLAVOR	CLOTHING & SHELTER	BEAUTY & SYMBOLISM
by 8000 B.C. Yams are likely cultivated as a staple food in Africa. **ca 6500 B.C.** Lentils and fava beans found at Yiftah'el, a Neolithic village site in Israel. **by 5000 B.C.** Date palms likely cultivated in Iraq, Iran. **ca 1700 B.C.** Pearl millet cultivated in sub-Saharan Africa.	**by 5000 B.C.** Flax, from which linen is made, is under cultivation in Syria and Turkey. **ca 2200 B.C.** Acacia wood is used in Egypt for roofing and for ship hulls and masts. **ca 1260 B.C.** Egypt's Queen Nefertari presents gifts of linen cloth and garments to the Hittite queen.	**ca 2600 B.C.** Dates are buried with royals in the ancient Sumerian city of Ur. **1325 B.C.** Seed remains prove that many plants, including wheat, coriander, garlic, watermelon, safflower, and dates, were buried with Tutankhamun in ancient Egypt.
2800 B.C. *Fah Shên-chih Shu,* Chinese text on farming, names five sacred grains. **510 B.C.** Persian soldiers find sugarcane along the Indus River: "the reed that gives honey without bees." **327 B.C.** In India, Alexander the Great first tastes bananas.	**ca 2600 B.C.** Madder is used to dye cotton red in the ancient Indus Valley city of Mohenjo Daro, located in today's Pakistan. *The "female" mandrake* (Atropa mandragora)	**ca 475 B.C.** The *dizi,* a bamboo flute, becomes a popular instrument in China. **A.D. 815** Saicho, a Buddhist monk, brings tea seeds to Japan from China, considering the drink an aid to meditation. **1422** Birth of Murata Shuko, Zen monk credited with inventing the Japanese tea ceremony.
by A.D. 360 Romans have selectively cultivated wheat for so long that hard and soft types of grain exist. **by mid-1300s** A popular Venetian cookbook, *Libro per cuoco (Book for the Cook),* includes a recipe combining chicken, dates, pine nuts, and spices.	**ca 500 B.C.** Etruscan flax is woven into sails; dense linen cloth, soaked in linseed oil, is worn by Roman soldiers. **A.D. 400** In Norse mythology Frau Holle spins flax into linen and helps industrious housewives.	**ca 776 B.C.** Victors in Greece's Olympics are crowned with wreaths made of olive or laurel. *Cyclamen* (Cyclamen europaeum), *used extensively by ancient physicians*
by 5500 B.C. Gourds, beans, and peppers are cultivated and harvested or gathered wild in Mexico. **by 5000 B.C.** Maize is cultivated in Mesoamerica. **by 5000 B.C.** Potatoes are cultivated in South America.	**by A.D. 1300** Cotton is cultivated in Mexico.	**A.D. 500** Animal effigy pipes for smoking tobacco buried in Hopewell ceremonial mounds. **1051** In the Nuttall Codex, a Mixtec manuscript from Mexico, a bride and groom drink chocolate to celebrate their marriage.

S INCE THE BEGINNING, PLANTS HAVE FORMED A MAJOR PART OF THE HUMAN diet. The earliest humans obtained food by hunting and gathering, the degree of emphasis on either activity depending on local conditions and the time of the year. Early peoples collected parts of wild species that could be gathered with little or middling effort, such as fruits, nuts, leaves, seeds, and tubers, to complement reliance on game. Over time, the hunting-gathering balance shifted and plants gained even more importance nutritionally.

Among some animal species, plant choice seems hardwired in the genes, perhaps explaining the steadfast reliance of the monarch butterfly on the milkweed. Like other animals with more varied diets, humans learned about potential plant foods by trial and error, gleaning recognition of which species were palatable, which gave more energy, and which contained toxins or held other properties that produced unpleasant or harmful physiological symptoms—or even death.

A hotly debated topic, the origins of control of fire may date back hundreds of thousands of years to the presence of *Homo erectus* in Africa. Regardless of the time span, controlled fire greatly and undisputedly improved early human life and expanded the value of plants in the human diet. Fire gave heat on demand and various options to prepare plant and animal foods, and led to the acquisition of new knowledge about plants. Stone Age hunters became aware of which species of trees burned longer and stronger—roasting their kill, creating warmth, and keeping dangerous animals at bay—and which other plant species made good tinder to get the fire started.

Eventually, humans learned that some kinds of wood could impart pleasant flavors to meat and, further, that wood smoke itself could preserve animal flesh so that it could be stored for future use. They also learned that some plants used as seasoning could improve taste in general and mask the off flavors of foods turning from fresh to fetid. And, quite important, they found that although certain parts of some plants could be toxic and dangerous, cooking could transform a number of toxins and render them harmless.

SPEARS INTO PLOWSHARES

EVEN WITH THEIR BURGEONING KNOWLEDGE OF THE PLANT WORLD, EARLY HUNTER-gatherers seemed to remain, at heart, hunters. Plants did not appear among the sophisticated figures of game animals drawn in vibrant colors on cave walls by people of the Upper Paleolithic in France and Spain some 25,000 years ago. But they did provide the artists' media—charcoal stubs, the by-products of slow-burning wood fires, were used to sketch out and realize the riveting figures. Evidence elsewhere, though, suggests more of a connection to the plant world among early peoples. Neanderthals, the first to bury their dead, as early as 70,000 years ago, apparently placed flowers in

Fig
Ficus carica

Figs have been cultivated since antiquity. Their significance in Hebrew life shows repeatedly in the Bible; a fig-harvesting scene appears on the wall of an Egyptian grave, dating from about 1900 B.C. The Romans considered the fig a gift of the god Bacchus. Americans today consider it a delicacy, but in parts of Europe it is known as the poor man's food. Spanish missionaries planted figs in California in 1769, but the choicest varieties would not fruit until 1899, when the U.S. Department of Agriculture imported a particular species of wasp to pollinate them.

Tab. LXXIII.

FICVS *foliis palmatis*
*Ficus sativa fructu majori violaceo oblongo: cute
lacera* Tourn. Linn. Amoen. Acad. Vol. I. p. 218.

the grave of a disabled man in Iraq, judging by the pollen found there. Thousands of years later, by 10,000 B.C., plant remains in the dwelling sites of people in southern Chile displayed solid knowledge of food and medicinal species.

Little more than a hundred years ago, some scholars posited a single source for the development of agriculture, the intentional manipulation and domestication of plant

Myrrh
Commiphora myrrha

Since biblical times myrrh has been a standard remedy in Middle Eastern medicine for mouth sores, infected wounds, digestive ailments, and lung complaints. Myrrh has a long history of use as a healing and rejuvenating herb in Indian Ayurvedic medicine as well. More recently, myrrh has been employed in eastern Africa and Saudi Arabia as an anti-inflammatory and antirheumatism drug. Most of the myrrh used commercially today is collected from wild trees in Ethiopia, Somalia, Sudan, and Yemen.

The dried resin of a spiny bush originating in northern Africa, myrrh has been used for embalming and fumigation and as incense, perfume, and holy oil. At times in myrrh's history it was so highly valued, it was worth its weight in gold.

Burseraceae.

Balsamodendron Myrrha Nees v. Es.

and animal species that led to vast changes in the way humans would live in the centuries and millennia to come. A few even attributed the momentous shift to one fledgling farmer, a lone genius who in their scenario had figured out the whole process himself—a characteristic thought in invention-crazy Victorian times, but not a realistic one.

We now know that agriculture arose independently in a number of areas across the planet, ranging from the Fertile Crescent of the Middle East to eastern Asia to Mesoamerica, Andean South America, and eastern North America. Nascent farmers in these regions gradually transformed wild grasses such as wheat, barley, corn, millet, and rice, and legumes such as beans and lentils, into varieties more suited to controlled cultivation. Many of the domesticated cultivars came to bear little resemblance to their forebears. Corn *(Zea mays),* for instance, probably originated as teosinte, a grass with its seeds embedded in earlike spikes at the top of the plant. Centuries of domestication transformed the food source into the fat, kernel-studded ears of today. In the case of highland South America and some parts of Africa, growing conditions were more suited to root crops and tubers, such as the potato and yam, which became staples in these areas. In North America, the sustaining trinity of corn, beans, and squash would come to feed diverse cultural groups across a wide area.

The presumed start-up date for agriculture has been a moving target in recent decades, the hypothetical date changing as new evidence comes to light. The earliest verified traces of crop agriculture come from the Fertile Crescent at the eastern end of the Mediterranean about 10,500 years ago, with various dates for its origin elsewhere. Rice consumption seems to date back about 8,000 years in China, based on findings in the Middle Yangtze Valley, with domestication occurring about 6,000 years ago.

By about 4000 B.C., though, agriculture was firmly established in most regions where the climate could support it. By then, agricultural crops and techniques had

The aromatic seeds of black cardamom have long been prized for their culinary and medicinal qualities. Their fragrance is potent enough that the seeds have been used to make perfume.

long been following the paths of borrowing and dissemination that sent plants scattering in all directions. The establishment of agriculture bestowed the ability to feed large numbers of people, free up many to perform other tasks, store food for the future, and generally pave the way for all the advancements, as well as the pitfalls, of civilization. In tandem, though greatly reduced in scope, the hunting and gathering way of life has survived to the present.

DIVINE FLORA

As humans developed notions of the supernatural, plants became sacred objects. On the Indian subcontinent, people continue to worship species such as the Indian lotus *(Nelumbo nucifera),* tulsi *(Ocimum tenuiflorum),* and two fig trees, the bo *(Ficus religiosa),* and banyan *(F. benghalensis),* as they did as far back as 6000 B.C. Ancient Egyptians associated the sycamore fig *(F. sycomorus)*—an all-purpose tree that among its many gifts provided welcome shade from the desert sun—with the goddesses Isis, Hathor, and Nut.

Cardamomum majus, grain de Paradis. Paradis-Körner.

The Greeks also assigned trees to their deities, and thus the oak was dedicated to Zeus, the olive to Athena, and the myrtle to Aphrodite. Groves of trees held sacred associations as well, often in proximity to burial places. More than 2,500 years ago, animist Celtic peoples of Iron Age Britain conducted many of

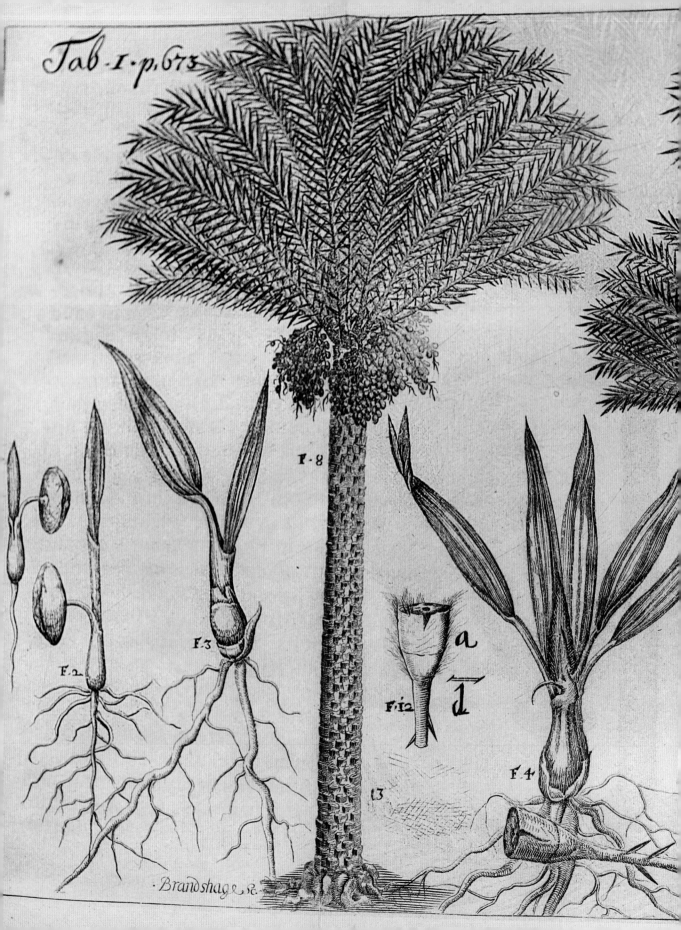

DATE PALM

Phoenix dactylifera

The date palm—a statuesque tree bearing clusters of bright red fruit—has been important to North Africa and the Middle East for millennia. The fruit provides essential vitamins and protein, which has allowed desert Arabs to live healthily on a simple diet of dates and milk. Dried dates are easily stored and carried. Their high energy content—nearly 70 percent sugar when dried—makes them an ideal food for nomads, who most likely spread them in their travels throughout the southern Mediterranean.

All other parts of the tree yield useful products as well: The fruit can be made into syrup, alcohol, and vinegar; the trunk is harvested for timber; fibers from the frond stems can be used to make rope; leaves can be woven into baskets and furniture. When this palm was first harvested is unknown, but it was probably one of the first trees domesticated. Date seeds found in lower Mesopotamia indicate cultivation by around 4000 B.C.

Wall carvings and paintings depict ancient Egyptians eating and tending dates as early as 3500 B.C. Around 450 B.C. the Greek historian Herodotus observed that in Assyria, "Date-palms grow everywhere, mostly of the fruit-bearing kind," and the fruit supplied the Assyrians

A palm laden with dates figures prominently in murals that grace the walls in the tomb of Pashedu in Deir el-Medina, on the west bank of Egypt's Nile River.

"with food, wine, and honey." Marcus Gavius Apicius' *De re coquinaria (On Cooking),* a collection of recipes from the first century A.D., considered the world's first cookbook, describes how to make *dulcia domestica,* a dessert, from dates, nuts, honey, and a pinch of salt.

Palms have been so important to human life, they have assumed symbolic meaning in a number of religions. Date palm seeds have been found in burials from both the ancient Mesopotamian and the Egyptian cultures, including the tomb of Tutankhamun. Christians wave palm fronds on Palm Sunday, recalling the procession of Jesus into Jerusalem, and the Prophet Muhammad urged Muslims to tend palms and eat the dates. The Spanish most likely brought date palms to the New World to continue their religious practices. In 1770 a Franciscan monk planted trees at his mission in San Diego, thus bringing palms into California even before the Colonies gained their independence.

Recently scientists germinated a date palm seed thought to be 2,000 years old. Israeli archaeologists soaked the seed in a hormone-rich solution and planted it. Six weeks later, much to their astonishment, it sprouted. The plant, nicknamed Methuselah after the oldest man in the Bible, has continued to grow. ∎

DATE PALM THROUGH TIME

ca 6000 B.C.	**5000-4000 B.C.**	**2650-2550 B.C.**	**2035 B.C.**	**A.D. 1513**	**1770**	**2008**
Dates found at Mehrgarh in Pakistan may be the oldest.	Dates under cultivation: Seeds at sites in Iran and Iraq.	Burials in the royal cemetery of Ur include dates.	Sumerian cuneiform tablets record date palm orchard yields.	Spanish bring seed to Cuba.	Franciscan missions in California import seed from Mexico.	Scientists sprout 2,000-year-old seed from Israeli site.

their rituals in sacred groves, a practice that some modern-day revivalists carry out in Britain today.

Sometime around 1470 B.C., a trade expedition set sail from Upper Egypt for the land of Punt on Africa's eastern coast, a bygone destination usually correlated with present-day Somalia. The undertaking was launched by Hatshepsut, a regent for her stepson, Thutmose III, who despite her gender took on full pharaonic status and ruled as de facto king of Egypt for 15 years.

Hatshepsut's mostly peaceful reign allowed her to focus on trade. Her shopping list for Punt included precious gold and ebony and an almost equally precious ingredient that was indispensable to royal Egyptian preparations for the afterlife: the fragrant resin of the myrrh tree *(Commiphora myrrha)*. The Egyptian traders returned with myrrh in both its processed form and as live trees, which Hatshepsut had planted in the gardens of Deir el Bahri, her magnificent mortuary temple at Thebes. Chronicles of this trading voyage appear in relief on her temple walls—documentation of the world's first known botanical expedition and proof that some 3,500 years ago, trade in herbs, spices, and whole plants reflected their value in ancient cultures, including the spiritual realm, and pointed to a willingness to obtain them, whatever the cost or effort.

Healing Herbs

Each indigenous culture on Earth, from Stone Age tribe to great civilization, has incorporated plants into its healing arts. Spiritual dimensions as well as intimate connection to plant life permeated the world's oldest medical systems, developed independently in India and China as far back as 6,500 years ago.

Indian traditional medicine, known as Ayurveda, from the Sanskrit *ayu,* or life, and *veda,* or knowledge, most likely preceded its Chinese counterpart by almost two millennia. It has passed down intact to the present day with the help of ancient authoritative texts such as the *Charaka Samhita,* dating to the third century B.C. Ayurveda encompasses a complex system that places life, health, and disease on an integrated spectrum along with the mind, body, and spirit. It also takes account of lifestyle and diet in assessing an individual's needs. Ayurvedic herbal therapies draw from some 3,000 native medicinal plant species and offer treatments that are both curative and preventive in an enduring system that is represented still by upwards of 300,000 practitioners in India, and countless others around the world.

A long-used herb in the Ayurvedic tradition is withania *(Withania somnifera),* or *ashwagandha* (smelling like a horse) in Sanskrit, a shrub in the nightshade family. Despite the word *somnifera,* or bringing sleep, in the plant's Latin name, ashwagandha has been widely prescribed for 3,000 years as a tonic covering a range of debilitating conditions including the weakness of advanced age and sexual dysfunction, effectively making it ancient India's equivalent of today's little blue pill.

> *"Therfor the Lord God took man, and settide hym in paradis of likyng, that he schulde worche and kepe it."*
>
> — Genesis 2:15, *Wycliffe Bible,* ca 1395

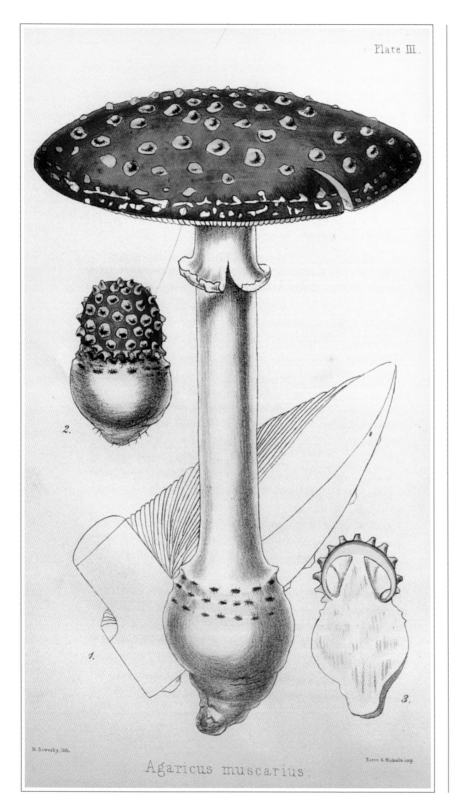

Plate III.

2.

1.

3.

H. Sowerby, lith.

Reeve & Nichols imp.

Agaricus muscarius.

The quintessential fairy-tale toadstool, Amanita muscaria *is in fact a poisonous and psychoactive mushroom, commonly known as fly agaric since it was once used to make an insecticide to kill flies.*

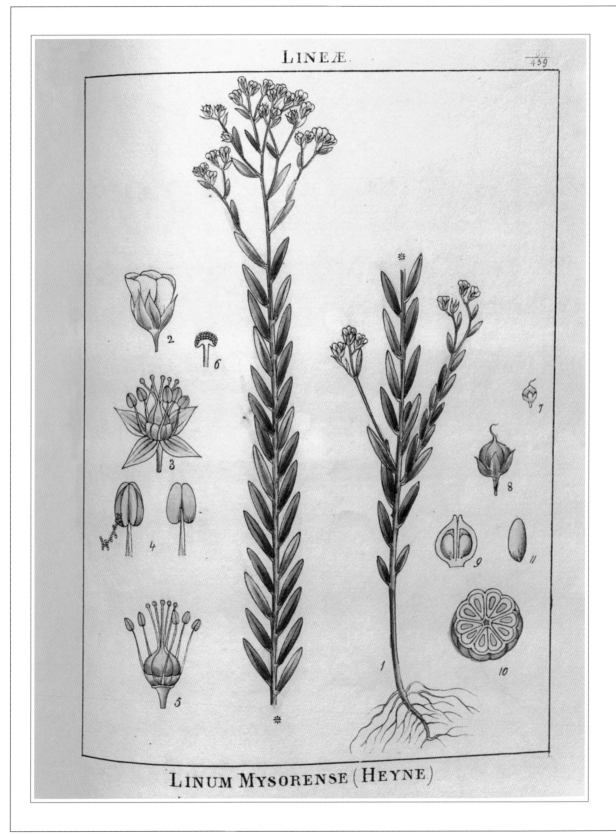

LINEÆ.

439

LINUM MYSORENSE (HEYNE)

Chinese herbal medicine also extends back as far as its civilization, some 5,000 years, and written documentation of its practices has existed for some 2,000 years. The last two millennia have produced more than 400 herbals, or manuals listing medicinal herbs, their properties, and instructions for their use. One classic, attributed to the legendary emperor Shen Nong, touts the fever-reducing capacities of *chang shan,* or the blue evergreen hydrangea *(Dichroa febrifuga),* now a proven antimalarial herb.

What has come to be known as Traditional Chinese Medicine, or TCM, elevates itself above localized herbal medical practices, with an approved list of some 500 official herbs that today are distinguished from the 4,500 or so used by local non-TCM practitioners, many from China's ethnic minorities. The approved list of medicinal plants—a feature first found in the *Ben Cao Jing* by Shen Nong, considered the world's oldest herbal—ranks the growing parts of plants according to their effectiveness, with roots ranking first, seeds and fruits second, and leaves last.

Asian ginseng root *(Panax ginseng)* sits near the top of the list as one of the most prescribed herbal medications and carries the distinction in TCM of being prescribed alone and not in a combination of up to 100 complementary herbs. The genus name *Panax* means "cure-all," announcing the plant's prominent status as an adaptogen (as is ashwagandha), a substance that makes the body function better as a whole. For thousands of years ginseng has been widely prescribed as a tonic targeting and replenishing the body's chi, or vital energy.

As early as 500 B.C. the Chinese also recognized the analgesic properties of the white willow *(Salix alba),* which contains the active ingredient salicin. This chemical was

Flax
Linum usitatissimum

Flax is one of the world's oldest crop plants, having been cultivated since at least 5000 B.C., first by the ancient Mesopotamians and then by the Egyptians. Hippocrates recommended flax for colds, and the herb is a centuries-old remedy to relieve coughs and soothe sore throats. In modern herbal medicine, flaxseed oil is recommended as a safe, gentle laxative for chronic constipation, irritable bowel syndrome, and diverticulitis. Flax plants are cut when mature to extract the fibers they contain, which are spun into linen thread and woven into linen fabric.

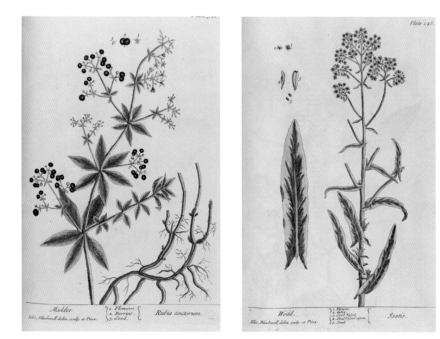

Stronger than cotton, though less elastic, linen from the flax plant (opposite) has been used by humans for more than 5,000 years. Madder (far left) and wold (near left) were favored dye plants, madder shading fabric red, and wold, yellow. Madder was also considered "good for the Jaundice, Dropsy, Stone and Stranguary."

Gramineae (Hordeae.)

Triticum vulgare L.

W.Müller n.d.Nat

WHEAT

Triticum spp.

Humans may have domesticated wheat, but wheat also domesticated humans. Wheat was one of the first wild plants to be tamed and grown for food, and with these early successes in agriculture came significant social and technological advances, leading to the rise of city-states and the complex social organization that they involve. Thus wheat symbolizes a key turning point in human history.

Archaeological evidence dates the first stage of agriculture to 10,500 years ago, in southwestern Asia's Fertile Crescent. At that time, wheat grew as a wild plant across most of Asia. But the Mediterranean climate of the Near East, characterized by cool, short winters and warm, dry conditions during the rest of the year, was perfect for growing wheat and essential to its domestication.

Wheat provides a nutritious grain, high in amino acids and therefore in plant protein. Complementing wheat with legumes, seeds, or animal protein satisfies important human nutritional needs. Wheat's distinctive protein binds in ways that can result in either leavened or unleavened bread.

Archaeologists have found wheat seeds at many sites in the Fertile Crescent, in Syria, Jordan, Turkey,

A wheat harvest symbolizes the month of July in the Très Riches Heures du Duc de Berry, *a medieval book of hours created in 1416.*

and Mesopotamia, dating them to 7000 B.C. Seed remains occur throughout the region: at sites in Turkey like Çatalhüyük, east through Mesopotamia to Abu Hureyra, and south into Egypt. By 2875 B.C., Egyptian farmers had established elaborate irrigation techniques along the banks of the Nile. They are credited as the first people to build ovens and bake bread.

By the height of the Roman Empire, wheat was being grown across Europe, wherever temperature allowed, and bread formed a staple of the European diet. Those living in regions where wheat could not be grown, such as in parts of Gaul and along the Danube, imported it from elsewhere and built an industry that fueled the great empire.

With the fall of Rome, wheat production shrank significantly, but it did not fade away. Through the Middle Ages, wheat was mixed with rye and made into a type of bread called maslin.

Only in the 18th century did wheat become the dominant crop it is today. Recently developed dwarf strains mean even higher yields and disease-resistant varieties, securing for wheat its position as the world's top cultivated grain, with nearly 600 million metric tons produced annually at the end of the 20th century. ∎

WHEAT THROUGH TIME

by 7000 B.C.	1325 B.C.	330 B.C.	by A.D. 360	1529	1788	1970
Wheat, barley, and goats domesticated in Mesopotamia.	Wheat is buried with Tutankhamun in Egypt.	Pytheas, Greek explorer, sees wheat in southeastern Britain.	Roman farmers differentiate between hard and soft wheat.	Wheat is brought to the New World by the Spanish.	Wheat cultivation begins in Australia.	Dwarf strains double tropical wheat production.

Often associated with China, where they symbolize immortality, peaches (Prunus persica) *reached the Mediterranean by way of Persia (now Iran), hence their species name. The lily of the valley* (Convallaria majalis, *opposite) carries a sadder meaning, despite its enchanting fragrance: Christian legend purports that the flower sprang from the tears shed by Eve after she was forced to leave the Garden of Eden.*

Pêcher à fruits lisses.

isolated more than two millennia later—in the 19th century—and transformed into acetylsalicylic acid, or aspirin.

THE BASIC NECESSITIES

WITHIN THE TRIAD OF LIFE'S NECESSITIES, SHELTER AND CLOTHING ALSO CARRY STRONG links to the planet's plant life. Human ancestors descended from the shelter of trees but always remained in close proximity to them, creating dwellings of limbs and branches, bark, or animal hides. From these basic uses rose more durable techniques such as woven branches, or wattle, often chinked with mud, or daub, and timber-frame construction, in place by Neolithic times in Britain. The plant world also provides a wealth of roofing materials: Palm fronds, reeds, rushes, and grasses have been used for thousands of years and are found still in indigenous dwellings all over the world. Thatching, the built-up layering of dry vegetation, creates an impermeable and durable roof that, depending upon conditions, might not need replacement for centuries.

Over time, permanent shelters acquired furnishings, and plants provided many of the raw materials for them. Of the various woods used in furniture construction, the cedar of Lebanon (Cedrus libani), native to the Mediterranean area, was one of the most prized. Of great utility also were the grass, rush, and reed fibers employed in weaving baskets, the all-purpose receptacles and carrying bags that long predated pottery vessels in human civilization. Kapok and similar plant materials, often the fibers that surround and protect seeds as they develop within the pods, were harvested and stuffed into mattresses and pillows. Egyptian tombs, with their dry atmosphere, yield some of the best examples of ancient furniture making, at least for the culture's elite, such as the piles of spectacular gilt, inlaid, and veneered wooden furniture and accessories placed in the tomb of King Tutankhamun, the ill-fated boy pharaoh who ruled Egypt during the 14th century B.C.

From the earliest times, human attempts to launch themselves on rivers, lakes, and seas involved the use of many plant materials, the most important being trees. The long, strong timbers of the cedar of Lebanon were fashioned also into fine ships that sailed waters from the Mediterranean to the Persian Gulf, Arabian Sea, and beyond. Among the earliest type of vessel is the raft made of limbs lashed together with vines. Conifers mainly provided the hulls of dugout canoes, which were crafted using stone tools, or a combination of digging out and burning, about 10,000 years ago.

Trees also supplied the necessary poles, paddles, and oars to propel these simple vessels. As watercraft progressed through various stages of boats and ships, plants continued to provide raw materials for the main structures and other key components, such as sails. Early on, papyrus (Cyperus papyrus), a reed native to Africa, was used for that purpose, as well as for making baskets, rope, and sandals, although the versatile fiber is best known as the source of a kind of paper that was used until the eighth century A.D.

One of the most fragile and elusive of early human artifacts, cloth appears in the archaeological record as far back as 7000 B.C., as a scrap only three inches long discovered in southern Turkey. The fragment is of coarse linen, possibly woven from a wild precursor to the lustrous-fibered flax

Peach
Prunus persica

Some ancient Chinese writers called the peach the tree of life, some the tree of death; others thought it symbolized longevity. The pink peach blossom was associated with feminine promiscuity, and growers were warned not to plant peach trees near windows of a lady's boudoir. The English word "peach" derives from the Latin word for Persian, as does the tree's species name, *persica*. In fact, peaches used to be called Persian apples, but most botanists now agree that China was the native home of the peach.

plant *(Linum usitatissimum)*. By 5000 B.C. there is firm evidence of flax cultivation in Mesopotamia and in Egypt, where linen provided mummy wrappings as well as finely woven garments for the living. Tomb paintings and carvings there celebrated this important plant, whose seeds and oils were also used by the ancients for food and medicines. The Egyptians also grew cotton *(Gossypium* spp.), which came to them from Asia and ultimately from Pakistan, along with Central America one of its two likely centers of independent origin. Cotton fabric itself reached Europe about A.D. 900 and spread eastward to China, Japan, and Korea some 400 years later.

Until quite recently, plants contributed to the rich colors seen in plant-based fabrics, as well as in wool and animal hides. For example, the roots of the madder plant *(Rubia tinctorum)* produce a strong red, yellow can be made from the skin of the pomegranate *(Punica granatum)* or from the dried pistils of the saffron crocus *(Crocus sativus),* and blue from the leaves of various indigo plants *(Indigofera* spp.). Natural dyes can also be derived from mineral and animal sources, such as the vivid red that comes from crushed beetle carapaces.

RE-CREATING PARADISE

BIBLICAL SCHOLARSHIP PLACES THE GARDEN OF EDEN IN THE VICINITY of Mesopotamia, the land that is watered by the Tigris and Euphrates Rivers. In the Judeo-Christian tradition, the Garden of Eden was a place of wholesome earthly delights that symbolized innocence and perfection but that came undone because of human disobedience, or sin. It appears that all early cultures and civilizations came to value gardens—places designed to invite the admiration of plants for their own sakes, aesthetically and without immediate regard to practical or commercial uses. Collections of plants were gathered into tranquil spaces apart from everyday life to provide a place for respite and reflection.

Royalty and the well-to-do incorporated the most esteemed plants into their own versions of paradise, a word with origins in ancient Persian, denoting a walled enclosure. Different cultures had different notions of which varieties of trees, shrubs, and flowers belonged in these pleasure gardens; how the plantings should be laid out and displayed; and which other kinds of elements, be they water features or sculpture, should accompany them. The science and art of horticulture, or the cultivation of ornamental plants, grew along with development of the pleasure garden and created a demand for the services of talented gardeners. Societies in contact borrowed freely from each other, and, as in other aspects of culture, waves of conquest rode in with fresh ideas in plants and garden design.

The globe artichoke (Cynara cardunculus) *is a perennial thistle. What we serve as a vegetable dish is actually the opening flower, which the ancient Greeks and Romans considered an aphrodisiac.*

ARTICHAUT *Commun*

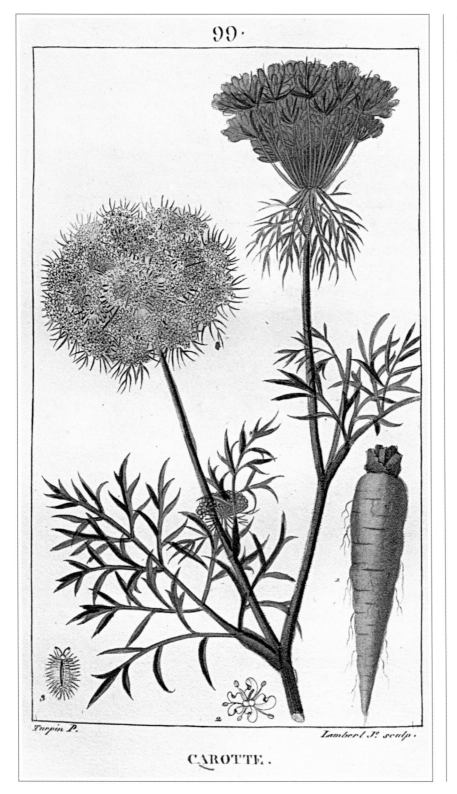

99.

Turpin P.

Lambert J.ᵉ sculp.

CAROTTE.

Carrot
Daucus carota

As with a number of vegetables, the first interest in carrots developed from their supposed medicinal value. Greek physicians around the first century A.D. wrote of their value as a stomach tonic. The carrot was certainly cultivated in the Mediterranean area before the Christian era, but it was not important as a food until much later. By the 16th century, Europe's botanists were describing many kinds: red and purple in France, yellow and red in England. European voyagers carried the carrot to America soon after discovery of the New World, and Native Americans rather promptly took up carrot culture.

Generations of discerning gardeners pushed the carrot (Daucus carota) *toward the sweet, plump, orange root we know today. Wild carrots— still with us as the wildflower Queen Anne's lace—and early cultivated varieties were purple or yellow and slender, with a bitter taste.*

RICE

Oryza sativa

The origin of rice, as with many of the most important plants in human history, remains a mystery. Most agree that rice cultivation began about 6000 B.C. and was fully under way 2,000 years later. Rice cultivation may have begun in several locales independently, some of the earliest along the rivers of southern China and later along the Ganges River in India. The mythical Chinese emperor Shen Nong stated that "the most precious things are not jade and pearls but the five grains"—the first of which was rice.

Rice has a number of qualities that made it attractive to early farmers: It yielded more than other early domesticated grains, such as wheat and barley; the low moisture content of its seeds allowed for easy drying and long storage; and the tough seeds resisted bruising and were easily transported.

Rice is fairly adaptable as to its growing needs. Most types are grown in submerged fields called paddies, but not all. There are four main types of rice, each adapted to a different climate or terrain: dry, upland rice, which does not require surface water; rain-fed lowland rice; irrigated rice; and semiaquatic deepwater rice, grown mostly in floodplains.

An 1855 Japanese woodcut depicts people working in rice paddies under the watchful eye of Mount Fuji.

Rice cultivation spread from eastern Asia gradually, very likely facilitated by the ancient Persians, whose empire stretched from Central Asia into western Europe. The ancient Greeks knew *oryza,* as they called it, by about 300 B.C., though to them it was an expensive import, not a dietary staple. Rice is not mentioned in the Bible, but it was a favorite of the Prophet Muhammad, and the plant may have spread with Islam from the Middle East into North Africa and Europe. When first introduced in Britain, rice was valued as a medicine. In the 15th century, England's King Charles I ate rice boiled with milk, sugar, and cinnamon. In those days, many considered it an aphrodisiac.

Rice reached the Americas by the 1650s, most likely on trade ships from Madagascar. African slaves may have grown and eaten rice in their native lands, and their familiarity with its agriculture turned it into a major cash crop in the Carolinas within a century. Soon rice was being grown widely in the marshlands of the southern United States and South America.

Today, rice is a dietary staple for about half of the world's population. Developed into more than 8,000 varieties, including genetically engineered varieties, it is traded as a commodity on local and world markets. ■

RICE THROUGH TIME

6000 B.C.	2800 B.C.	ca 330 B.C.	A.D. 1519-1522	1690	1740	by 1980
Rice is being grown in China.	Rice is one of the five sacred crops of China.	Alexander the Great brings rice wine from India.	Magellan's crew sees rice in the Malay Archipelago.	Carolina Gold flourishes in North Carolina, a New World industry.	U.S. rice trade out of Charleston, South Carolina, booms.	Ten percent of all rice grown is IR36, genetically engineered.

Early Mesopotamia's most celebrated secular garden, the Hanging Gardens of Babylon, has appeared on the short list of wonders of the ancient world for two millennia. Ironically, it is the only one of the seven original wonders that has left no trace of its existence. Extensive renovation of Babylon's ruins and a thorough combing of the thousands of cuneiform texts found in ancient Mesopotamia's preeminent city—now in modern Iraq—have turned up nothing to substantiate many "eyewitness" accounts of the time. They described rising terraces of densely planted shade trees, fruits, and flowers ornamented with dancing fountains that were built by Nebuchadnezzar II to please his wife, homesick for the forested mountains of her native Media. This noticeable absence now has some scholars thinking that the celebrated gardens actually belonged to the city of Nineveh, the great Assyrian capital on the Tigris River, located today in the suburbs of war-torn Mosul.

> "And all things are ordered together somehow, but not all alike,—both fishes and fowls and plants."
>
> — ARISTOTLE, *METAPHYSICS*, FOURTH CENTURY B.C.

A CLASSICAL PERSPECTIVE

THE GREEKS AND ROMANS OF THE CLASSICAL AGE SHOWED themselves to be confident exponents of all branches of learning at a time when the knowledge in the Western world was beginning to be systematized. New discoveries, experimentations, and conjectures were reported continually, combined with received traditions, and set forth in ambitious treatises to inform and instruct. Though we tend to think first of philosophy, math, and physics, botany and other natural sciences also came under intense scrutiny in the classical age.

Aristotle, who lived and taught in Athens during the fourth century B.C., never overlooked a chance to teach, and he used the garden of his academy as a vehicle. This garden contained plants common to the Mediterranean region as well as those collected in Asia and sent back on the orders of Aristotle's pupil Alexander the Great, such as cotton, pepper, cinnamon, and the banyan tree.

At the philosopher's retirement, study and supervision of the garden passed to another student, Theophrastus, along with leadership of the Lyceum. Although he carried forward all of the Aristotelian subjects, Theophrastus made his own enduring contribution in the field of botany. He wrote two treatises that marked the beginning of Western botany, *Historia plantarum (History of Plants)* and *De causis plantarum (On the Causes of Plants)*, a pair of trailblazing works on description, classification, and cultivation of plants. One of the topics Theophrastus pursued was the proper planting techniques for roses, and

Part doctor, part cook, part soothsayer, the medieval herbalist drew upon ancient lore, most likely combined with local trial-and-error knowledge.

he extolled their scent, demonstrating that the perennially popular flower was well established in classical Greece. The Greeks may have passed their penchant for roses on to the Egyptians, who in short order managed to corner the rose trade throughout the Mediterranean.

From a modern perspective the writings of Theophrastus earned him the sobriquets father of western botany and father of taxonomy. His works remained important in the botanical canon as late as the 17th century and were made widely available to both Western and Eastern scholarship in printed versions not long after Johannes Gutenberg's invention of the printing press. Pedanius Dioscorides, writing in the first century A.D., was an army surgeon who understandably had great interest in the medicinal value of plants. His compilation, written in Greek but known by its Latin title, *De materia medica,* immediately became the go-to work on the subject, and, like the writings of Theophrastus, retained its authority for some 1,500 years.

Roman contributions to the foundations of botany include the writings of Pliny the Elder, who consolidated his own version of the scope of the natural world in his first-century *Historia naturalis (Natural History).* Quite fanciful in places, it nevertheless shed light on botany and horticulture in the vast Roman Empire, at that point highly influenced by all things Greek. His writings described what was later learned by the archaeologists who uncovered the buried cities of Pompeii and Herculaneum, that

One of the first printed herbals, Gart der Gesundheit— Garden of Health—*displayed plants drawn from life, a revolutionary practice in 1487. The written text was still based on ancient knowledge, often erroneous, gathered through the centuries.*

Exotic plant species often traveled along caravan trade routes such as the Silk Road or across stretches of water, carried by the early explorers. Seeds were often the only way to transport the nascent plants, since seedlings were almost impossible to keep alive en route.

Romans of the age were garden crazy, and no villa was too small for its own patch of green, which might include aviaries, sculpture, fountains, pools, and streams, as well as view-expanding frescoes lush with reality-mirroring flowers, trees, and birds.

Roman garden design reverberated throughout the empire, as seen, for example, in remains uncovered at the Fishbourne Roman Palace in Chichester, West Sussex, in the British Isles, and carried through centuries, ultimately to influence the formal gardens of the Italian Renaissance.

MEDIEVAL CLINICS: THE BROTHER IS IN

AFTER RISING BEFORE DAWN AND SAYING HIS MORNING OFFICE, A 14TH-CENTURY ENGLISH monk leaves the quiet confines of the monastery and heads outside to a dewy garden just a few steps away. He will spend the rest of the day there, carefully tending the beds of herbs under his care. From time to time, a visitor interrupts his work, seeking relief from a cramping stomach, a chronic fever, a painful boil, or an inability to sleep soundly. The monk takes the patient into a shed and pulls the appropriate plant parts from baskets of leaves, bark, roots, flowers, seeds, and berries to concoct just the right mixture, telling the sufferer to go home and brew a strong infusion or prepare a poultice with the plants in his prescription.

Monastery gardens, large and small, served as botanical and medical headquarters throughout the Western world during the Middle Ages. Monks grew and harvested plants, conducted research on their properties and uses, and practiced the healing arts, dispensing herbs as medication to commoners and royalty alike. For botanical knowledge they drew mainly on classical authors such as Theophrastus and Dioscorides, and they helped keep the information in these venerable works alive while updating it with their own findings. They additionally wrote and illustrated their own herbals, or botanical manuals.

Monks tended to grow a wide variety of medicinal herbs but relied very heavily on some all-purpose species. For example, catnip or catmint *(Nepeta cataria)* was a commonly prescribed plant to treat a wide array of maladies ranging from coughs to bruises to colic. It also was consumed as a basic tea before China tea *(Camellia sinensis)* arrived in the West. Altogether, dozens of uses have been assigned to this unpretentious herb, which—although tending to have a calming effect on humans—now serves largely as a recreational stimulant for bored housecats in many parts of the world.

A recreational substance of another kind native to Central Asia, cannabis *(Cannabis sativa),* also commandeered a lot of growing space in monastery gardens. The flowers of this plant contain several chemicals known for their psychoactive properties. Today cannabis can be prescribed legally only in some locales and only for the treatment of specific conditions, such as chemotherapy-related nausea, the spasms of multiple sclerosis, and the optical pressure of glaucoma; but in the Middle Ages, monks recommended it routinely for all manner of ailments, including insomnia, muscular pain, and even skin cancers. Cannabis also held strong commercial value, and forms of the plant, known as hemp, were fashioned into durable rope and also woven into the rugged cloth known as canvas, a name derived from cannabis.

CLEARING THE AIR

OUR MODERN LIFE—WITH ITS ANTISEPTICS, DEODORANTS, scented candles, and odor-masking sprays—leaves us hard-pressed to imagine just how smelly life used to be. Up until little more than a century ago, life routinely reeked, especially in urban areas, where the lack of plumbing and sanitation joined forces with countless animals and a large and basically unwashed population.

In the Middle Ages, with urbanization beginning to hit full stride, every stroll down the street served up a walloping assault on the nostrils. The remedy, as in the case of illness, was herbal. Doctors and lawyers carried herbs

"Those who wrote about herbs, or about plants in general, taught about the observable nature of these plants . . . and they claimed that some of them have a power either when taken into the body or applied to the outside."

— GALEN, ON HIPPOCRATES' ON THE NATURE OF MAN, CA A.D. 180

The saffron crocus (Crocus sativus) has long been valued for many things but especially for the bright yellow seasoning made from the flower's stigmata, ripe with pollen. Medieval herbals note medicinal qualities of the plant as well.

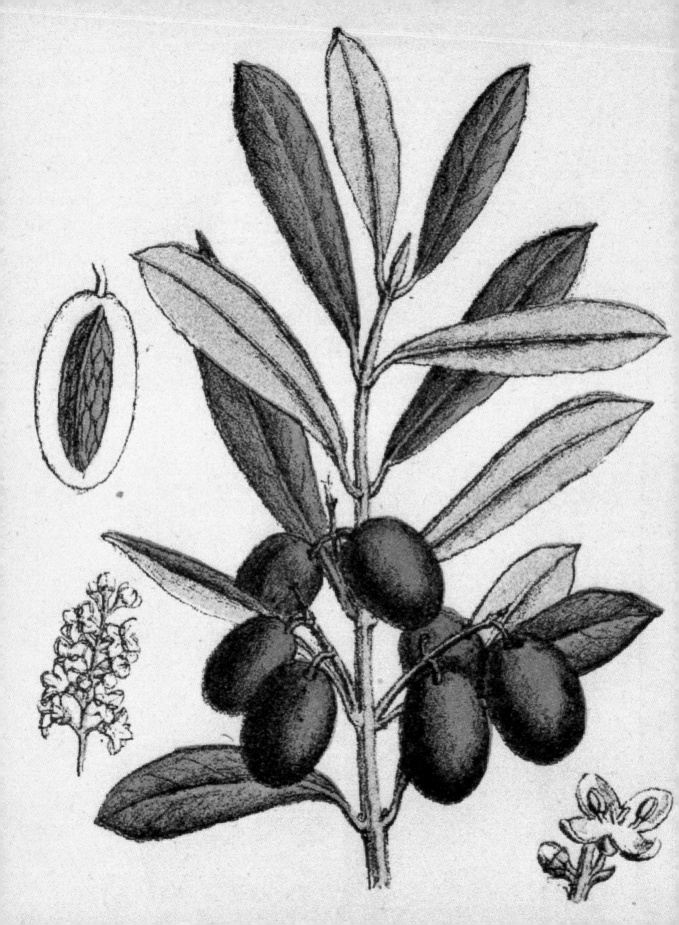

OLIVE

Olea europaea

The origin of the olive tree is unknown, yet its roots are deeply embedded in the Middle East. Cultivation probably started in the eastern Mediterranean, where the fruit quickly became important. Evidence for daily use is common in the archaeological record: Ceramic oil lamps that burned olive oil are found throughout the region, dating back to the late Bronze Age.

Olives found their way into the region's many religions, both pagan and monotheistic. According to ancient Greek mythology, Athena and Poseidon held a contest to determine who would be Athens's protector. Both had to produce something valuable for the people of the city, and the god offering the more valuable gift would win. Poseidon produced a saltwater spring, while Athena offered the olive tree. She won the competition and became benefactor of the greatest city of Greece.

In the Christian tradition, Noah sent a dove out from the ark during the Flood, and it returned, bearing an olive branch in its beak—a sign that the floodwaters had receded and a new life was soon to begin. The olive branch is still a symbol of peace today.

Considered one of the oldest domesticated trees,

In a 15th-century painting by Flemish painter Hans Memling, an angel holds an olive bough, a centuries-old symbol of peace.

the olive tree was probably more shrublike in its wild state. Today's cultivated trees grow 10 to 14 feet high. They have long, spear-shaped leaves and produce fruits called drupes by botanists: a berry with a thin skin, fleshy middle, and a single pit.

Since olive trees require a hot, dry climate they thrive between latitudes 30° and 45° north and south. Their hearty trunks resist decay, and olive trees several hundred years old are still in production. The fruit is not edible straight off the tree, and a variety of methods for curing olives have evolved through the centuries, varying according to the ripeness when harvested as well as cultural preferences.

Both black and green olives come from the same tree, but they are picked at different stages of growth. Green olives are picked, or beaten, off the tree when very immature; black olives are picked when they are very ripe, containing 20 to 30 percent oil by this stage.

Today more than two million metric tons of olive oil is produced worldwide. The largest portion comes from countries in the Mediterranean: Spain, Italy, Tunisia, Greece, Portugal, Turkey, Morocco, and Syria. Argentina, Australia, and the United States—California—also contribute to the world olive market. ∎

OLIVES THROUGH TIME

4000 B.C.	3000 B.C.	1600 B.C.	850 B.C.	A.D. 160	1800	1990
Olive cultivation begins in Syria or Palestine.	Olives are Crete's chief commodity.	Vessel carrying olive oil wrecks near Turkey.	Greek athletes use olive oil to clean themselves after exercise.	Cato describes cultivation in *De agricultura (On Farming)*.	Jefferson cites importing olives as one of his great civic services.	Spain and Italy lead the world in olive oil production.

to counteract the smells and disease of patients and defendants; the wealthy wore costly pendants filled with fragrant oils and herbs to create a personal stench-free zone; and others who had to venture into the crowds sniffed sweet herbs packed into the tops of their canes. These kinds of defensive measures continued into the Victorian era, when nosegays, or tussie mussies, were still carried on outings. Trendsetters of the Middle Ages, of course, wanted the newest and most exotic plants and oils, which created demand and kept the trade routes humming.

THE GARDENS OF ISLAM

WHILE MUCH OF WESTERN BOTANY AND PHARMACOPOEIA REMAINED ENSCONCED IN THE Christian monastic tradition, the expansion of Islam beginning in the seventh century A.D. carried with it a renewed infusion of botanical specimens, aesthetics, and knowledge. The spread of Islam was swift and wide-ranging: Within the space of a few centuries, its influence extended from India to the Iberian Peninsula, the latter transformed by Islam into Al Andalus.

Islamic botanists incorporated knowledge of the Western classical world and the sophisticated notions of garden design refined in Persia, and enhanced it with a fertilization of plants and ideas that came through Arab ports and inland routes and swept along the Silk Road. This fabled corridor, in use for some two millennia, linked the Near East with India, China, and many points in between. It marks the path traveled by the prized cloth created from fibers that the Chinese, somewhere around 3000 B.C., had learned to harvest from silkworms, the larvae of the silk moth.

To start the silkmaking process, silkworms gorge on the leaves of the mulberry tree, and as they ready for their transformation, their saliva glands produce the gossamer filaments that can stretch more than a mile. These they spin into thick cocoons. The Chinese learned to collect unbroken strands by boiling the cocoons before metamorphosed moths could break free. The mulberry itself, along with earthly delights of peach, plum, and apricot, and the versatile giant grass bamboo, represent a mere fraction of the plant life that traveled along the Silk Road and into the Western world, as did the Chinese invention of paper from paper mulberry tree *(Broussonetia papyrifera)* pulp mixed with other fibers.

Islam's prohibition against the depiction of the human form heightened the cultural importance of plants in its art and all aspects of Islamic design in general. The flora of Persian gardens, echoed in stylized carpet designs, fit the need for symbolic elaboration and provided the blueprint for the Islamic vision of paradise, with its fragrant roses and tangy citrus, nourishing date palms, pomegranate, and fig trees, and refreshing water in abundance.

The ancestor of today's garden pansy, the wild violet (Viola spp.) was also known as heartsease, referring, perhaps, to its promise to treat ailments of the heart—or to aid in romance.

The Table of Vertues.

"From Aleppo to Tripoli is forty leagues. . . . The sugar-cane grows here luxuriously, as likewise orange and citron trees; also the banana, the lemon, and the date."

— Nasir-i Khusrau,
Diary of a Journey Through Syria and Palestine, ca 1052

One of the most famous of English herbals was John Gerard's, first published in 1597. A 1636 edition of The Herball, or, Generall Historie of Plantes, *"very much enlarged and amended," included this table of "the nature and vertues of all the Herbes, Trees, and Plantes," listed by ailment.*

This kind of heaven on Earth, its details refined in the Koran, was laid out in the gardens of the Alhambra, the Moorish fortress in the city of Granada, last stronghold of their presence in southern Spain. The Alhambra gardens, known as the Generalife, brought together plant species that reflected the breadth of Islamic domination. When Islam waned in the West, it pushed eastward, bringing similar splendors to the mountains and plains of northern India under the Mughal emperors.

A WORLD ON THE BRINK

BY THE MIDPOINT OF THE 15TH CENTURY, CIVILIZATIONS OF THE EAST AND WEST HELD increasingly substantial notions of what each other offered in the realm of botanical riches, and traders had developed the means to obtain them through overland and sea routes. Both also knew what they wanted in the way of valuable spices that grew mostly in the southern reaches of Asia—in the southern Arabian Peninsula, India, Sri Lanka, and the Moluccas, or so-called Spice Islands, in present-day Indonesia.

With so much demand coming in from all corners of the known world, profits were enormous not only for spice traders and the major port cities, such as Alexandria in Egypt, but also for middlemen who brokered the elaborate distribution dance of the berries, nuts, seeds, flowers, and bark that form the majority of the most coveted spices, including black pepper, cinnamon, nutmeg, cardamom, allspice, and clove. Much of this enormous trade fed the finicky palates of the well-to-do, but the most valuable spice—black pepper *(Piper nigrum)*—was aspired to, if not attainable by, people in all walks of life.

This master spice, as pepper was called, mitigated the overwhelming flavor of heavily salted meat, the only form of long-term preservation in those times. When the wreckage of the *Mary Rose,* Henry VIII's warship, was pulled from the waters off Portsmouth in the 1980s, it revealed that nearly every sailor who went down with her in 1545 had carried a small cloth bag of peppercorns.

The lust for spices fostered a kind of early commercial espionage among traders in the lands where the spices flourished. Far-fetched stories were invented to keep the curious from seeking proprietary sources. In the fourth century B.C., Herodotus described the "winged animals much resembling bats, which screech horribly, and are very valiant"— and apparently have the ability to take one's eyes out—that guard groves of pungent cassia, a spice in the genus *Cinnamomum* that was collected by Arabian spice hunters.

All these stories were a ruse to keep competitors out and keep prices up. You could pay your rent, you could seal a marriage, or you could ransom your city with the right amount of pepper, as the Romans did from the Visigoths and the Huns on a number of occasions. Spices were, and had been, undisputed luxury items and status symbols for millennia, and the competition to control the trade in these lucrative plant parts was just warming up. ◁

"The Crowne Imperiall for his stately beautifulness, deserveth the first place in this our Garden of delight."

— JOHN PARKINSON,
PARADISI IN SOLE PARADISUS TERRESTRIS, 1629

Lush and exotic, the crown imperial (Fritillaria imperialis) was introduced to Europe in the second half of the 16th century by way of Constantinople, where it was a prominent garden flower.

Fritillaire Impériale.

P. J. Redouté _ 59.

DISCOVERY

1450–1650

Change was breathtakingly imminent on the eve of the voyages of discovery of the late 15th century. Not only would people soon come to think about the world in completely new and different ways, but also the natural and cultural balance of the world and its component parts was about to change irrevocably and to an extent never before imagined. These changes involved human issues of wealth, power, and domination; disease and decimation; and in the natural realm, the wholesale redistribution of the planet's plant life. The newfound ability to effect these changes opened the floodgates, putting plants at the center of economic greed, individual and national rivalries, and—in a more productive vein—an increased desire to understand the old in light of the new. By the end of this era of exploring the world, notions of botany retained from classical Greek and Roman writers were slowly giving way to understandings gleaned from empirical research on plants collected in their native habitats, and gardens were evolving from the practical and medical to the elaborate and ornamental. The appearance of Johannes Gutenberg's printing press at the beginning of the era fostered the distribution of burgeoning knowledge at accelerated pace to a wide and receptive audience. ∼

The banana is a remarkable plant, as big as a tree but botanically an herb, since it does not grow a trunk over years. Alexander the Great is credited with bringing the banana west from India in 327 B.C. Today's sweet, yellow fruit is a mutant strain of green and red cooking bananas.
PRECEDING PAGES: The first passionflower brought from South America to Europe flowered in Rome in 1619.

	KNOWLEDGE & SCIENCE	POWER & WEALTH	HEALTH & MEDICINALS
AFRICA & MIDDLE EAST	**1592** First pictures of coffee published in Prospero Alpini's *De plantis Aegypti (Plants of Egypt)*. **1593** Portuguese build Fort Jesus in Mombasa Harbor.	**1497** Vasco da Gama establishes Portuguese route around Cape of Good Hope, breaking the Spanish monopoly on spice trade. **1498** Portuguese ships arrive at Africa's eastern coast, establishing a stopping point for spice trade. **1598** France and Germany impose laws against indigo imports to protect local industry, which used woad as a dye plant.	**1473** A diplomatic gift from Qaitbay, Mamluk sultan of Egypt, to Lorenzo de' Medici of Florence, Italy, includes Chinese porcelain; fine textiles, including a ceremonial tent; a giraffe and a lion; sugar; spices; aromatics; and medicinal herbs from the Middle East and Asia.
ASIA & OCEANIA	**1578** Li Shih-chen completes *Pen-ts'ao kang-mu (The Great Pharmacopoeia)*, including more than a thousand plants with medicinal uses. **1597** Chinese *Materia Medica Pharmacopoeia* is published, compiling traditional medical plant preparations.	**1505** Portuguese envoys land on Sri Lanka (Ceylon), promising to defend local leaders in exchange for cinnamon. **1512** Portuguese take possession of Indonesia's Moluccas. A treaty with the sultan of the island of Ternate secures trade in cloves. **1514** Nutmeg is discovered by the Portuguese in the Banda Islands, breaking the Venetian monopoly.	**1563** Garcia de Orta, Portuguese physican living in Goa, publishes his *Colóquios* on medicinal plants of India.
EUROPE	**1471** Printed edition of 13th-century Italian work *Opus Ruralium Commodorum*, a compilation of ancient works on agriculture, is published in Germany. **1523** Anthony Fitzherbert publishes *Boke of Husbandrie*, first agricultural manual. **1525** In England, Richard Banckes publishes his *Herball*, first ever printed. **1549** Leonhard Fuchs publishes *Plantarum effigies* in five languages with plant drawings from life. **1597** John Gerard's *Herball*, listing some 800 species, is published in England.	**1519-1522** Ferdinand Magellan voyages around the world. Magellan is killed en route; Juan Sebastián de Elcano completes the journey, bringing spices to Spain and receiving a coat of arms bearing cloves, nutmeg, and cinnamon. **1580** Sir Francis Drake completes circumnavigation of the globe, bringing spices to England. **1637** Tulip market crashes in Europe.	**1514** First professorship in medical botany is established at the University of Rome. *Dragonfly from a German hand-colored engraving*
THE AMERICAS	**1547** Gonzalo Fernández de Oviedo y Valdés's *Historia General y Natural de las Indias (Natural History of the West Indies)* is published, reporting on New World botany based on his 20 years in Panama, Colombia, and Hispaniola.	**1516** The first shipment of sugar from Santo Domingo reaches Spain.	**1552** Martín de la Cruz compiles an encyclopedia of medicinal plants and remedies among the Aztec, collecting information in the Aztec language that was then soon translated into Latin.

"God Almighty first planted a garden.
And indeed it is the purest of human pleasures."

—SIR FRANCIS BACON, "OF GARDENS," 1625

SUSTENANCE & FLAVOR	CLOTHING & SHELTER	BEAUTY & SYMBOLISM

ca 1475 Kiva Han, the world's first coffee shop, opens in Constantinople, Turkey.

ca 1500 Portuguese traders bring native American peanuts to Africa, where they soon become a valued food crop.

ca 1590 The Bagh-e fin, Iran's oldest surviving garden, is completed.

1718-1730 The Ottoman Empire enjoys peace and prosperity, called the Tulip Period. Tulips, symbolizing wealth and privilege, ornament buildings, fabrics, and artworks.

1480 Josafa Barbaro reports drinking *chiai Catai* (tea of China) during his travels earlier in the century.

1505 A Chinese herbal presented to the Ming emperor includes corn (maize), called *yi yi-ren* (Job's tears).

1488-1499 Zen monks build renowned dry garden at Ryoan-ji, a temple in Kyoto, Japan.

1645 Gardens completed at Katsura Rikyu, residence for Japan's imperial family.

Crown imperial and tulips, all originating in Turkey

1544 Italian Pietro Andrea Mattioli publishes first European description of *pomi d'oro*—golden apples, or tomatoes.

1594 Four years of bad harvests cause great famine in Europe.

1607 American sassafras root tea becomes popular in England.

1466 King Louis XI of France declares Lyon the capital of silk trade.

ca 1600 French King Henry IV plants mulberry trees, hoping to stimulate French silk industry.

1572 Luís Vaz de Camões writes *Os Lusíadas (The Luciad)*, an epic poem recounting da Gama's ventures on behalf of Portugal, calling newfound lemons "fair as . . . the virgin's breasts."

1633 Tulipomania in Netherlands sends bulb prices up astronomically.

1493 Christopher Columbus transports sugarcane plants to the West Indies.

1516 Friar Tomás de Berlanga, bishop of Panama, is said to have brought banana rootstock to Santo Domingo from the Canary Islands.

1519 Aztec in Mexico introduce Hernán Cortés to *xocoatl*, a drink made of chocolate and vanilla. Both pods are carried back to Spain.

Nasturtiums: Peruvian wildflowers yet undiscovered by Europeans in 1600

Chocolate
Theobroma cacao

Cacao—*Theobroma*, food of the gods, as Carolus Linnaeus named it—has a long history as a medicinal. In Mesoamerica, cocoa drinks treated intestinal complaints, calmed the nerves, and acted as stimulants; cocoa butter soothed burns, wounds, chafing, and skin irritations. European herbals and medical manuals from the 16th to the 20th century list dozens of uses. In modern herbal medicine, cocoa powder is used to treat angina (chest pain) and high blood pressure. Cocoa butter is still widely used for irritated skin and burns. Cocoa and chocolate are rich sources of antioxidants.

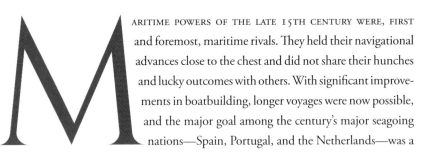

MARITIME POWERS OF THE LATE 15TH CENTURY WERE, FIRST and foremost, maritime rivals. They held their navigational advances close to the chest and did not share their hunches and lucky outcomes with others. With significant improvements in boatbuilding, longer voyages were now possible, and the major goal among the century's major seagoing nations—Spain, Portugal, and the Netherlands—was a more direct sea route to the East Indies, with their spices, gold, and other known or presumed riches. A longer-ranging voyage meant greater profits for European traders, as it eliminated some of the need to conduct business at entrepôts, trading areas where valuable spices and other goods changed hands without the need to pay duties, but where others, such as Arab middlemen, profited from such handoffs.

In August 1492, with the backing of the Spanish monarchs Ferdinand II and Isabella I, an Italian navigator led an expedition from southwestern Spain, three ships heading west. Christopher Columbus's mission was to find a shorter route to the East Indies, via China and Japan, by sailing west—an idea that would upstage the penetration of Portuguese navigators along the western coast of Africa. His failure to make it that far, which he never acknowledged, put him in the Western Hemisphere, whose northeastern regions had been reached by Viking Leif Erikson in the early 11th century. Columbus most likely landed on Hispaniola in the Caribbean, which he steadfastly maintained was Japan, and then on Cuba, which he proclaimed Cathay, or China. Despite his persistent denials, Columbus had found his way to a New World that as a result would never be the same.

Figures in a mural in the ancient Maya city of Calakmul, Campeche, Mexico: One prepares and the other one sips the beverage called xocoatl.

Everywhere else that Europeans ventured in search of things botanical there were established relations, rules of commerce and protocol—in other words, systems for doing things that had been honed by millennia of trade and exchange. It is not that entitlement and exploitation were unknown within the realm of the known world, but they did not approach the scale of the wanton disregard that marked the treatment of New World peoples, their leaders, and the environment by Columbus and those who followed him. The highly developed civilizations and cultures that the conquistadores found in the New World—notably those of the Maya, Aztec, and Inca—elicited curiosity and some individual regard, but that did not counteract the general sense that everything was there for the taking or for alteration in any way that suited their needs. This wholesale appropriation was applied to all the resources of the New World: human, animal, mineral, and botanical. It extended in the other direction as well, to the importation of anything that enabled the Europeans to establish a presence of the familiar amid the unfamiliar.

A New World to Explore

Riding the acclaim of his first voyage, Columbus soon planned a second one, a journey that once and for all blurred the distinctions between an Old and New World. He arrived in a flotilla of 17 ships, carrying hundreds of crew and passengers and cargoes of domestic animals such as cows, pigs, and horses, and plants, including wheat, barley, wine grape vines, and sugarcane. The last would become merely the first in a series of plant appropriations and redistributions that would enslave humans and degrade the environment of the New World.

Within a few short decades, the New World was awash with Spanish, Portuguese, and later Dutch and English explorers. In 1519 Hernán Cortés staged his expedition to Central America from a base in Cuba. He approached the land of the Aztec from the Gulf of Mexico, and marching inland, was able to advance upon Moctezuma's capital, where the Aztec leader and his people mistakenly awaited the return of the great god Quetzalcoatl in the form of the opportunistic conquistador and his army.

Cortés's party marveled at the sophistication of the Aztec capital, Tenochtitlan, established on an island in the valley where Mexico City stands today. Everything impressed the Spanish, especially the *chinampas,* raised beds of vegetables and flowers

Produced in Mexico in 1552 and colorfully illustrated, the Codex Badianus was the first herbal of the Americas. Aztec physician Martín de la Cruz wrote it, and then another native, Juan Badiano, translated it in to Latin.

that appeared to float in the water but actually were mud platforms excavated from the lakeshore. The chinampas as well as the irrigated terraced fields in the surrounding mountains provided food for the sprawling Aztec city, several times larger than contemporary London. And, unlike the Hanging Gardens of Babylon, which left no foundations or diagrams to support its alleged magnificence, the botanical wonders of Tenochtitlan appear on a detailed plan drawn by the conquistador himself.

Some dozen years later, Francisco Pizarro would repeat a similar process of conquest, leading to the defeat of the Inca and appropriation of all that their civilization had to offer. In the Andean highlands the Inca grew many varieties of potatoes as well as maize. These crops flourished even at 8,000 feet on the steep terraces of Machu Picchu, which was connected to the vast Inca empire by a well-developed system of highland roads. As the decades of discovery continued on, each subsequent incursion into the New World by explorers and conquerors from the old one revealed a growing panoply of botanical riches.

EAST IS EAST

IN MAY 1498 VASCO DA GAMA AND HIS CREW COMPLETED THE FIRST DIRECT SEA VOYAGE from Europe to Asia. His countryman Bartolomeu Dias had paved the way by inching down the coast of western Africa and rounding the Cape of Good Hope ten years earlier. Upon coming to shore in Calicut on India's Malabar Coast, da Gama's men were reported to shout, "For Christ and spices!"

Malabar already had a large Christian population because of its settlement by Syrian Christian traders centuries earlier, so it soon became, to an even greater degree, all about the spices—and, more precisely, all about the black pepper. The demand in Europe was so great that black pepper at various times had a one-to-one exchange rate with gold. And no place on Earth grew (or still grows) a finer *Piper nigrum* than the Malabar Coast.

Da Gama's feat streamlined the spice trade between Europe and the East Indies and solidified, for a time at least, Portuguese dominance of trade with the East, diminishing the role of Venice, which had formerly been the major player in pepper dealing. Twenty years later, Ferdinand Magellan followed Columbus's lead and sailed west from Portugal, with the goal of circumnavigating the globe. Although he died en route, one of Magellan's ships went the distance and, reaching the Indies, was able to bring back to Portugal enough cinnamon, clove, nutmeg, mace, and fragrant sandalwood to more than finance the whole expedition.

"Nutmegs cause a sweet breath, and mend those that stinke, if they be much chewed and holden in the mouth."

—JOHN GERARD,
THE HERBALL, OR, GENERALL HISTORIE OF PLANTES, 1597

Plants with aromatic oils in the seeds (like nutmeg, above) or in the wood and roots (like sandalwood, opposite) were coveted in a time without refrigeration or sanitation.

Santalaceae
(Osyrideae)

Santalum album L.

BLACK PEPPER

Piper nigrum

The original purpose of spices was to mask bad flavors, in contrast to their purpose today of providing good ones. For many centuries, black pepper—considered the king of spices—was prized for its ability to hide the taste of rotting food while providing a pleasant zest that made meals more exciting. The high demand for pepper set many ships a-sail and fueled the age of exploration, which dramatically changed the known world. Black pepper is produced from the dried berries of a climbing vine found growing along the Malabar Coast of India. Full-grown berries are picked while still green and left to ferment overnight, then sun dried for several days as their skin darkens. White pepper comes from the same berries, picked a bit later and processed differently; green pepper comes from immature berries.

Though pepper has been under cultivation in India since prehistoric times, there is little mention of it outside that region until the time of the Greeks and Romans, when pepper and other spices were traded overland through Asia. Its rarity and the high cost of transporting it over such a distance at first made black pepper exorbitantly expensive, consumed only by the wealthiest. The first time Alaric the Goth led his Germanic forces into Rome, in about A.D. 400, he agreed to retreat only if the Romans met his demand: 3,000 pounds of black peppercorns. Even into the Middle Ages, black pepper was used as currency to pay rent or boost a dowry.

As the exotic ingredient gained popularity, it played a large part in the development of the Italian city-states of Venice and Genoa, which prospered from their trade relations. In 1381 Venice claimed a naval victory over Genoa, securing a trade monopoly that lasted for the next several centuries. All Europe relied on the Venetians for their spices, which meant that they could charge extortionate prices.

By the 15th century, tired of this monopoly and developing nautical capabilities of their own, other European countries sent out expeditions to find alternative routes to the spices in the Indies. Christopher Columbus voyaged westward, Vasco da Gama voyaged eastward—and his sail around the Cape of Good Hope ultimately resulted in toppling Venice's spice supremacy.

In this way, we can thank the tantalizing flavor of black pepper for the extraordinary age of discovery. Because of it, new lands were found, new spices discovered. Even today, black pepper is the king of spices. Consumed around the globe, it is rivaled only by its frequent tabletop partner, salt. ■

The black gold of ancient times, peppercorns were an exotic and valuable treasure in the days when ocean travel took long and risked lives.

BLACK PEPPER THROUGH TIME

460 B.C.	80 B.C.	A.D. 92	1179	1498	1600	1976
Hippocrates lists black pepper as a medicinal.	Traders enter Alexandria, Egypt, by the city's Pepper Gate.	Rome includes a city street called Via Piperatica— Pepper Way.	London's Guild of Pepperers is founded.	Vasco da Gama sails east to Asia and pepper prices fall.	British East India Company is founded, trading in spices.	World pepper trade sets a new record: 220 million pounds.

SUGAR AND SHAME

IN 1505 A SHIP MADE PASSAGE TO THE NEW WORLD CARRYING CARGO THAT DID NOT involve a transfer of plant life from the Old World to the New. Instead, it was the first voyage to transport slaves from West Africa to the Caribbean, to work the labor-intensive exploitation of natural resources in the Americas—including backbreaking agricultural tasks such as the cultivation of sugarcane. The male slaves were often shackled together to lie belowdecks in tightly packed rows to prevent dissent or suicide. The overall mortality rate, especially in the earlier centuries of the slave trade, was very high—approaching 50 percent. Some estimates correlate the loss of one slave life to every ton of sugar produced.

Columbus himself, quickly sizing up the potential for sugarcane production in the American tropics, had carried scions of these plants to Santo Domingo on his second voyage in 1493. Europeans were already hooked on sugar, even though many of the now standard uses for the product, such as sweetening tea and coffee, had not yet come

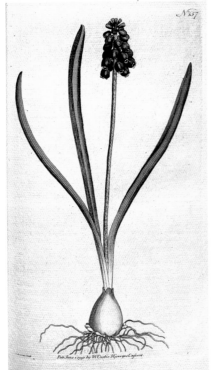

Grape hyacinth (Muscari botryoides), *a native of southern Europe, grew in gardens belonging to both John Gerard and John Parkinson, two giants in early English botany.*

into vogue. The crop required a great deal of manpower, unavailable among the rapidly declining populations of indigenous peoples who were dying at an exponential rate from imported diseases, or among the conquering Spanish. The answer to the dilemma was slaves—by the millions over time—with estimates ranging from 2.5 to 6 million for the sugar plantations alone.

The voyage from West Africa to the Caribbean, known as the Middle Passage, became one leg of a shipping triangle that ran sugar, molasses, and rum to Britain and cloth, guns, and other supplies to Africa to be traded for the slaves. The total of imported slaves for all enterprises in the New World over a span of more than 350 years has been estimated at 13 million. The plantation system that brought great profits from the cultivation of sugarcane, which became known as white gold, was repeated many times over with other plants in the decades and centuries that followed—tobacco, cotton, tea, coffee, and rubber, to name only a few—promoting slavery and other unconscionable forms of human exploitation.

CHANGING TASTES

THE ROSTER OF PLANT FOODS INTRODUCED TO THE OLD WORLD FROM THE Americas is a long one and includes maize (corn), potatoes, sweet potatoes, tomatoes, manioc, peanuts, peppers, beans, squashes, and cacao. Europeans generally were slow in warming to the food potential of some of the fruits and vegetables introduced from the Americas. Some felt the foreign foods should be avoided because they hailed from pagan lands and were unlike anything known in the Christian world, which had largely

123

Publish'd as the Act directs June 1.1790 by W.Curtis St Georges Crescent.

"*The people have plenty of roots called* zanahorias, *with a smell like chesnuts; and they have beans of kinds very different from ours. . . . There are a thousand other kinds of fruits which it is impossible for me to write about, and all must be profitable.*"

—CHRISTOPHER COLUMBUS, JOURNAL, NOVEMBER 4, 1492

A native of North Africa, Gibraltar candytuft (Iberis gibraltarica) flourishes among the limestone slopes of its namesake rock. It became a greenhouse ornamental when brought into northern climes.

LEONHARTVS FVCHSIVS
AETATIS SVAE ANNO XLI.

"Magellan said to the overseer of the House of Commerce in Seville that 'if they gave him the ships he asked for, and men and artillery, he would . . . discover new lands . . . from which he would bring gold, cloves, cinnamon, and other riches.'"

— GASPAR CORREA,
LENDAS DA INDIA, CA 1560

German physician Leonhard Fuchs, considered one of the fathers of botany, wrote the 1542 herbal De historia stirpium *(Notable Commentaries on the History of Plants). For it he hired three artists to draw plants from life. The book set a precedent for accuracy in botanical illustration.*

adopted the lists presented as comprehensive by classical Greek and Roman scholars. They figured that if the plants did not exist in the Old World, there was a good and godly reason for it.

By this thinking, species such as corn, potato, and tomato were eyed suspiciously. But that didn't stop Europeans from prizing the plants for their novelty or finding uses other than food for some of them. When the French first came in contact with the potato, for example, they treated it as an ornamental for its lovely leaves and vines; the nutritious part under the ground was of no consequence.

Eventually, though, Europeans started to eat these New World foods. The Spanish were the first to give corn a chance, and other nationalities followed suit. Soon corn was sailing to the Philippines with Magellan in 1521, landing also in Africa, where it became a reliable staple that enabled population growth there—and ironically would help fuel the slave trade.

Potatoes would become a staple in northern Europe, providing higher yields per acre than any grain crop. Potatoes afforded an additional advantage during times of war, when occupying armies routinely commandeered food stores. Unlike grain, potatoes did not have to be harvested; they could be left in the ground, making it very inconvenient for soldiers to accumulate them quickly. In time potatoes would become the mainstay of peasant farmers, especially the Irish, and would lead to the catastrophic potato famines of the 19th century.

Italians, not surprisingly, were the first to give tomatoes a try. Yet they knew about them for more than a hundred years before they consumed them in the mid-17th century, so wary were Europeans of this strange fruit. Today, it is almost impossible to imagine Italian cuisine without abundant *pomi d'oro,* or golden apples. Europeans did not underappreciate only New World foods, they rejected some of the offerings of the East as well. Until the discovery of sweet and juicy oranges in Ceylon in the mid-15th century, Europeans tended to value citrus more for its fragrance than for its taste.

SOME LIKE IT HOT

OTHER CULINARY NOVELTIES WERE RECEIVED WITH MUCH MORE enthusiasm. Not surprisingly, many fell into the category of new and interesting spices. The variety of spicy fruits that Columbus also dubbed pepper (*Capsicum* spp.), part of his seemingly stubborn denial of not reaching the Indies, drew significant attention from European visitors to the New World.

Friar Bernardino de Sahagún, who arrived as a missionary in Mexico in 1529, noted that the Aztec elite ate "frog with green chillis; newt with yellow chilli; tadpoles with small chillis; maguey grubs with a sauce of

A showy shrub with luxuriant, pendulous flowers native to the Caribbean, this plant was named fuchsia in honor of Leonhard Fuchs by Charles Plumier, a monk turned royal botanist who sailed three times to the New World in the late 1600s.

Gramineae.

Saccharum officinarum L.

SUGARCANE

Saccharum officinarum

ugar is a luxury item whose history begins in the tropical region of India. It comes from the sugarcane plant, a member of the grass family that reaches a height of 15 feet, requires plenty of sun and water to grow, and is ready to harvest within ten months. The stalks are crushed to extract the juice, which is clarified, concentrated into syrup, and then crystallized. The species of sugarcane used today is probably a hybrid, bred for higher yield.

The taste for sugar dates to before recorded history, and for centuries desires were satisfied simply by chewing on pieces of the stalk. Early Sanskrit sources document that sugar was made using presses by 500 B.C. Persian soldiers coming upon it growing along the Indus River called it "the reed that gives honey without bees." Its original use was medicinal, but recently such uses have been forgotten.

Animals and African slaves provided the muscle power to run the mills in tropical colonies where cane stalks were crushed, their sweet juice extracted.

From India, sugar spread to the east and west. Returning from his travels in the 13th century, Marco Polo described Chinese sugar refineries as the greatest marvel he saw in that land. Medieval crusaders brought sugar back from the Holy Land to Europe with them, and the sweet commodity soon played an increasingly important role as ships plied the world's oceans, headed west and east from Europe, during the 15th century.

Columbus is credited with bringing sugarcane to Haiti in 1493, and the production of sugarcane in the Caribbean islands soon rivaled production in India. As demands for sugar and its by-product, molasses, increased, a transcontinental triangle of trade emerged. Sugar grown in the Caribbean was transported to England; English goods were loaded on ships and sent to Africa; and those goods were traded for slaves, who were then transported by the same ships to the Americas to work on sugar plantations. The trade triangle led to great wealth for a few and slavery for many.

In 1811 the Royal Navy of Great Britain blockaded the French empire and its access to the New World, cutting off the sugar supply and forcing French emperor Napoleon Bonaparte to search for alternative sources for the sweetener that his people had come to love. Sugar beets proved to contain similar percentages of sugar, and by the end of the 19th century the tonnage of sugar produced from sugar beets had surpassed that produced from sugarcane around the world. ∎

SUGARCANE THROUGH TIME

by 500 B.C.	A.D. 600	1099	1493	1520	1650	1747
Sugar is grown in India, according to Sanskrit records.	Sugar spreads east to China, west to the Levant.	Sugar is first brought to England by returning crusaders.	Columbus transports sugarcane to Hispaniola.	Portuguese sugar plantations are developed in Brazil.	Rum is made from sugar by-products in Barbados.	Technique to extract sugar from beet roots is developed.

small chillis; lobster with red chilli." We now know that the culinary technique of using hot spices to make palatable some of the more gustatorily challenging protein sources is culturally widespread, and that the varieties of chili pepper, sent on as seeds by the Spanish padres to their Iberian homeland, were embraced before migrating northward and eastward. So rapid and complete was the incorporation of chilis into the cuisines of South and Southeast Asia that later visitors to those regions assumed local origins for the *Capsicum* peppers found there.

Vanilla or Chocolate?—A Win-Win Combo

THERE WAS NO ARM-TWISTING INVOLVED TO GET EUROPEANS TO ACCEPT VANILLA, THE dried pods of the orchid *Vanilla planifolia,* which the Aztec used as a flavoring, especially in their highly prized chocolate beverage known as *xocoatl.* Hernán Cortés had tasted the combination in Moctezuma's capital and brought it back to Spain.

Europeans welcomed vanilla's sweet and appealing flavor and scent, which curiously does not appear in unripe beans. It takes a number of months of curing and drying before the organic compounds, including the aromatic vanillin, accumulate in the orchid pod. As that happens, small crystals of the vanillin mixture will actually appear

The Botanic Garden at Padua was founded in 1545, making it the oldest known university garden in the world. Dedicated to growing medicinal plants for experiments and teaching, it played a key role in the study of exotic plants in Europe. A wall built around the garden helped keep out thieves.

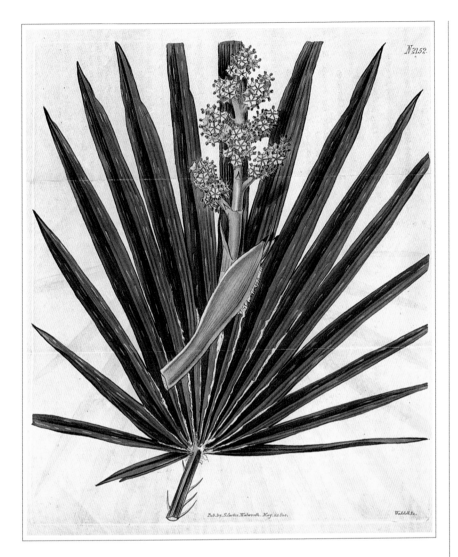

Nº2152.

Still living after all these centuries, the same Mediterranean fan palm (Chamaerops humilis) *has grown in the garden at Padua since 1585—the oldest plant in the garden. A ginkgo and a magnolia tree date back to the mid-1700s.*

"This [cacao] drink is the healthiest thing, and the greatest sustenance of anything you could drink in the world, because he who drinks a cup of this liquid, no matter how far he walks, can go a whole day without eating anything else."

—Reported by one of the retinue of Cortés, 1556

on the surface of high-quality beans. As pleased as they were to discover and attempt to exploit the potential of the vanilla orchid, Europeans were stymied about its cultivation. It took more than 200 years for them to figure out that pollination of the delicate flower required the services of a very small bee, as happened naturally in the wild in Central America, or human assistance with a slender device such as a wooden needle. This eventually was realized on the French colonial island of Bourbon in the Indian Ocean in 1841, and once known, commercial exploitation of the vanilla orchid on a larger scale could get under way.

The main ingredient of the Aztec drink xocoatl excited Europeans even more than the vanilla flavoring did, and in the short run proved easier to cultivate. In 1502 Columbus was the first to encounter chocolate, the product of the pods of the tropical cacao *(Theobroma cacao)*, or cocoa, tree, but Cortés was perhaps the first European to

taste it. He was offered the chocolate beverage ceremonially in a solid gold cup by one of Moctezuma's attendants, as it was a drink reserved for the elite.

For about a century, the Spanish withheld knowledge of the secret beverage they had imported. They drank it hot and flavored it with both vanilla and cinnamon. Even after its delights were shared with the rest of Europe, chocolate remained a delicacy that only the rich could afford until the mid-19th century. In the meantime, the French and the Spanish established cacao plantations in their respective colonies in the Caribbean and the Philippines. Cultivation of the cacao tree was well understood, unlike that of the vanilla orchid, and cacao was well suited to cultivation in moist, shaded, tropical environments.

NEW AND OLD WORLD HERBALS

IF THE WESTERN WORLD DID NOT YET HAVE AN UNDERSTANDING OF MUCH OF AMERICAN flora, the indigenous peoples of the Americas certainly had a good grasp of their native plants. At the same time that the first European physic gardens—gardens specifically designed for teaching and research on medicinal plants and usually attached to a university—were established in Italy at Pisa in 1543 and Padua in 1545, the great Aztec

city of Tenochtitlan in Mexico already boasted a botanical garden, perhaps the largest in the world. The Aztec had also produced written records of their plant species, including a 1552 manuscript by two students at the College of Santa Cruz de Tlatelolco in Mexico. Considered the first American herbal, it has an Aztec text and illustrations created by Martín de la Cruz and translated into Latin by Juan Badiano, whose name in latinized form—Badianus— later became attached to the document.

This work did not pique the interest of the rest of the world until it was published in English in 1940 after it had come to light in the Vatican Library a decade earlier. Europe did take note of the 1555 English version of the *Natural History of the West Indies* by Spaniard Gonzalo Fernández de Oviedo y Valdés. Oviedo had a difficult time reconciling New World plant discoveries with classical scholarship and ancient botanical knowledge—sources being questioned by Renaissance Europe anyway—and he noted that the European plants introduced to the Americas were already displacing the native flora, a development that disturbed him.

As scientific thinking advanced past the recycled works of antiquity, botany acquired a new impetus, spurred on by advances in printing and engraving. These changes

Vanilla
Vanilla planifolia

Vanilla is a tropical orchid valued for its sweet, aromatic seed pod, mistakenly called a vanilla bean. The Totonac, who inhabited Mexico's Gulf Coast, were likely the first to cultivate vanilla; they considered it a gift from the gods. Vanilla was transported to Europe in the 16th century, but until the 19th century, Mexico remained its primary source. Today it is grown in tropical regions around the world, including Madagascar, Indonesia, Uganda, and Tonga.

New flavors flooded the European market from around the world as sea-going vessels rounded the continents. Not until the details of propagating the vanilla orchid (opposite) became known, however, in 1841, did that mellow flavor join the array.

Gramineae
(Andropogoneae)

Zea Mays L.

MAIZE

Zea mays

When humans began populating the Americas, around 20,000 years ago, the ancestors of maize, particularly a strain called teosinte, grew wild in Central and South America. By 5000 B.C. native peoples were cultivating maize in Mexico; by 3000 B.C. the practice had reached South America and, soon after, North America.

Maize—or corn in the United States, from the British English for grain or small seed—is the third largest plant food source in the world, behind wheat and rice. Because of its hardy nature, the tall, stout grass, called king of the grasses, can grow as far north or south as latitude 50°—and it is cultivated nearly everywhere that it can grow.

Wild maize self-propagates: Its seed, relatively small compared with today's kernels, can sprout and reproduce the same plant type. That capability has been lost by modern species. Scientists have deduced that maize was disseminated throughout South America only after early farmers deliberately selected varieties that were suitable for human consumption. Early maize seeds were not sweet, and they grew in a variety of colors and designs: red, blue, black, and pink; banded, spotted, and striped.

Fuchs's 1542 herbal represents the earliest known illustration of maize, mistakenly named Turkish corn, since he believed it came from the Middle East.

By the time Christopher Columbus reached the New World, maize was a staple for Native Americans, whose practice of combining it with beans, squash, and some animal protein improved on its nutritional deficiencies. Shipped back to Europe, maize dashed across Europe and the Middle East, finding its way to China, where it became a part of the diet within a century of its transport from the New World.

The reproductive strategy of corn is distinctive. Tassels, or male flowers, stand at the top of the grassy stalks, distributing pollen into the wind. Silk, the female flowers—long, thin strands of plant matter emerging from inside the developing ear—receive the pollen. Each fertilized embryo matures into a single seed, and rows of seeds plump up into an ear of kernels. Maize may be versatile, but it does not compare nutritionally with wheat or rice. The poor across the world who rely on maize as their core staple often suffer from pellagra, caused by a deficiency of niacin and protein. Today nearly two-thirds of all maize grown goes into animal feed instead.

Recently maize took on a new future. A primary ingredient in ethanol, a motor fuel with high octane and low carbon emissions, maize may provide one answer to the urgent quest for sustainable biofuels. ■

MAIZE THROUGH TIME

by 5000 B.C.	A.D. 1492	1527	1550	1877	1911	1970s
Central Americans are cultivating maize.	Columbus finds New World natives growing maize.	Muslim travelers sight maize on Africa's west coast.	Maize reaches China by overland routes from Europe.	Corn is first cross-pollinated successfully to increase yield.	Mazola corn oil comes on the market.	High-fructose corn syrup is developed for food and drink.

showed up early in the herbal, an illustrated manual of medical plants that described their appearance, uses, and best methods of cultivation. Earlier herbals were mainly the work of monks and were written in Latin, the language of the church and of learning at the time. Often these herbals contained large chunks of classical Greek and Roman writings that the new authors would amend based on their own knowledge and experience. Illustrations tended to be plain and didactic, and in a printed herbal were created mainly by simple woodcut.

But in the early 16th century, vernacular herbals written by secular botanists began to appear, some with original content and some translated from works in other languages, often without proper attribution. In 1526, for example, Englishman Peter Treveris published *The Grete Herbal,* which was a translation of a contemporary French herbal. Twenty-five years later, physician William Turner put out *A New Herball,* also in English, in which he questioned some of the more far-fetched and antiquated claims his predecessors had made about plants.

The Herball, or, General Histories of Plantes, published in 1597 by apothecary and botanist John Gerard, is one of the most famous of the English herbals, although it drew heavily on the work of Flemish physician Rembert Dodoens. Nevertheless, Gerard's *Herball* grabbed the attention of Elizabethan England with its straightforward and pithy prose. Regarding the almighty black peppercorn, Gerard summarized: "All Pepper heateth, provoketh urin, digesteth, draweth, disperseth, and clenseth the dimnesse of the sight, as *Dioscorides* noteth," invoking the first-century Greek physician whose influence continued well into the Renaissance.

At this same general time, botanical art also was evolving from the plain and practical woodcuts of the earlier herbals to artistic representations of flowers as flowers in all their aesthetic beauty. This shift acknowledged the enthusiasm for the exotic plants that were coming into Europe from both the East and the West. Collected into gardens, they advertised the wealth and savvy of their collectors. Their images were also collected into a book called a florilegium, a "gathering of flowers." A fine early example is the florilegium of German botanist Basil Besler, the *Hortus Eystettensis* (1613), which celebrated the greatness of the garden—and therefore of the man himself—of his patron and employer, the prince bishop of Eichstätt. Florilegia proliferated over the next two centuries, becoming more magnificent still with each advance in painting, engraving, and printing.

Heeding the Signs

HERBAL MEDICINE OF THE 17TH CENTURY ALIGNED ITSELF STRONGLY WITH THE CONCEPT of resemblance: that the appearances of natural objects gave clues to their purpose. In the 16th century a Swiss physician with the flamboyant self-styled name of Paracelsus ("greater than Celsus," a first-century Roman doctor) von Hohenheim took the notion

"What greater delight is there than to behold the earth apparelled with plants, as with a robe of embroidered worke, set with Orient pearles and garnished with great diversitie of rare and costly jewels?"

— JOHN GERARD, THE HERBALL, OR, GENERALL HISTORIE OF PLANTES, 1597

Cashew
Anacardium occidentale

The cashew is a fast-growing evergreen tree native to the Americas. The cashew nut dangles down outside the bright red or yellow fruit, which is in fact a swollen stalk holding the true fruit, inside which is the familiar cashew nut. An acrid substance surrounds the nut, so that it must be roasted before eating. When French naturalist André Thévet first saw cashews in Brazil in 1558, he asked the natives for their name. They answered *acajou*, meaning that the unroasted nuts pucker up the mouth—and he therefore named them "caju."

of resemblance and elaborated it as the Doctrine of Signatures, holding that the clues were obvious signs, or signatures, directly from God indicating the essence and purpose of an organism.

A half century later, Jakob Böhme, a shoemaker from the German town of Görlitz, experienced a mystical vision that illuminated for him the relationship between God and humans. He explained his vision and its revelations in a book he called *De signatura rerum,* or *The Signature of All Things.* The medical practitioners of Böhme's day adopted this doctrine wholesale and applied it to the role of plants in healing human illnesses. By their shapes, colors, smells, taste, and other qualities, plants advertised their potential uses. We find direct evidence of these signatures in many of the common and scientific plant names that come down to us from this time. The basal leaves of *Hepatica,* for

The intriguing cashew (Anacardium occidentale) grows a sweet-tasting false fruit called the cashew apple—actually the stalk— from which hangs the true fruit, containing the protein-rich cashew nut inside. The fruit's outer skin contains the same irritating allergen as poison ivy and has been used as a wart remover.

"And for that high concernment we all seek after, Health, what hath the great preserver of all things rendered more soveraigne then the vertues of Herbs and Plants?"

— WILLIAM COLES,
ADAM IN EDEN, OR, NATURE'S PARADISE, 1657

*A native of Mexico, the sunflower (*Helianthus annuus*) was prized not only for its size—John Gerard sprouted 14-foot plants in his garden—but also for its diurnal motion, as the broad flower tracks the sun across the sky through the day.*

SOLEIL ANNUEL

example, being liver shaped, were used to treat liver disorders. The spotted, organ-shaped leaves of the European lungwort *(Pulmonaria officinalis)* were believed able to vanquish pulmonary diseases, and so forth.

The doctrine extended beyond shape; the yellow sap produced from the herb celandine *(Chelidonium majus)* evoked the yellowed skin of jaundice sufferers, and it also was used to treat liver disorders. Not infrequently, the perceived signature pointed to the right remedy; celandine has been proved to stimulate the secretion of bile in the liver. But not all of the signatures were valid from a medical point of view. The milky white mottling on the leaves of the milk thistle *(Silybum marianum),* interpreted as a sign that it would promote the flow of milk in nursing mothers, appeared to have no such effect, although it was later demonstrated to aid liver health and repair.

Böhme's influence continued after his death in 1624. Writing in the mid-17th century, botanist William Coles, for example, extolled the value of walnuts for head ailments, as they represented a perfect signature of the head: "The Kernal hath the very figure of the Brain, and therefore it is very profitable for the Brain, and resists poysons." The essential thought behind the Doctrine of Signatures, minus the Christian theology, appears in traditional Asian as well as Native American medicine. It persisted in the Western tradition and even made its way into medical texts into the 19th century, before it was rejected in favor of more scientifically based evidence.

By the time of Queen Elizabeth I, gardening had become a national passion in England. A woodcut illustration from the popular 1594 book The Gardener's Labyrinth *depicts a variety of garden tasks: pruning, training, and weeding.*

ADAMI

POMVM

COMMVNE

CITRUS

Citrus spp.

The genus *Citrus* includes many familiar fruits: oranges, grapefruits, lemons, and limes. Citrus fruits are characterized by a leathery rind pocked with aromatic oil glands and, inside, by symmetrically organized sections. In fact, they are specialized berries called hesperidia by botanists. The term comes from Greek mythology, from the three beautiful-voiced maidens, the Hesperides, who guarded Hera's golden apple tree. The Trojan War took place because fruit was stolen from this tree, and Hercules stole from it again when performing his 12 labors—mythical details suggesting that the famous "golden apples" might have been oranges, brought to Greece by Alexander the Great around 300 B.C.

Grown in subtropical and tropical climates, citrus fruits are thought to have originated in the region of Asia between the Malay Archipelago and India. Citrus cultivation became important early on in China. The genus name recalls the citron—a small, thick-skinned, lemon-like fruit used primarily for candied rind and marmalade—suggesting that this was the first cultivar to reach Europe. Citrus fruits are depicted in Roman mosaics and wall paintings from the first century A.D., but their broad dissemination probably

In Hieronymus Bock's 1546 herbal—illustrated with woodcuts, printed in Germany, and hand-colored—a lemon tree bears abundant fruit.

occurred as the Arabs conquered North Africa and Spain, beginning in the sixth century. The movement of the orange across Asia can be traced linguistically: *naranga* in Sanskrit was corrupted into *narang* and *naranj* in Persian and Arabic respectively; the Spanish called it *naranja,* from which the English word "orange" derives.

Once the Muslims were expelled from Spain in the 15th century, citrus fruits carried a stigma associated with Islam. Returning crusaders brought lemons from Palestine, however, and helped disseminate the fruits in Europe. Citrus fruits were first valued in Europe more for their fragrance than their flavor—until Vasco da Gama returned to Portugal from China, carrying sweet oranges. Their early landing in Portugal is still apparent in the Greek and Turkish words for orange: *portokáli* and *portakal.* Christopher Columbus took citrus seeds across the Atlantic, and from them a booming citrus industry grew.

British sailors carried citrus with them aboard ship—hence their nickname, Limeys—but not until the 1930s did scientists determine that the fruit's vitamin C prevents scurvy. Citrus now represents a multibillion-dollar global industry, with Brazil and the U.S. leaders in production. ◾

CITRUS THROUGH TIME

2400 B.C.	A.D. 1178	1493	1693	1753	1804	1971
Chinese texts name oranges and pomelos.	Han Yen-Chih's *Chu Lu* lists 27 varieties of orange.	Columbus takes seed on his second voyage to the West Indies.	The first grapefruit is recorded in the West Indies.	Scottish physician James Lind discovers citrus can cure scurvy.	First sweet orange orchard established at a California mission.	Florida produces more than 200 million boxes of fruit.

TULIPOMANIA, OR FLOWER POWER

THE 1630S PRODUCED A STRANGE AND STARTLING FINANCIAL SPECULATION IN THE PLANT
realm that rivaled or surpassed any other before or since. In its brevity and out-of-
control escalation, followed by spectacular collapse, it resembled 21st-century subprime
mortgages, although the basis for speculation was not a substantial 3,000-square-foot
house but a mere one-ounce tulip bulb.

The tulip had come to Europe around 1559, sent from Turkey to the Flemish
botanist Carolus Clusius, aka Charles de L'Écluse, who oversaw the Viennese gardens
of Maximilian II, the Holy Roman Emperor. When Clusius decamped to Vienna to
teach at the University of Leiden in Holland in the early 1590s, he took tulips with
him, becoming the main source for the distribution of the prized flower throughout
much of Europe. (Tulips can grow from seeds, but once established, this perennial's
bulb can be more easily moved and replanted and will continue to bloom successfully
for several years, even after the parent bulb dies, when the bulblets that develop around
its base begin to produce their own flowers.)

Most of Europe quickly became enamored of the appealing flowers that displayed
such variation in color, pattern, and petal shape, some due to mutations caused by a virus
that was transmitted by aphids. In the parlance of tulip growing, the mutations "break"
the appearance of the normally solid-hued blooms. Although most plant viruses create
harmful economic effects, the seemingly infinite possibilities of broken, or variegated,
tulips added to their value. Many still lifes of the period depict fringed blossoms, worth
a king's ransom as a vase of cut flowers, in reverential splendor. Eventually, though,
there was a kind of Faustian bargain to be paid for all this beauty. Each generation of a
broken tulip became weaker, even as its compounding mutations produced ever more
amazing and varied patterns, until the bulb eventually died.

Entering a period of peace and unification, the attention of the Dutch—and their
spending—soon was diverted to the growing hobby of tulip collecting. By the 1630s
the situation was well on its way to getting out of hand. Tulip enthusiasm did not stop
with the wealthy, but it trickled down to the middle classes, who could ill afford to
put up a year's income just to own a single bulb. Nonetheless, people flocked to tulip
auctions, which often were held in taverns where alcohol added to the already heady
atmosphere, betting homes and estates on bulbs that were not even present at the sale.
They remained in the ground, to be sold and resold many times over without ever
actually changing hands.

For three years Dutch tulipomania continued unabated; at its height, the highly
prized red-and-white variety known as Semper Augustus brought the princely sum of
4,600 florins plus a coach with two dapple gray horses. How much was that by modern
standards? A financial analyst recently calculated the top price of a Semper Augustus
bulb at about $35,000. In hindsight, overspeculation compounded by bubonic plague

Narcissus Tazetta   *Narcisse a plusieurs Fleurs.*

Starting as a Mediterranean wildflower, the narcissus has been grown, selected, and hybridized for centuries, to the point that today there are more than 25,000 different registered cultivars.

in the low country led to the disaster that occurred in 1637, when the bottom fell out of the tulip market, bankrupting thousands. The Dutch government got involved in straightening out the mess, but it was some time before it was resolved.

Sobered by the Dutch debacle, the rest of Europe dialed back on its own enthusiasm for the tulip. The Dutch never gave up on the flower, but learned to cultivate it with deliberate genetic variations. They continue to sell both bulbs and cut flowers, activities that contribute about four billion dollars to the Netherlands' economy today.

North American Plant Hunters

While the voyages of discovery and high-stakes trade in economically important plants such as sugarcane, vanilla, and cacao kept much activity focused on the Middle Passage of the Atlantic, the knowledge of plant life of northeastern North America began gradually to unfold. This happened not as the result of planned expeditions—these would not be mounted until well into the 18th century—but because of the curiosity of individual explorers who either collected data themselves or had the foresight to enlist the aid of experts on their far-reaching travels. In some cases it made strategic sense to

John Parkinson's book Paradisi in sole paradisus terrestris, *published in 1629, offered information on growing plants in the flower garden, the kitchen garden, and the orchard. The title was a play on words: Paradisi in sole means, roughly, park in sun.*

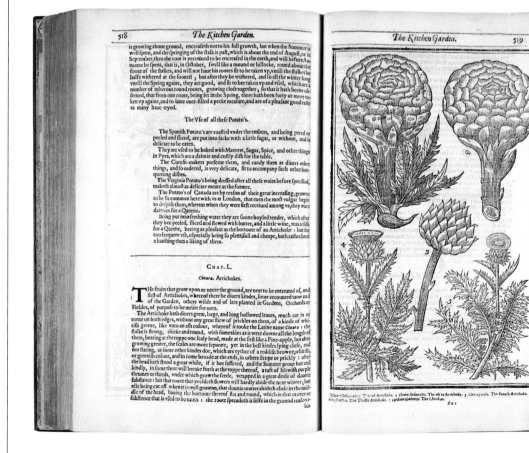

include a few experts, or at least the scientifically inclined, who could make detailed inventories of New World resources and help sell the backing of future enterprises to investors. Sir Walter Raleigh seemed to fit into the latter category.

Raleigh enlisted the aid of a mathematician and astronomer as well as a portrait painter among those he sent to Roanoke Island, at the northeastern end of North Carolina's Outer Banks. Two attempts to establish a permanent settlement there failed, but the second yielded a report from Thomas Harriot, *A Briefe and True Report of the New Found Land of Virginia,* in 1588 and a set of paintings published by John White two years later.

Farther to the north as early as the 1530s, French mariner Jacques Cartier tried unsuccessfully to get a settlement going in Quebec, but nevertheless managed to record detailed impressions of New World flora and fauna. Some 70 years later, Samuel de Champlain accomplished much more during the course of several voyages to the New World.

Among his many activities, Champlain successfully settled Quebec; "discovered" Lake Champlain; established a fur trade; fought the Iroquois, Huron, and Algonquin on and off for years—and created a botanical garden where he grew both North American and European plants. He also sent seeds, cuttings, and live plants to Paris, where botanist Jean Robin and his nephew Vespasien Robin added these North American flora to their own garden. Some of these were shared with the wider world when Paris physician and botanist Jacques Cornut included a few specimens, such as the yellow lady's slipper orchid *(Cypripedium calceolus)* in his 1635 work *Canadensium plantarum . . . historia (History of the Plants of Canada),* the first botanical volume to describe and illustrate plants native to the American Northeast.

John Parkinson's life story chronicles changing times in the world of plant science: Alive from 1567 to 1650, he served as apothecary and chief herbalist to England's King James I and then as royal botanist to King Charles I.

Tradescant's Ark

By the mid-17th century, European botany and horticulture seemed to be well on its way to becoming a family affair. There were the royal gardeners for Henry IV, Jean and Vespasien Robin of Paris, and next there were the Tradescants of London.

A father-son team, like the Bartrams of the next century, John Tradescant and John Tradescant the Younger collectively positioned themselves as indispensable horticulturists in service to the English aristocracy and to royalty, including the Earls of Salisbury, the Duke of Buckingham, and King Charles I. In fact, the Stuart king appointed the elder Tradescant Keeper of His Majesty's Gardens, Vines, and Silkworms (silkworm cultivation was attempted in Britain but never succeeded on any significant scale) at the palace home of his consort Henrietta Maria in Surrey, England. The younger Tradescant

TULIP

Tulipa

A cousin to the onion, the simple, unassuming tulip grew naturally across Asia Minor and probably started its journey to stardom in Persia. Originally the plant was called *dulband*—turban—and then *tuliband* by the Ottomans. Courts across Turkey quickly became fond of these colorful, scentless flowers and filled their gardens with them, so jealously that at one point, it is reported, they banned their export. Botanists in these Turkish courts discovered that wild tulips were susceptible to change through selective breeding, and beautiful colors and forms resulted from their experiments.

There is no mention of tulips in early Greek or Roman texts, and it is unclear how they made their way to Europe. Popular belief attributes that mission to Oghier Ghislain de Busbecq, the ambassador of Ferdinand I, Holy Roman Emperor and King of Bohemia and Hungary, to Süleyman the Magnificent of Turkey. De Busbecq apparently sent seeds home to Europe around 1550.

Tulip cultivation began in earnest during the 1570s, with Carolus Clusius, the court gardener at the Holy Roman Emperor's gardens in Vienna. In 1593 Clusius left Vienna to teach at the University of Leiden, in

Early tulips, short and simple, fascinated imperial botanist Carolus Clusius, who recorded their growing habits in a 1583 volume published in Antwerp.

Holland, and took tulip seeds with him. The flower moved through royal court gardens, continuing to receive favor, which made the seeds highly desired. They sold for extraordinary prices.

No place was crazier about tulips than Holland, where the flower instantly became popular. By the early 1600s, tulipomania had taken over Holland. The demand for new colors, in particular for flowers with color streaks known as breaks, exceeded supply, and prices for a single bulb shot skyward. By 1610 a new tulip variety was perfectly acceptable as a dowry, and houses and businesses were often mortgaged to facilitate the purchase of a coveted flower.

Tulipomania reached its peak in 1633. The end came just as swiftly, in 1637, when no one bought bulbs at an auction in Haarlem. The tulip market crashed almost overnight, causing many people to blame the flower for nearly bankrupting an entire country.

Although the tulip may never again generate the same high-pitched passions it inspired during those few decades of 17th-century tulipomania, horticulturists around the world, especially the Dutch, grow exquisite varieties commercially, and it is still one of the world's most popular garden flowers. ∎

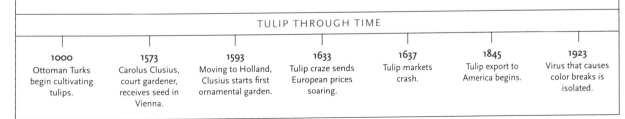

TULIP THROUGH TIME						
1000 Ottoman Turks begin cultivating tulips.	**1573** Carolus Clusius, court gardener, receives seed in Vienna.	**1593** Moving to Holland, Clusius starts first ornamental garden.	**1633** Tulip craze sends European prices soaring.	**1637** Tulip markets crash.	**1845** Tulip export to America begins.	**1923** Virus that causes color breaks is isolated.

Tab. 7.

3

1650–1770

EXPLORATION

Primula Sinensis 2987

Waddell sc.

EXPLORATION
1650–1770

O nce long-distance sailing ships regularly plied the world's oceans, the six green continents were visited not only by explorers but also by entrepreneurs for whom the plant world blossomed with commercial opportunities unimagined centuries earlier. Most explorers saw the benefit of including botanists and illustrators in their expeditions, as did the plant hunters and traders, if they did not hold these skills themselves. On a parallel track, the discipline of botany grew amid the scientific revolution of the 17th century, spurred on by greater understanding of plant physiology, especially the reproductive roles of flowers. At the same time, the passion and need to categorize and catalog the world's botanical wealth culminated in the watershed intellectual achievements of Swedish botanist Carolus Linnaeus, whose system of nomenclature still provides the international underpinnings of identification and discourse in the life sciences. During these two centuries botanical illustration continued to improve, with refined renderings and colors highlighting more realistic plant appearance. Garden design underwent major changes and became even more competitive—and thanks to the explorers, there was always some new plant to desire. ∽

	KNOWLEDGE & SCIENCE	POWER & WEALTH	HEALTH & MEDICINALS

AFRICA & MIDDLE EAST

1691 French botanist Michel Adanson publishes a natural history, including flora, of Senegal.

> *"To make thee truly sensible of that happinesse which Mankind lost by the Fall of Adam, is to render thee an exact Botanick . . ."*
>
> —WILLIAM COLES, ADAM IN EDEN, OR, NATURES PARADISE: THE HISTORY OF PLANTS, FRUITS, AND FLOWERS, 1657

ASIA & OCEANIA

1768-1771 James Cook and the artist Sydney Parkinson sail around Cape Horn and through the Pacific, studying plants and animals.

The pineapple, a New World discovery

1667 With the Treaty of Breda, the English relinquish any hold on sugar in Suriname and nutmeg in Indonesia; the Dutch gain a monopoly on both.

1678-1693 *Hortus Indicus Malabaricus*, a comprehensive pharmacopoeia of Indian medicinals, is published in Utrecht.

1700s Ginkgo tree seeds are transported from China or Japan to Europe, and later to North America.

1727-28 Roots and seeds of ginseng are brought from Korea to Japan, where cultivation of ginseng begins.

EUROPE

1661 British physicist-chemist Robert Boyle explains that plants need air to grow.

1665 English scientist Robert Hooke observes plant cells.

1675 Italian anatomist Marcello Malpighi proposes that plants have circulatory vessels analogous to human veins.

1682 English botanist Nehemiah Grew describes the reproductive parts of flowers.

1753 The British Museum is established, with botanical specimens collected by Hans Sloane a core part of the collection.

1753 Carolus Linnaeus's *Species Plantarum (Species of Plants)* is published.

ANANAS CONIQUE.

1658 Advertisements appear in London newspapers for "Jesuits powder, which cureth all manner of Agues"—namely, cinchona bark, so named because priests sent it from Peru.

1673 London's Worshipful Society of Apothecaries founds a garden to study "simples," medicinal plants; it becomes the Chelsea Physic Garden.

THE AMERICAS

1687-88 Hans Sloane catalogs some 800 plant species in Jamaica.

1699-1701 Maria Sibylla Merian studies plants and insects in Suriname.

1712-1726 Mark Catesby collects flora in the American Southeast and the Bahamas.

1728 John Bartram purchases a farm near Philadelphia, which becomes America's first botanic garden.

1765 Bartram is appointed botanist to England's King George III.

1652 In Boston, John Hull opens the American mint and begins striking coins with trees, including the famous pine tree shilling.

1676 British soldiers attempting to quell Bacon's Rebellion in Virginia eat jimsonweed, "Jamestown weed" (*Datura stramonium*), and experience hallucinations.

A Brazilian armadillo

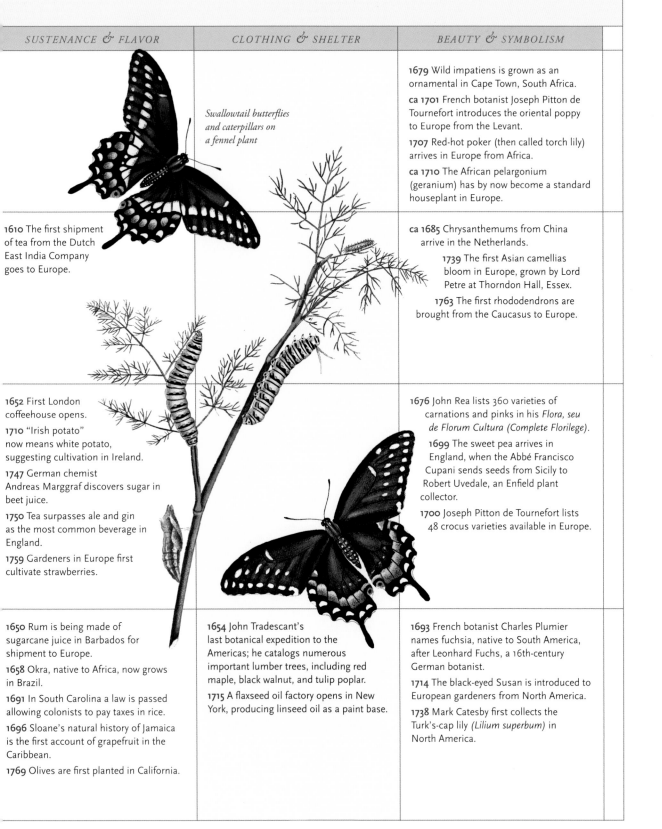

SUSTENANCE & FLAVOR	CLOTHING & SHELTER	BEAUTY & SYMBOLISM

Swallowtail butterflies and caterpillars on a fennel plant

1679 Wild impatiens is grown as an ornamental in Cape Town, South Africa.

ca 1701 French botanist Joseph Pitton de Tournefort introduces the oriental poppy to Europe from the Levant.

1707 Red-hot poker (then called torch lily) arrives in Europe from Africa.

ca 1710 The African pelargonium (geranium) has by now become a standard houseplant in Europe.

1610 The first shipment of tea from the Dutch East India Company goes to Europe.

ca 1685 Chrysanthemums from China arrive in the Netherlands.

1739 The first Asian camellias bloom in Europe, grown by Lord Petre at Thorndon Hall, Essex.

1763 The first rhododendrons are brought from the Caucasus to Europe.

1652 First London coffeehouse opens.

1710 "Irish potato" now means white potato, suggesting cultivation in Ireland.

1747 German chemist Andreas Marggraf discovers sugar in beet juice.

1750 Tea surpasses ale and gin as the most common beverage in England.

1759 Gardeners in Europe first cultivate strawberries.

1676 John Rea lists 360 varieties of carnations and pinks in his *Flora, seu de Florum Cultura (Complete Florilege).*

1699 The sweet pea arrives in England, when the Abbé Francisco Cupani sends seeds from Sicily to Robert Uvedale, an Enfield plant collector.

1700 Joseph Pitton de Tournefort lists 48 crocus varieties available in Europe.

1650 Rum is being made of sugarcane juice in Barbados for shipment to Europe.

1658 Okra, native to Africa, now grows in Brazil.

1691 In South Carolina a law is passed allowing colonists to pay taxes in rice.

1696 Sloane's natural history of Jamaica is the first account of grapefruit in the Caribbean.

1769 Olives are first planted in California.

1654 John Tradescant's last botanical expedition to the Americas; he catalogs numerous important lumber trees, including red maple, black walnut, and tulip poplar.

1715 A flaxseed oil factory opens in New York, producing linseed oil as a paint base.

1693 French botanist Charles Plumier names fuchsia, native to South America, after Leonhard Fuchs, a 16th-century German botanist.

1714 The black-eyed Susan is introduced to European gardeners from North America.

1738 Mark Catesby first collects the Turk's-cap lily *(Lilium superbum)* in North America.

"By the help of
Microscopes,
there is nothing
so small, as to
escape our inquiry;
hence there is a
new visible World
discovered to the
understanding."

— ROBERT HOOKE,
MICROGRAPHIA, 1665

BOTANY CAN BE PRACTICED ANYWHERE, ON ANY SCALE, AND BY ANYONE at any point on the spectrum of botanical expertise. Someone has to collect specimens, to be sure, but not necessarily the persons who study them. Botanists can study specimens collected by others, either as live plants or dried ones mounted in herbaria, and subject them to rigorous investigation. Thus, in the 17th and 18th centuries, with many people paying attention to plants in many different ways, botany stood at the forefront as scientific thought, methods, and knowledge advanced. Science was now firmly an international endeavor in which all the participants kept in remarkably close touch with each other and botanical specimens traveled reciprocally within a tightly woven network. To promote science in official capacities, the Royal Society of London was formed in 1660, and the Académie des Sciences in Paris in 1666.

As this age of great botanical exploration commenced, the disciplines of botany and medicine were still intertwined, although with each passing decade botany became more of a scientific entity in its own right. Plants were viewed increasingly with an eye to their own intrinsic biology and less concern for their medical applications and healing properties, although that aspect, obviously, would remain very strong until the advent of synthetically derived medications.

MINUSCULE DISCOVERIES

SEVERAL KEY SCIENTIFIC DISCOVERIES AND INVENTIONS AIDED THE STUDY OF BOTANY, AS they did the life sciences in general. One was the understanding of organisms at the cellular level. Robert Hooke, an all-around master of multiple forms of scientific investigation in the mid-17th century, had assembled a very functional compound microscope and illumination system, which he used to examine life-forms as varied as insects, sponges, and plants, as well as bird feathers. Observing the honeycomb structure of thin slices of cork (the bark of certain oak trees), he described "microscopial pores." These he named cells, as if they were connected rooms in a monastery.

Hooke found similar structures in wood itself and in other kinds of plant tissues. These are clearly seen in his illustrations of cork for his 1665 work *Micrographia,* so compelling a read that it kept diarist and government official Samuel Pepys intensely engrossed one night until two o'clock in the morning. Although he held an academic position in London for the rest of his life, Hooke did not achieve the kind of fame that his many accomplishments would merit.

Hooke nevertheless laid the groundwork for Anton von Leeuwenhoek, an amateur Dutch microscopist and draper by trade with no higher education or scientific training, but with a well-realized inquiring nature and considerable ingenuity. Leeuwenhoek fabricated more than 500 microscopes in his lifetime, but they were simple instruments with simple lenses, not much more than powerful magnifying glasses. But thanks to Leeuwenhoek's gift for grinding very clear lenses—and a knack for illumination—he achieved a factor of magnification up to ten times as great as Hooke did with his more complex devices.

Leeuwenhoek examined all manner of substances, including plant tissue, and even some obtained from his own body or from family members or willing volunteers. He scraped the teeth of an old man who reportedly had never once in his life attempted to clean them and observed living bacteria. He also examined red blood cells as well as sperm cells in their motile state. Leeuwenhoek was no artist, but he hired an illustrator to draw the things he saw. He sent his findings and illustrations to the Royal Society of London, which published them for its members with his native Dutch translated into English or Latin. He was elected to the society in 1680, but he never made it to England to add his signature to the register alongside those of the other scientific superstars of the day, including Hooke, Boyle, and Newton.

In the early 18th century, the understanding of plant reproduction was advanced by an unlikely experimenter, Cotton Mather, a Puritan minister perhaps best remembered for his connection to the Salem witch trials. Harvard-educated Mather actually

In 1665 Englishman Robert Hooke published Micrographia, *the world's first book on microscopy. He devised a compound microscope—an instrument using two or more lenses—peered into a world invisible to the naked eye, and saw the form of things such as molds and fungus as never before imagined.*

The proper name of it amongſt the Indians is *Picielt*, The name
For the name of *Tabaco* is giuen to it by our Spaniards, by of it.
reaſon of an Iſland that is named *Tabaco*.

It is an hearbe that doeth growe and come to bee very The deſcri-
greate: many times too bee greater then a Lemmon tree. tion of it.
It caſteth foorth one ſteame from the roote which groweth
vpright, without declining to any parte, it ſendeth foorth

J 2   many

TOBACCO

Nicotiana spp.

A member of the nightshade family, tobacco grows leaves that are consumed by smoking, chewing, or inhaling as snuff, but they can be poisonous in large quantities. Though plenty of people enjoy its effects on the nervous system, tobacco is a carcinogen and contains a highly addictive alkaloid, nicotine.

Tobacco first grew in the mountains of South America. It was probably under cultivation as early as 3000 B.C., and its use spread throughout the Americas. Christopher Columbus and his men witnessed locals smoking dried rolls of tobacco leaves in the late 1400s.

When Rodrigo de Jerez, one of Columbus's crew, took his new habit back to Spain, he became (so it is said) the first non-American tobacco smoker. No European had ever witnessed anyone smoking anything before, but perplexity soon turned into addiction. Claims were made for tobacco's medicinal properties. In 1571 Spanish physician Nicolas Monardes proclaimed the herb to fulfill "so general a human need, not only for the sick but for the healthy."

By the early 17th century, people were smoking tobacco in most parts of the world. Opposition spread just as quickly, and soon tobacco products were banned in many localities. In his 1604 *Counterblaste to Tobacco*, England's King James I called tobacco "loathsome to the eye, hateful to the nose, harmful to the brain," and "dangerous to the lungs." Tobacco became more popular over the next few centuries, nevertheless, and fashions constantly changed. Starting with pipe smoking, trends soon shifted to snuff: inhaled powdered tobacco. In 1600 cigars were introduced to Spain from Cuba, and before long, cigarettes became popular. By the 1790s tobacco consumption was the norm, with millions of tons of leaves grown and processed in the eastern U.S.

Tobacco's popularity peaked right after World War II. Soldiers in Europe had been given free cigarettes, leading to widespread addiction, and stigmas about women smoking in public disappeared as well. Soon medical researchers began linking increases in cancer with tobacco use, however, and in 1964 the U.S. Surgeon General issued a public statement about the health risks of smoking tobacco. Tobacco use is now on the decline in some parts of the world. Almost half of all Americans who smoked since 1965 have quit, for example, but that percentage is matched in only one other country in the world—Zambia, in East Africa—according to the World Health Organization. ∎

Considered a medicinal plant when it was first introduced to Europe, tobacco from the New World was originally included in many European pharmacopoeias.

TOBACCO THROUGH TIME

1000 B.C.	A.D. 1492	1556	1600	1612	1998	2004
Pipes and cigars smoked in Central and South America.	Arawak in the Bahamas give tobacco to Columbus.	Jean Nicot brings tobacco to France; nicotine named for him.	Tobacco reaches Japan.	John Rolfe establishes tobacco harvest in Virginia.	U.S. courts cite companies in smoking-related illnesses.	Ireland bans smoking in public indoor spaces.

the garden's more-than-300-year history and current work. Stroll down the path to the southern end and gaze out across the Embankment to the steel gray Thames, once London's main thoroughfare for every kind of traffic—including the barges of the venerable and resilient Chelsea Physic Garden.

A statue of Hans Sloane, the garden's 18th-century patron, presides over it, not far from a pond surrounded by Britain's oldest rockery, built using lava from Iceland, surplus stones from the Tower of London, and other materials such as the shell of the giant Pacific clam. The chubby, bewigged figure may draw some smiles now, but he was a shrewd operator for his age—or any age.

Trained as a physician, Sloane gravitated toward the botany side of medicine. During a stint to Jamaica as personal physician to its governor, he used the opportunity to collect some 800 new species of plants that he cataloged in his natural history of Jamaica. Returning to England, Sloane purchased the Chelsea estate that included the garden land and took an active role in the garden's management. He also expanded his botanical and other scientific circles and kept feelers out for botanical matters all over the world.

At Isaac Newton's death, in 1727, Sloane became president of the Royal Society, and at his own, in 1753, the British Museum was established to house the prodigious collection of specimens, paintings, books, and documentation that he left behind. His most far-reaching act with regard to the Chelsea Physic Garden, certainly appreciated by today's apothecary students who take practical training there—as well as those who seek a tranquil, green, and inspirational spot amid London's bustle—was to create a leasehold for the garden's acreage that his heirs could not break and that could be satisfied in perpetuity for the payment of a mere five pounds a year.

A Feminine Eye

For long periods during the late 1730s, the focused figure of a gentlewoman could be found making sketches at various spots around the Chelsea Physic Garden. Her name was Elizabeth Blackwell, and she was working feverishly to produce both the text and images for publication of an herbal. She had trained as an artist, so the work interested her greatly, but she was in it more for the money; she needed the proceeds to support her family and secure her husband's release from debtor's prison, where he was serving time for bankruptcy.

Isaac Rand, curator of the Chelsea Physic Garden, supported her efforts and saw that she was afforded whatever cooperation or accommodation she needed. Every night she took her day's work to the prison so that her husband, a physician, could supply the Greek and Latin and write the plant descriptions. She finished her project in record time, engraving and coloring the plates herself, and published the first volume of the work in 1737 under the somewhat cumbersome title *A curious herbal, containing five*

"The first Discovery of the West-Indies, to me seems to have been accidental, as has happen'd in most other great Discoveries."

— Hans Sloane
A Voyage to the Islands Madera, Barbados, Nieves, S. Christophers and Jamaica, 1707-1725

Cedars of Lebanon (Cedrus libani) *were planted at London's Chelsea Physic Garden in 1683, probably the first to take root in Britain. Known for their magnificent growth habits, these evergreen conifers can live more than a thousand years. In ancient Mesopotamia, forests of these trees were considered the abode of the gods.*

hundred cuts, of the most useful plants, which are now used in the practice of physick. The second half of the work came out two years later. *A curious herbal* sold well both in its first edition and in an updated version some 20 years later. Not long after he was released, Blackwell's husband left the country for Sweden and eventually wound up losing his head—literally—on a charge of conspiracy against the Swedish monarchy.

XXI

F. Keller Sculp   Marquaas

Blackwell's art was more didactic than aesthetic. It lacked the life and grace that was beginning to characterize other botanical illustration of the 18th century. But it was accurate and served the traditional purpose of the herbal as a teaching tool—and it placed Blackwell firmly in the growing ranks of talented women who were involved in the field.

INSECTS AND FLOWERS

THE ERA OF WOMEN IN BOTANICAL ILLUSTRATION HAD BEGUN EARLIER IN THE CENTURY, when Maria Sibylla Merian, a 52-year-old painter and embroidery teacher originally from Frankfurt, Germany, made the brave decision to join her daughter and son-in-law in Suriname, in northern South America, to study the insects of that tropical Dutch colony. As the daughter of a natural history publisher, Merian was drawn to entomology. Newly married in Nürnberg, she had studied closely and painted field studies of the metamorphic transformation from caterpillar to moth and butterfly. By depicting caterpillars on their host plants, Merian added the rather novel dimension of ecology to her work. She compiled her observations and art into a two-volume work, *Caterpillars, Their Wondrous Transformation and Peculiar Nourishment From Flowers*, also known as *The Caterpillar Book*.

Having left her husband and moved to Amsterdam, and now accompanied by her younger daughter, Merian left for Suriname in 1699. Enduring oppressive heat, humidity, and dangers of the jungle, she put in two long years at her task before ill health forced her to return to Europe. Her daughter Dorothea Maria helped her prepare her work for publication, with Maria Sibylla doing some of the engravings herself, and the result in 1705 was the remarkable *Metamorphosis insectorum surinamensium*, or *The Metamorphosis of the Insects of Suriname*.

Despite the emphasis on butterflies and moths, *Metamorphosis* was a botanical tour de force, as Merian had again painted each species on its host plant, providing a wealth of information about plant life in the South American outpost also known as Dutch Guiana. Her compositions were painterly and lively, and her plants were rendered equally as lushly as, or even more lavishly than, her insects. A portion of her original watercolor paintings (a canny marketer, she made at least two sets of "originals") wound up in the collection of King George III, and some were purchased by Peter the Great of Russia as well. Merian's daughters, artists in their own right, continued the family tradition of innovation in natural history illustration after Maria Sibylla's death in 1717.

THE CATESBY CONNECTION

ONE WAY OR ANOTHER, HANS SLOANE AND THE CHELSEA PHYSIC GARDEN HAD A HAND IN most things English and botanical in the 18th century. The same could be said about

"The number of plants now cultivated in England are more than double those which were here when the first edition of this book was published [in 1731]."

— PHILIP MILLER, *THE GARDENERS DICTIONARY*, 3RD EDITION, 1768

Naturalist Maria Sibylla Merian traveled from Amsterdam to Suriname, a Dutch colony, in 1699. She lived there two years, studying the natural world and creating unprecedented works of art. Depicting insects on host plants—here, the flag-legged bug on the passionflower vine—she revealed much about the relationship between plants and insects. Her work represents a first step as botanical illustration crossed over into art.

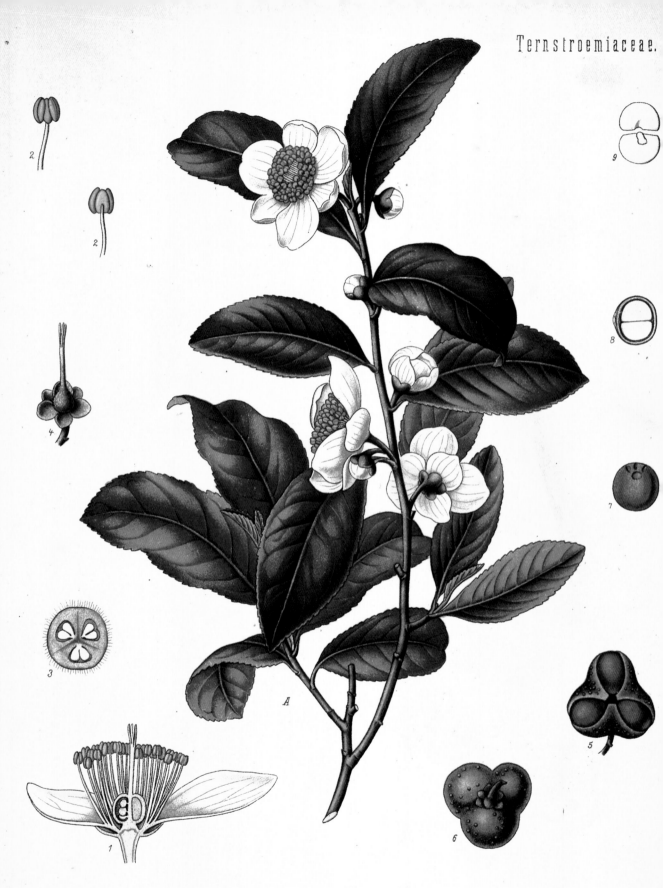

Ternstroemiaceae.

Camellia Thea Lk.

TEA

Camellia sinensis

Green tea or black tea, Darjeeling or Oolong—all tea begins as the leaves and flower buds of the tea bush *Camellia sinensis*. Two varieties of the plant have been identified, among other regional variants. The first, central to the Chinese tea culture, is *Camellia sinensis* var. *sinensis*, native to western China. A second, *Camellia sinensis* var. *assamica*, native to South and Central Asia, came into use later, although whether centuries or millennia later is unknown.

Legend has it that tea drinking in China began in 2737 B.C., when leaves from a tree blew into water that was boiling for the mythical emperor Shen Nong, and he found the drink refreshing. Texts by the fourth century A.D. mention tea frequently, and by the Tang dynasty (A.D. 618-907), tea was China's national drink, the teahouse a popular destination. Tea leaves were harvested and dried, pressed and baked into blocks. Chunks of these were then cut off, ground into a powder, and added to boiling water. Tea consumption dwindled under the Mongols but resumed with the Ming dynasty in the 14th century, when tea was brewed simply by adding loose leaves to boiling water.

In the early 1600s, East India trading ships brought tea to the rest of the world. Colonial America got a taste for it first, around 1650, a full decade before the trend hit England. When Portugal's Princess Catherine of Braganza, a tea lover, married Great Britain's King Charles II, all London took up the teacup—and the British have not put it down since.

Soon Britons were drinking more tea than either ale or gin. In 1750 the British East India Company imported 4,727,992 pounds of tea leaves. High taxes encouraged smuggling, biting into the profits of the company. To compensate for this, the British slapped huge duties on imports to the American Colonies, including tea. Outraged colonists dressed as Native Americans chucked tea chests into Boston Harbor in what was later dubbed the Boston Tea Party, the first rebel action leading up to the American Revolution.

Tea has a way of inspiring customs and traditions, which changed over the centuries and between cultures. People began adding milk and sugar; teacups gained handles; in Britain, afternoon tea evolved into a meal. The biggest 20th-century breakthrough was an accident: New York tea importer Thomas Sullivan stitched tea into small silk bags for delivery, and his customers simply poured boiling water over them. Thus was born the modern tea bag. ■

The Chinese character for tea could be pronounced tay, which is the word that English traders heard and brought home, the source for our tea.

TEA THROUGH TIME

780	815	1589	1610	1773	1898	1904
Lu Yu's *Ch'a Ching* describes tea ceremony.	Saicho, a Buddhist monk, brings seed to Japan from China.	Venetian Ramusio writes of drinking tea in Asia.	Dutch East India Company makes first shipment to Europe.	American colonists lob 342 tea chests into Boston Harbor.	Queen Victoria knights Thomas Lipton for his tea.	First iced tea served at the St. Louis World's Fair.

naturalist and explorer Mark Catesby. Catesby had a sister living in Williamsburg, and he took the opportunity of a seven-year visit to Virginia and the West Indies to collect specimens and seeds, which he sent back to England. His fame as a plant investigator spread, and he was soon on his way to the Colonies again, on a collecting expedition to Carolina sponsored by the Royal Society. Many of his specimens were sent to his patron Sloane at Chelsea.

Catesby returned to England in 1726 and began the preparation of his magnificent folio edition, *The Natural History of Carolina, Florida and the Bahama Islands,* a comprehensive account of the flora and fauna of North America. Financially pinched, he prepared the plates himself, pairing plants and animals in natural combinations, prefiguring the style of Audubon, and also introducing elements of charm and whimsy.

Catesby's work was vast in scope, covering much new ground, and was very well received. In 1768 England's King George III purchased Catesby's original art, as he had done with the work of Maria Sibylla Merian. He may have been mad in his later life, the result of a genetic disease, but the long-reigning king was a true patron of all things botanical.

The Isle of Green Thumbs

The modern notion of the English as a nation of avid gardeners who spend their weekends puttering among their roses and vegetable marrows is more than a stereotype. Gardening in Britain is a deep-seated passion, developed over the past 500 years. By the 17th century, it was abundantly clear that Britain's climate could accommodate a very wide range of plants, encouraging its busy and entrepreneurial horticulturists and plant hunters, who both created and supplied a demand for ornamental plants from all over the world.

In the earlier part of the century, John Parkinson had thoughtfully compiled and illustrated all the species of plants that currently grew in the British Isles in his 1629 *Paradisi in sole paridisus terrestris,* or *Park in Sun's Terrestrial Paradise,* which contained in its Latin title a pun on his name. It was the first comprehensive horticultural guide that anticipated all the knowledge an English gardener would need to have to establish a flower, kitchen, or orchard garden, such as what kind of plants to plant and tools to use and how to amend the soil, sow seeds, and make grafts. He later published *Theatrum botanicum (The Botanical Theater),* a work of almost 1,700 pages that included more than 3,800 plants. Parkinson had set the stage for ornamental gardening by the dedicated amateur gardener.

In the 18th century, the notion of elaborate stylized gardens with deep roots in the Italian Renaissance, French excesses inspired by the Sun

"I had principally a regard to Forest-Trees and Shrubs, shewing their several mechanical and other Uses, as in Building, Joynery, Agriculture, Food, and Medicine."

— Mark Catesby,
The Natural History of Carolina, Florida, and the Bahama Islands, 1754

Mark Catesby captures a critical moment shared by a nightjar and a mole cricket (below). Catesby often portrayed plants and animals together in a natural setting, a frog (opposite) leaping through a bog where the purple pitcher plant grows, for example.

LXX.

Rana Aquatica. *Saracena.*

King, Louis XIV, and Dutch styles such as clipped topiary brought over by William and Mary began to fade in favor of a more natural effect. Into the discussion came Lancelot "Capability" Brown, a gardener to a number of aristocratic families before hanging out his own shingle in London in 1751.

Brown earned his quirky nickname from a habit of telling potential clients that their gardens possessed "great capabilities," especially if he were hired to develop them. Brown created a gardening revolution, sweeping aside formal, regular, and angular plantings in favor of natural-looking clumps, sinuous lines, serpentine lakes, sumptuous lawns, and long vistas accented by small architectural features such as bridges and temples. Of course, this version of natural did not come naturally; it was nearly as contrived as the formal gardens it replaced, but it celebrated an idealized nature and nurtured growing romantic yearnings for the natural world.

A New World Order

Carol von Linné. Caroli Linnaei. Carolus Linnaeus. By any name, Linnaeus made an indelible mark on the botanical world—and science in general—when he published in 1735 at the age of 28 the first version of what would become his *Systema naturae (System of Nature),* a scheme of hierarchical classification for three designated kingdoms of nature: plants, animals, and rocks and minerals. He built his system from the ground up, starting with individual species and progressing through ever wider ranks, including genera, classes, and kingdoms. He also standardized naming through a system of binomial nomenclature (genus, species) that put botanists and other scientists on the same page, literally and figuratively, in discussions and publications. In the largest sense, Linnaeus imposed order on impending chaos.

The whirlwind of botanical discovery in the 17th and 18th centuries had created a conundrum, and Western scientific thinking had been struggling to keep up. The question was how to categorize, and what to call, the hundreds of plants coming into Europe from all parts of the globe so that everyone knew what the other was talking about.

Dividing the plant world into categories was not a new idea—Aristotle had done so—and Linnaeus was working in an active field in which others had laid promising and more modern groundwork. Rembert Dodoens, the 16th-century Flemish physician whose work was largely appropriated by John Gerard in his 1597 *Herball,* had already begun to question the classification systems of the ancient Greeks and Romans. English naturalist John Ray, who is credited

Swedish scientist Carolus Linnaeus first used the number and arrangement of flowers' stamens to work out his system for classifying plants—a decision with lasting impact on botany and botanical illustration.

CAROLI LINNÆI CLASSES S.LITERÆ.

"I would give any thing could I one day or other be with you, too see your dried Plants, and to give the all a nice Inspection and therough examination. But since thesse Wishes of mine are in vain, I earnestly beg the Favour of you to spare me a dried Specimen of those you have in greater plenty."

— CAROLUS LINNAEUS
LETTER TO PATRICK BROWNE,
IRISH SCIENTIST,
AUGUST 19, 1756

with coining the term "species," championed botanical classification that took into account an observation of physiological similarities and differences instead of pre-conceived categories.

Linnaeus advanced the task of organizing the vastness of the plant world by suggesting that the construction of the reproductive parts of a plant—the stamens and pistils on flowering plants, for example—provided an architecture for categories that could be applied universally. Some of his contemporaries expressed shock at the focus on reproduction—one accused him of "loathsome harlotry"—and yet the

In 1731 the young Linnaeus went to Lapland to study and collect plants, hence this endearing portrait of him in traditional Lapp clothing, carrying a shaman drum.

Rubiaceae.

COFFEE

Coffea arabica

Ethiopian tradition has it that a goatherd named Kaldi discovered coffee one day while tending his flock. Noticing how excited his goats became after eating the red berries of a particular plant, he decided to try one himself—and felt that same sort of lift. Soon people all over the country were chewing on the red berries.

It may be a folktale, but coffee is still tracked back to roots in Ethiopia. Coffee culture as we know it, though, really sprang up across the Red Sea, in Yemen. The plant takes its name from the Arabic *qahweh,* which may mean "wine of the bean." Pilgrims to Mecca carried coffee seeds with them, and in that way the plant traveled through the Arab world. By the 15th century, coffee was widely enjoyed in Turkey, Persia, Egypt, and across North Africa.

The Ottoman Turks, who controlled Yemen by the first part of the 16th century, took great pains to maintain their monopoly on coffee. Exportation from Yemeni ports was closely watched, and seeds leaving the country were dropped in boiling water to prohibit germination. By 1616, however, seeds had been smuggled out of Yemen to India, where the Dutch acquired them

Only men were served in London coffeehouses like this one in the early 1700s. Some women objected, not to their exclusion but to their husbands' long absences from home as they sipped, read, visited, smoked, and debated.

and began coffee cultivation on the island of Java. A Venetian merchant introduced the stimulating drink to Europe, which went crazy for coffee.

By the late 1600s coffeehouses could be found in every major European city. London coffeehouses were male-only institutions, places to sit and sip and read shared newspapers and argue politics. King Charles II tried to ban them for being "the great resort of Idle and disaffected persons," but patrons went up in arms, and the ban was lifted before it ever went into law.

In the early 1700s a young French naval officer named Gabriel Mathieu de Clieu stole some clippings from the king's garden in Paris and carried them to the Caribbean island of Martinique. From them the South American coffee industry grew. Coffee shrubs grew so successfully in Brazil that by 1800 huge harvests flooded the markets around the world, making the drink affordable to the masses. Today coffee is a global commodity. Nearly one-third of the world drinks it, either hot or cold, still appreciating that caffeine lift that Kaldi's goats felt. In fact, next to water, coffee is the most consumed drink on the planet. ■

COFFEE THROUGH TIME

ca 920	1511	1615	1688	1825	1930	1971
Arab physician Rhazes calls coffee hot, dry, and good for the stomach.	Mecca governor enforces short-lived ban on coffee-houses.	Pope Clement VIII baptizes coffee as a Christian drink.	Edward Lloyd opens London coffee-house, becoming Lloyd's of London.	Coffee planted in Hawaii.	Nestlé invents instant coffee under contract with Brazil.	First Starbucks opens in Seattle, Washington.

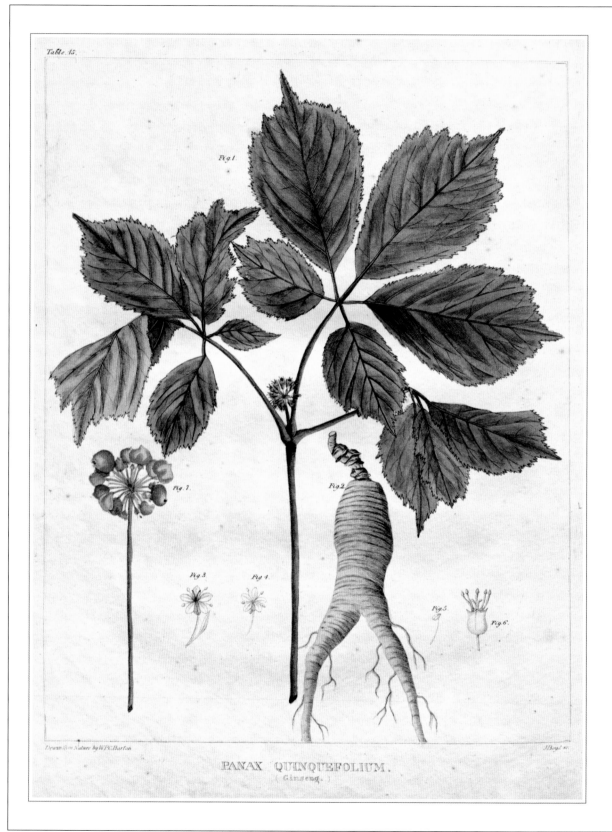

PANAX QUINQUEFOLIUM.
(Ginseng.)

practice worked well, despite some complications, and has served the life sciences admirably to the present day. (Rocks and minerals were dropped from the classification scheme eventually.)

Thanks to Linnaeus, for example, an unwieldy descriptive classification such as *Palma Brasiliensis prunifera folio plicatili seu flabelli formi caudice squamato* (Brazilian palm tree with a scaly trunk bearing fruit on a fan-shaped leaf), offered by Hans Sloane for the thatch palm of Jamaica, became, according to the Linnaean system, *Acrocomia spinosa* (spiny top-hair)—simple, elegant, more easily remembered, and more easily discussed. Advances in genetics also inform modern taxonomy, but Linnaeus's contributions retain their trailblazing status.

Born in Sweden in 1707, Linnaeus gravitated toward botany but trained as a physician, receiving his medical degree in the Netherlands. He traveled widely in search of botanical and ethnographic specimens on the Scandinavian Peninsula, visiting the northern reaches of Lapland. For his magnum opus, which he updated and expanded throughout his life, Linnaeus mainly relied on others to collect specimens for him or to share their own collections in his attempt to be as inclusive as possible. He was in constant contact with hundreds of botanists, other scientists, explorers, artists, and philosophers—in fact, with most of his era's greatest minds. Some species he knew only through art created by others, such as the insects of Suriname painted by Maria Sibylla Merian and a number of North American birds in the illustrations of Mark Catesby.

THE FAR REACH OF CAROLUS LINNAEUS

LINNAEUS LEARNED FROM BOTANICAL ARTISTS, AND he also taught them how to paint in a way that made their work more useful to botanists. He profoundly influenced Georg Dionysius Ehret, a German painter who would establish a style much emulated among future generations of botanical illustrators. Ehret collaborated with Linnaeus on documenting the amazing collection on the estate of George Clifford, a Dutch East India Company director, near Haarlem in the Netherlands. The botanist convinced Ehret of the value of including the smallest details of plant anatomy in his paintings, which were published in the 1738 masterpiece *Hortus Cliffortianus (Clifford's Garden)*. Although at first Ehret resisted, not wanting to detract from the overall image, he relented—and the world of botanical illustration is all the better for it to this day.

American ginseng
Panax quinquefolium

At least ten species of ginseng grow worldwide. The genus name, *Panax*, derives from a Greek word meaning "panacea" or "cure-all." American ginseng (*P. quinquefolium*) is closely related to Asian ginseng (*P. ginseng*). Ginseng is considered an adaptogen—a substance that helps the body adapt to stress with few side effects. Though ancient texts refer to ginseng's use for cooling and calming, digestive distress, and nutrition, ginseng is widely used today to strengthen the immune system, treat diabetes and cancer, and for energy, strength, stamina, and vigor.

New World riches: The root of American ginseng (opposite) is prized for its curative properties. With a new source in America, traders could fill the demand in the East that had already stripped Asian forests of a related plant. When the Chilean strawberry (left), noted for large berries, was accidentally bred with a flavorful wild American strawberry, the result was the strawberry grown commercially today.

Ehret moved from the Netherlands to London, where he contributed to the illustrations of key plants in the *The Gardeners Dictionary,* published in 1768 by Philip Miller, the Scottish horticulturist who served as head gardener at the Chelsea Physic Garden. Ehret also married Miller's wife's sister, further solidifying his relationship with those in London botanical circles.

Linnaeus carried on an enormous correspondence with at least 600 different individuals of many nationalities, writing his letters as well as his publications in Latin, the lingua franca of learning and science. With input from all these sources he published the capstone of his botanical work, *Species plantarum (Plant Species),* in 1753.

Despite his scientific approach, Linnaeus espoused a divine influence on the nature of hierarchical classification. Writing in the preface to a late edition of *Systema naturae,* Linnaeus, the son of a Lutheran pastor, declared unabashedly: *"Creationis telluris est Gloria Dei ex opere Naturae per Hominem solum*—Earth's creation is the glory of God, as seen from the works of Nature by Man alone."

AMERICAN PLANT HUNTERS

THE ENGLISH WERE KEEN ON EXOTICS IN THEIR GARDENS, AND demand for North American plants had been well primed by what they learned from Catesby's *Natural History.* Into the picture came a father-son duo—in the tradition of the Tradescants of 17th-century London—Pennsylvania Quakers John Bartram and his young son, named William.

Like other Quakers there, the Bartrams were keenly interested in botanical matters, seen as fitting curricula in their schools. Farmer Bartram had started a botanical garden at his home in 1729 that drew many visitors from the Colonies and overseas. Possessed also of an entrepreneurial spirit, Bartram was quick to cash in on the potential of the European plant trade. With a patron in London who furnished European plants for the colonists and found customers for American species, the Bartrams created a thriving enterprise. In addition to moving plants back and forth across the Atlantic, they were able to sell sets of seeds containing about a hundred varieties each, which could create, in a manner of speaking, an instant North American flora for the successful gardener. Not surprisingly, the Bartrams also joined the rest of the international community of plant hunters in supplying Linnaeus with important specimens for his work.

The grapefruit (Citrus x paradisi), *believed to be a hybrid of the pomelo with the sweet orange, was first brought to Europe from Jamaica in 1693.*

59

Pub by J. Ridgway 170 Piccadilly Oct 1 1815.

Passionflower
Passiflora spp.

Native Americans of the eastern United States applied the crushed leaves of passionflower to heal and reduce swelling in bruises and wounds. Infusions of the pounded roots were used to wean babies and as drops for ear infections. A tea made from the vine was drunk to soothe nerves. Throughout the past few centuries, passionflower continued to be used in folk remedies as a "calming" herb. In 1978 the U.S. Food and Drug Administration listed it as "not generally recognized as safe and effective," although passionflower is still widely used in Europe.

The passionflower (Passiflora spp.) grows worldwide and has long been valued as a source of medicine and food. The common name refers to the Passion of Christ, and many flower parts have been connected to aspects of Jesus' life. The flower's radial filaments represent the crown of thorns, for example.

Plate 129.

3

4

1

2

2

Guinea Pepper

Eliz. Blackwell delin. sculp. et Pinx.

1. Flower
2. Fruit
3. Fruit open
4. Seed

Piper indicum

PEPPERS

Capsicum spp.

ewfound spices, and in particular black pepper from India, had smitten the taste buds of wealthy Europeans in the 15th century, but the love affair was becoming expensive. Venice held a monopoly on the spice trade, in large part an impetus for Spanish monarchs Ferdinand and Isabella to support Christopher Columbus's sail west in search of a new and cheaper route to the Indies, land of spices. When Columbus first made landfall, he assumed he had reached his desired destination and named those islands the West Indies. There Columbus found no black pepper, but he did find the locals flavoring their food with a spicy red fruit that they called *aji*. Columbus named the plant the "pepper of the Indies," assuming some relation between the two spicy flavors.

The plant that bears the fruit that we still call pepper today was common throughout the New World at that time. Bearing fruit of many shapes, sizes, and tastes, capsicum peppers most likely came under cultivation between 7,000 and 4,500 years ago, and scientists today believe that pepper species had been growing across Central and South America long before humans even arrived. They bear no botanical relationship to black pepper.

Fuchs's 1549 herbal showed three capsicum pepper varieties, two labeled Indianischer—*Indian.*

Columbus transported capsicum peppers back to Spain, where they received little attention, but they did make their way into the hands of botanists in Portugal. Shortly thereafter, Vasco da Gama set sail in search of new routes to the Indies, and, by rounding the Cape of Good Hope, he reached India—and black pepper. He carried New World peppers with him, and their pungent flavor, caused by the nitrogen compound now named capsaicin, intrigued those who tasted it in India. The capsicum pepper fruit was quickly adapted to local cuisines, and within 30 years several varieties were being grown across Eurasia.

In 1542 the capsicum pepper returned to Europe, this time coming in from the east. The plant and its marvelous culinary uses had traveled west from India, across the Middle East, and through Turkey, influencing many cuisines along the way. The German botanist Leonhard Fuchs was so sure that the plant, like other spices, originated in the Indies, he named it the Calicut or Indian pepper. Today more than 200 species and varieties of peppers grow around the world, essential to many cuisines, from paprika in Hungarian goulash to jalapeños in Mexican salsa, from cayennes in Thai curries to chilis in Peruvian ceviche. ■

PEPPERS THROUGH TIME

ca 2500 B.C.	1493	1530	1585	1615	1869	1912
Peppers eaten in South and Central America.	Explorers take seed back to Spain.	Three chili varieties are grown near Goa, India.	Peppers being grown in Italy, Germany, England, and the Balkans.	Conquistadores collect New World plants, called *chilli*, red, in Nahuatl.	Tabasco sauce first manufactured for market on Avery Island, Louisiana.	Scoville heat unit invented to rate hotness.

The Bartrams gained other fans in high places. Ever the plant lover, King George III appointed John Bartram as his North American botanist, and spurred on by his London agent, an aging John set off in 1760 with William for points south in search of more unusual species than those native to their usual botanizing grounds of the mid-Atlantic seaboard.

The expedition provided the Bartrams with a number of firsts, including the discovery in the swamps of southeastern Georgia of a flowering tree, which they named the Franklin tree *(Franklinia alatamaha)* in honor of their good friend and fellow Pennsylvanian Benjamin Franklin. Unfortunately for both Franklin and future biodiversity, the species had a precarious range, from which it disappeared altogether sometime around 1790. A relative of the camellia, it is now known only from cultivars, including descendants of specimens brought by the Bartrams back to Pennsylvania.

William Bartram made a solo expedition to the South in the 1770s, covering more ground than he had with his father. His path took him as far as Mobile, Alabama, and Baton Rouge, Louisiana. Along the way, the younger Bartram collected some 200 plants, which he sent to a new Quaker patron in England. His account of the more than three-year-long journey was published in *Travels Through North & South Carolina, Georgia, East & West Florida,* with his own competent illustrations. In the corner of one of his plates appear the tooth-edged leaves of the Venus flytrap *(Dionaea muscipula),* the first capture of the species in illustration. He also drew and described several American species of pitcher plant. Not surprisingly, European botanists and horticulturists were fascinated by North America's carnivorous plants.

Although enthusiastically received, *Travels* contained many exaggerated descriptions that could fall into the well-known American tradition of tall tales. In his later life William stopped botanizing and traveling entirely and retired to the family home, giving over the care of even the garden to a brother. Part of his collection later went to Joseph Banks, the English botanist and organizer for the first expedition by Captain James Cook across the Pacific, and many of his specimens and illustrations are now housed in the British Museum.

MAGNOLIA *foliis ovato oblongis ad basin et apicem angustis, utrinqs virentib.*

A magnolia's lush white flower and sturdy leaves are captured in vivid detail by Georg Dionysius Ehret, who drew from life, transferred the images to copper plates for engraving, and hand-colored them.

AROUND THE WORLD WITH CAPTAIN COOK

IN 1768 THE BRITISH ADMIRALTY DECIDED TO UNDERTAKE A SYSTEMATIC EXPLORATION OF the Pacific Ocean and its islands. The voyage followed the French transoceanic journey

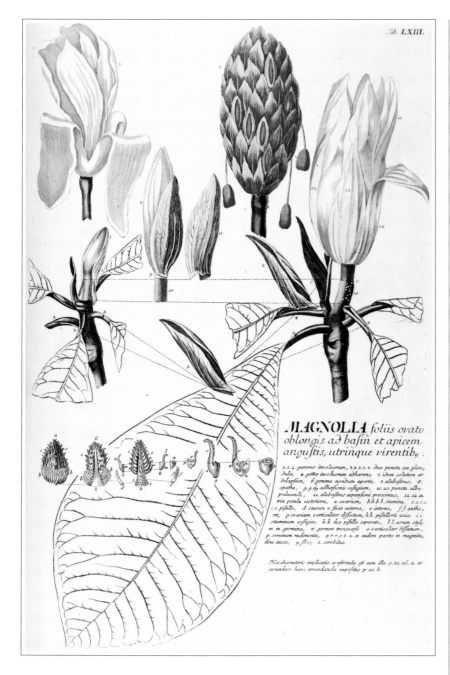

Tab. LXIII.

MAGNOLIA *foliis ovato oblongis ad basin et apicem angustis, utrinque virentib.*

1.2.2. gemmæ involucrum, 3.3.3.3. duo puncta seu glandulæ, 4. gestæ involucrum adhærens, 5. idem solutum et delapsum, 6. gemma nondum aperta, 7. alabastrus, 8. spatha, 9.9.9. adhæsionis vestigium, 10.10. puncta alba pedunculi, 11. alabastrus expansioni proximus, 12.12.12. tria petala exteriora, a. ovarium, b.b.b.b. stamina, c.c.c.c. pistilla, d. stamen a facie externa, e. interna, f.f. antheræ, g. ovarium verticaliter dissectum, h.h. pistillorū axis, i.i. staminum vestigia, k.k. duo pistilla separata, l.l. eorum stylo m.m. germina, n. germen transverso o. verticaliter dissectum, p. seminum rudimenta, q.r.r.s.t.u.x. eadem partes in magnitudine auctæ, y. flos, z. strobilus.

Hæc characteris explicatio conferenda est cum illa p. 81. col. a. et secundum hanc emendanda expositio p. 90. b.

"If I can any ways oblige thee with specimens seeds or plants or any information my poor Capacity can contribute, none can do it more Cherefully then thy sincear friend."

— John Bartram, letter to Carolus Linnaeus, March 20, 1753

A gardener turned artist, Ehret became the most famous botanical illustrator of the 18th century. He worked with Linnaeus and for George Clifford, an officer of the Dutch East India Company passionate about collecting plants. Ehret later moved to London and painted many plants held in botanical gardens there.

conducted by Louis-Antoine de Bougainville from 1766 to 1768 and included as physician and botanist Philibert Commerson, a student of Linnaeus's.

Cook's expedition was designed to coincide with the transit of Venus across the sun, an astronomical event whose observation and measurement would greatly aid the science of navigation. To that task they assigned a seasoned navy lieutenant—as a ship's commander he was referred to as Captain—James Cook, who had established

"Since then a plentiful perspiration is found so necessary for the health of a plant or tree, 'tis probable that many of their distempers are owing to a stoppage of this perspiration, by inclement air."

— **STEPHEN HALES**
VEGETABLE STATICKS, OR, AN ACCOUNT OF SOME STATICAL EXPERIMENTS ON THE SAP IN VEGETABLES, 1727

Caribbean plants were the special interest of French physician Michel Etienne Descourtilz, who lived in Haiti. His Flore médicale des Antilles *featured many plants little known in Europe: coconuts, mangoes, papayas, and this cactus, whose common name he reported to be* patte de tortue—*tortoise paw.*

Pl.68.

Théodore Descourtilz Pinx.

Gabriel Sculp.

CACTIER RETICULÉ.

his navigation credentials in a five-year survey of the coasts of Newfoundland, creating and refining techniques that would become standard in naval surveying.

Cook's mandate, which included orders to search for a fabled southern continent east of New Zealand, was broadened when a young gentleman-botanist named Joseph Banks successfully petitioned the Admiralty to join the expedition in order to document all that the sea—and land areas—had to offer in the way of flora and fauna. To that end Banks assembled a talented entourage of natural history experts.

What today might be called Team Banks was a diverse group of individuals with various kinds of expertise, each with a part to play in the well-planned expedition. Banks himself was educated at Oxford and at 25 already was an experienced plant hunter and the youngest person nominated to be a member of the Royal Society at that time. He and a prep school friend previously had sailed to Newfoundland and Labrador and collected some 340 plants, in addition to other specimens. The wealthy Banks, who came into his full inheritance when he turned 18 years old, bankrolled the necessary equipment for the *Endeavour* expedition, to the tune of some 20 tons and an estimated £10,000.

For artists, Banks recruited Sydney Parkinson, a Scottish Quaker who had acquired a reputation in London as a fine painter of flowers on silk, and Alexander Buchan, a portrait and landscape artist. Banks also signed on Daniel Solander, a Swedish naturalist and another student of Linnaeus's who had moved to England in 1760 on the taxonomist's suggestion to promote his system of classification. The expedition also acquired the services of astronomer Charles Green, as well as an assistant for Solander, the German secretary and draftsman Herman Spöring.

The Cook expedition set sail on the newly refitted *Endeavour* from Plymouth in August 1768 and made directly for Madeira, the Portuguese archipelago off the northwestern coast of Africa. During the short stopover, Banks and Solander managed to collect about 700 specimens—and they had not even left Europe.

Reaching Brazil more than a month later, the expedition ran into some governmental suspicion and red tape, and the duo had to sneak over the side of the ship in Rio de Janeiro and row to shore at night to make covert forays into the countryside to obtain plants. Cook was reluctant to make landfall elsewhere in South America, but adverse conditions in the area of Cape Horn made a break necessary. Banks and Solander wasted no time in getting to shore with other crew members, anxious to explore

Published in 1727, Stephen Hales's Vegetable Staticks *was the first significant book on plant physiology, explaining the movement of air and water in roots, stems, and leaves.*

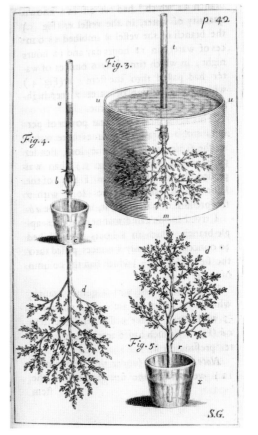

2.   3.   1   4.   5.

a. b.

CINCHONA

Cinchona officinalis

The European conquistadores brought many things to the Americas, including diseases. Malaria may have been one of them. Documented in China as early as 2700 B.C., the disease caused fevers, chills, and swift death. Its cause was a mystery, although many associated it with the fumes of swamplands—hence the name malaria, which comes from the Latin for "bad air."

Ironically, a plant known to native South Americans ended up curing the imported disease. While cinchona is not mentioned in the official pharmacopoeia of either the Inca or the Aztec, this tropical native went by the common name "fever-tree," suggesting indigenous knowledge of its medicinal use, but no one knows how its antimalarial properties were discovered.

Tradition tells of a European soldier in South America who fell ill and, left to die, drank from a water hole into which a cinchona tree had fallen. The bitter water cured him.

From the same tree bark, so another story goes, a curative tea was brewed for the Countess Chinchón, wife of the viceroy of Peru, when she fell ill with malaria. Soon samples of the precious bark were carried back to Europe. Most called the remedy "Peruvian bark,"

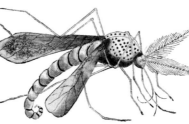

Not until 1898 was it known that mosquitoes transmitted malaria, but cinchona's effectiveness against the disease had been known for 200 years.

but ultimately Linnaeus renamed the plant after the Peruvian countess: Cinchona.

The remedy for malaria was not introduced to Europe until the 1630s, when it finally reached Spain from Peru, but by 1677 the bark was used as an antimalarial throughout Europe. In 1820 French pharmacists Pierre-Joseph Pelletier and Joseph-Bienaimé Caventou isolated the active malaria-fighting ingredient, a bitter alkaloid found in the bark of the cinchona tree. They named it "quinine," after the native term *quina quina,* bark of barks.

For more than a century, quinine was the only known cure for malaria, and for decades the precious substance was extracted from bark harvested in South America. Finally European entrepreneurs established plantations in Java, Ceylon, and India, planting South American seed. While posted in India, British sailors, commanded to drink the bitter tonic to stave off malaria, added gin to it—the origin of the cocktail that many still drink for pleasure.

The Japanese invasion of the Dutch West Indies during World War II cut off the supply of quinine to the Allies, spurring laboratory chemists to synthesize it in 1944. No synthetic quinine has proved as effective as the original botanical. ∎

CINCHONA THROUGH TIME

2700 B.C.	A.D. 1630	1638	by 1677	1820	1860	1944
Malaria symptoms first reported in China.	Spanish Jesuit priests in Peru learn of cinchona.	Fever tree bark said to cure the Countess Chinchón in Peru.	Peruvian bark used against malaria in England and Italy.	Pelletier and Caventou isolate quinine.	British and Dutch plant American seed in Java, Ceylon, and India.	Woodward and Doering synthesize quinine.

the alpine plants that grew in the craggy lands of Tierra del Fuego at the tip of South America. A summer blizzard caught them off guard, however, and two of the party died of hypothermia.

BOTANIZING THE PACIFIC

ROUNDING THE HORN, THE *ENDEAVOUR* SAILED TO TAHITI, WHERE THE VENUS TRANSIT was observed and recorded. Banks and Solander continued to collect plants efficiently and kept vivid journals, full of detailed and insightful observations of the Tahitian people and culture. The *Endeavour* sailed on, and the Cook expedition now laid open the treasures of New Zealand and the wondrous island continent of Australia.

In New Zealand Banks and Solander identified a kind of spinach that was cooked and pickled and taken on board to replace the sauerkraut that the innovative Cook insisted his crew eat to ward off scurvy. He made them drink lime juice for the same reason, before the consumption of limes was de rigueur for the British Navy. The botanizing duo also collected specimens of New Zealand flax *(Phormium tenax),* admired then for its fibers and now also as an ornamental plant in English gardens.

Landing on the east coast of Australia, Banks and Solander amassed a collection of more than a thousand plants including discoveries such as eucalyptus, acacia, mimosa, and the spectacular Illawarra flame tree *(Brachychiton acerifolius),* a species that grows up to 40 feet tall, covered in vivid red bell-shaped flowers. In recognition of the floral bounty acquired on this first landing, Cook named the spot Botany Bay.

Heading northward, the *Endeavour* was nearly lost when it struck coral in the Great Barrier Reef. Banks and Solander quite naturally used the time needed for ship repairs to collect fine specimens of timber trees as well as kangaroo grass *(Themeda triandra),* the source of nutritious seeds that could be baked into cakes.

The last leg of the *Endeavour* voyage took a heavy toll on the expedition. Despite the health precautions Cook had put in place, he was not able to prevent the outbreaks of fever, typhoid, dysentery, and tuberculosis that increased significantly toward the end. He lost more than 30 men, including Buchan, who died as the result of an epileptic seizure, and Spöring and Parkinson, both from fever.

Before his untimely death, Sydney Parkinson left more than a thousand paintings and sketches in various stages of completion. They had been supervised by Solander, and they were scientifically rigorous in their detail. Joseph Banks would later use his own money to have these illustrations completed, and 738 plates were engraved, but that is as far as it went. The plates as well as the illustrations and herbaria remained in the Banks collection at the British Museum. The first edition of Parkinson's Australian plants was not published until the early 20th century, and a complete *Florilegium* would not appear until the 1980s. Upon his return to England, Banks was lionized, receiving attention that upstaged Cook's own. By today's standards it is hard to imagine a

The crown flower (Calotropis gigantea), *native to Southeast Asia and Indonesia, takes its name from the complex configuration at the center of its waxy purple flowers. First grown at the Royal Garden in Hampton Court in the 1690s, this shrub was cultivated by the English as a hothouse curiosity.*

botanist as a kind of rock star, but Banks filled the bill. In his 1773 portrait by Joshua Reynolds he certainly looks the part—handsome, wealthy, powerful.

Banks tried to manipulate the adulation he enjoyed into an even grander role on the second Cook voyage, but his plan backfired. This was but a minor hiccup in a long and prestige-filled life that included a baronetcy in 1781 and 42 years in the longest ever presidency of the Royal Society, from 1778 to 1820. Banks also became botanical adviser to King George III, whose interest in plants and agriculture may have contributed to his somewhat mocking nickname, Farmer George. In many ways, the way in which Joseph Banks and his scientific passion would make a lasting difference was through the central role he was to play on one of the king's pet projects, the development of the gardens at Kew.

KEW: BANKS MAKES HIS MARK

THE TRACT NOW KNOWN AS THE ROYAL BOTANIC GARDENS AT KEW OCCUPIES 300 ACRES at a bend in the Thames River in southwestern London. Established in 1759 by the dowager Princess Augusta, widow of the Prince of Wales (the first son of King George II), Kew began as a private physic garden patterned on the one at Chelsea. At Augusta's death in 1772, her son George—King George III—obtained the property and spent a lot of time there. He put Banks in charge—albeit unofficially—and so Joseph Banks became the driving force behind the garden's acquisitions and development for the next 30 years, setting its trajectory on the way to becoming a world-class research garden.

Under Banks, Kew received many of the 7,000 or so new plants that came into Britain during his tenure. Kew continued as royal property before being turned over to the nation in 1840. From his position as the king's main adviser on matters botanical, Banks continued to wield major influence outside of Kew as well, deploying many individuals on botanical missions and even outfitting the new British penal colony in Australia (itself a Banks idea) with the plants he thought it needed.

Banks's good friend Carl Linnaeus, son of the famous Carolus, awed by the vastness of the plant discoveries made on Cook's first voyage, proposed that the territory of New South Wales in Australia be called Banksia. That was not to be, but Linnaeus did end up naming in his honor a genus of spiky-flowered trees and shrubs distinctive to the Australia landscape, plants that Banks himself had collected. Today, *Banksia* includes some 170 species. Later Banks's wife, Lady Dorothea, was honored with a thornless, double-blossomed and prolific climbing rose, native to China, the *Rosa banksiae*. And although botanical quests had already taken explorers and plant hunters into many new directions around the world, the natural history component of the first Cook voyage—orchestrated by Joseph Banks—was an unparalleled undertaking in its depth, breadth, and length, which set the bar for planning and scientific rigor and the scene for botanical endeavors to come during the Enlightenment. ⌒

"By mixing the useful and profitable parts of Gard'ning with the Pleasurable . . . My Designs are thereby vastly enlarg'd and both Profit and Pleasure may be agreeably mix'd together."

— STEPHEN SWITZER, *THE NOBLEMAN, GENTLEMAN AND GARDENER'S RECREATION,* 1745

The tallest of the lilies native to North America, the Turk's-cap lily (Lilium superbum) was first noted by Mark Catesby in 1738. The plant, a favorite in the perennial garden, has curving petals that must have reminded 18th-century observers of Ottoman turbans.

Tab. XI.

LILIVM *folius sparsis,* *multiflorum, floribus reflexis,*
fundo aureo, limbo auran- *tio, punctis nigricantibus,*
pedunculis singulis *unico folio instructis.*

FLORA

GRÆCA

Sibthorpiana.

CENTURIA PRIMA,

1806

MONS PARNASSUS.

ENLIGHTENMENT
1770–1840

During the last years of the 18th century, the scientific impetus of the Enlightenment promoted even more ambitious expeditions to further botanical knowledge. From the perspective of philosopher Jean-Jacques Rousseau, Nature was sacred and inspiring, and its contemplation and appreciation broadened the spirit. Botanical illustration shared such ideals when technical improvements in engraving that rendered detail more clearly and those in printing and coloring met the unbounded enthusiasm of illustrators who marveled at their subject matter. Illustrations provided viewers with armchair transport to increasingly exotic and intriguing destinations. By the early 19th century, though, real travel was beginning to replace vicarious experience, and weekend artists were creating their own flora and landscapes, reflecting the sentiments of the Romantic movement in poetry and painting. Art was certainly served by the beauty of the botanical illustrations of the late 18th century, as was science——and the marketplace. The illustrated natural histories, herbals, and florilegia were pored over in the manner of modern corporate reports, with an eye for clues to investment and entrepreneurial opportunities based on plants that were valuable for food, medicine, or their ornamental qualities. 〜

Flora Graeca, *a ten-volume opus based on fieldwork in Greece in the 1780s, was published between 1806 and 1840. Each volume contained a hundred botanical illustrations by Ferdinand Bauer, whose attention to detail replicated that of a scientist.* PRECEDING PAGES: Crinum augustum *was an amaryllis included among the "brilliant and fugitive beauties" collected in Africa for English gardeners by the 1830s.*

	KNOWLEDGE & SCIENCE	POWER & WEALTH	HEALTH & MEDICINALS
AFRICA & MIDDLE EAST	**1775** Francis Masson brings a cycad from South Africa to London's Kew Gardens, where it still lives today, one of the world's oldest potted plants. **1804-07** French naturalist A. M. F. J. Palisot de Beauvois publishes a two-volume book on the flora of West Africa, *Flore d'Oware et de Benin en Afrique.*	*"No occupation is so delightful to me as the culture of the earth, and no culture comparable to that of the garden."* — THOMAS JEFFERSON, LETTER TO CHARLES WILLSON PEALE, 1811	
ASIA & OCEANIA	**1772-75** Johann and Georg Forster, father and son, sail with Cook to the Pacific, Georg creating botanical illustrations. **1787** The British East India Company establishes a botanic garden in Calcutta. **1800-1810** George Caley botanizes in New South Wales, Australia, for Kew Gardens. **1818** In Sumatra, Joseph Arnold discovers the world's largest flower, named *Rafflesia* for the governor of the British East India Company there.	**1784** The first American ship to arrive in China, *The Empress of China,* carries American ginseng in trade for silk and tea. **1787** Food riots begin in Osaka, Japan, targeting rice warehouses, and soon spread to other large cities. **1823** China's monopoly on tea ends when indigenous Assam tea bushes are discovered in eastern India.	**1792** The bark of a native redwood of India, *Soymida febrifuga,* is used to treat fevers in a Danish colony in Tranquebar, India. **1793-1813** William Roxburgh, as superintendent of the British East India Company's botanical gardens, collects and studies native Indian plants and herbal remedies.
EUROPE	**1789-1791** Erasmus Darwin, grandfather of Charles, publishes *The Botanic Garden.* **1787** William Curtis begins publishing his *Botanical Magazine.* Ten years later its rival, *Botanist's Repertory,* appears. **1830s** The Wardian case—an early terrarium—makes transporting plants easier. **1831-36** Englishman Charles Darwin sails to the Galápagos aboard the H.M.S. *Beagle.*	**1820** On the death of Joseph Banks, a campaign begins to turn Kew into a natural garden. **1840** Kew is established as a national botanic garden.	**1790-94** William Woodville's encyclopedic *Medical Botany* is published as three volumes in London. Two more volumes are published after his death. **1821** John Lindley's *Monographia Digitalium* lists 23 different species of foxglove, not all known today.
THE AMERICAS	**1818** Thomas Nuttall's *Genera of North American Plants* is published in Philadelphia. **1837** The first volume of James Bateman's *Orchidaceae of Mexico & Guatemala* is published.	**1801** David Hosack establishes the 20-acre Elgin Botanical Garden in New York on site of today's Rockefeller Center.	*Foxglove* (Digitalis), *a late-discovered medicinal*

SUSTENANCE & FLAVOR	CLOTHING & SHELTER	BEAUTY & SYMBOLISM	

1772 Carl Pieter Thunberg collects bird-of-paradise *(Strelitzia)* in Africa and ships them to Sweden.

1816 Freesia is first brought from Africa to Europe.

18th-century garden design

1790 Joseph Banks brings tree peonies from China to London's Kew Gardens.

1796 London nurseries are growing irises brought from Japan.

1804 William Kerr brings the first tiger lily from China to Kew Gardens.

1818 Tea inspector John Reeves ships wisteria from China to London's Horticultural Society.

1791 Captain William Bligh carries breadfruit from Polynesia to the Americas.

1788-89 Crop failures mean prices for bread in France rise so high that many cannot afford it. Riots presage the coming French Revolution.

1810 Beet sugar factories open in France in response to British blockade of cane sugar.

1817 John Claudius Loudon invents the wrought iron glazing bar, soon used in building greenhouses.

South American hummingbird

1775 Richard Weston lists 575 hyacinth varieties available in England.

1799 France's Joséphine, wife of Napoleon, buys Malmaison and begins developing her rose gardens there.

1820s William Herbert develops daffodil, crocus, amaryllis, and gladiolus hybrids in England.

by 1830 European horticulturists have developed the pansy for gardens.

1785 Manasseh Cutler presents a paper on "vegetable productions," considered the first horticultural record of New England.

1818 German doctor Johann Siegert extracts angostura bitters from the bark of a South American tree, *Gallipea aspuria*.

1820 The primary pineapple cultivar—Smooth Cayenne, first found wild in Venezuela—is shipped from French Guiana to France.

1825 Coffee is first planted in Hawaii and in Central America, destined to be important growing locales.

1772 Pine Tree Riots in New Hampshire—colonists claiming ownership of mast-worthy white pine lumber—presage the American Revolution.

1793 Eli Whitney invents the cotton gin.

1826-27 David Douglas travels the American Northwest for the Royal Horticultural Society, discovering many species, especially coniferous trees.

1804 Alexander von Humboldt sends dahlia seeds from South America to Germany.

1823 The petunia is brought from South America to Europe, quickly becoming a favorite bedding and window plant.

*With Captain James Cook, Joseph Banks collected at least 800 plants in the South Pacific, 738 of which appeared as black-and-white engravings first, such as these of Australia's black bean (*Castanospermum, *near right) and* Banksia serrata *(far right).*

CAPTAIN JAMES COOK'S FIRST VOYAGE, ALTHOUGH IT HAD LASTED three years, was more or less a reconnaissance. Navigationally, Cook had not accomplished one of his main objectives: He had not definitively proved the nonexistence of a mythical southern continent, a Terra Australis that was not Australia or Antarctica but a continent farther south. From the natural history point of view, the time spent by Joseph Banks and Daniel Solander at Botany Bay in southeastern Australia while the *Endeavour* underwent emergency repairs had just whetted European appetites for knowledge of the continent's unusual flora and fauna. A second voyage, then, became a foregone conclusion. After the successes of the first one, it seemed natural that the indispensable Banks would be part of the second. But he made so many demands for specialized crew, equipment, and accommodation that he talked himself out of the enterprise. When Cook's second voyage sailed in 1772 with the ships *Resolution* and *Adventure,* it carried a different natural history team that included the father and son botanists Polish-born Johann Reinhold Forster and 18-year-old Georg Adam Forster.

CAPTAIN COOK SAILS AGAIN

DURING THE THREE-YEAR VOYAGE, INCLUDING TWO GRAND PASSES ACROSS THE PACIFIC, they collected hundreds of plant and animal specimens and the younger Forster made a similar number of drawings. In the group of islands west of Fiji that Cook named the New Hebrides, they discovered the exotic pine *Araucaria columnaris,* which

CASTANOSPERMUM AUSTRALE Cunn. & Fraser.

BOSTYLIS SERRATA Britten.

Distinctively Australian trees and shrubs with showy floral spikes now bear the name of the great botanical explorer Joseph Banks. All told, there are more than 150 different Banksia *varieties, including this magnificent* Banksia occidentalis, *which became a favorite greenhouse plant in Europe.*

became known as the Cook pine, and farther on toward New Zealand, the delicate and well-organized Norfolk Island pine *(Araucaria heterophylla)*. On their return to England, the Forsters quickly published their botanical findings in *Characteres Generum Plantarum (Descriptions of New Genera of Plants)*. A kind of bare-bones botanical record, *Characteres* also contained bare-bones illustrations, tiny engravings based on Georg's illustrations.

Cook's third voyage began in 1776, again on the *Resolution* and on the *Discovery,* a different second ship. His destination this time was mainly the northern Pacific and his goal the discovery of the Northwest Passage. Two visits to the Hawaiian Islands, making the crew the first European visitors there, could not have been more different.

Specimens of the flesh-colored justicia (Justicia carnea), *as it was then called, circulated among horticulturists in Scotland and England in the 1830s, after having been collected from its Rio de Janeiro home.*

On the first Cook was treated as a god. On the second his crew met with hostility and a small expedition boat was stolen, with the end result that Cook was mobbed and stabbed to death in 1779. This voyage carried the mild-mannered David Nelson, a gardener from Kew and a breath of fresh air compared with the obstreperous Johann Forster, but little of his collections survives, apart from some specimens such as *Kokia drynarioides,* or the Hawaiian cotton tree.

With the start of the American Revolution in the middle of the third voyage, Benjamin Franklin, who admired Cook's maritime and scientific contributions and the man himself, worried that the commander and his ships could come to harm if spotted or seized. To do what he could to prevent this, Franklin communicated with the captains of American warships not to interfere if they encountered the expedition, entreating that "Cook and his people" be regarded "as common friends to mankind."

Captain Bligh Redux

A DECADE AFTER CAPTAIN COOK'S LAST VOYAGE TO THE SOUTH PACIFIC, HIS MASTER FROM the *Resolution* set out to make a name for himself in the British naval world. Taking the advice and relying on the assistance of the ubiquitous botanist Joseph Banks, William Bligh was given the opportunity to sail to Tahiti to obtain a cargo of breadfruit *(Artocarpus communis)* for transport to Jamaica as a potential food staple for the growing population of African slaves on its plantations. A member of the mulberry family, the breadfruit tree produces large, starchy fruits that smell like bread when baked and potatoes when boiled. The transfer of this food crop seemed destined to meet the needs of the British plantation owners in the Caribbean.

The Admiralty footed the bill for refitting a 200-ton former coal-carrying ship for the voyage with a copper-reinforced hull to discourage parasites and increased hold space for a cargo of saplings. Captain Bligh sailed the newly christened H.M.S. *Bounty* to Tahiti in 1787, laying over there for almost six months while the young trees took hold. During the hiatus, most of his crew formed attachments with Tahitians and left only reluctantly when the time came. This and a number of other factors, including Bligh's inept managerial style, fomented a mutiny led by his friend and first mate, Fletcher Christian. Within a few weeks, the mutineers left Bligh and 18 others to fend for themselves in a launch with minimal provisions and some navigational aids. The original purpose of the voyage was abandoned, as some of the mutineers returned to their loved ones in Tahiti and others, including Christian, sailed to Pitcairn Island, where they created a permanent Anglo-Tahitian settlement on the isolated Pacific outpost.

Miraculously, Bligh was able to bring his men some 3,700 miles across the Pacific to Indonesia, where they obtained passage back to England. With his reputation tarnished but not ruined by the *Bounty* fiasco, Bligh received an opportunity for another attempt at the breadfruit mission. In 1791 he successfully completed the transfer of the plants from Tahiti to the Caribbean and went on to other commands in the British Navy. The breadfruit took well to its new environment, but the slaves in Jamaica gave the new food staple a lukewarm reception, greatly preferring a diet of bananas and plantains.

"The natives reckon eight kinds of the breadfruit tree, each of which they distinguish by a different name."

— WILLIAM BLIGH, *A VOYAGE TO THE SOUTH SEA . . . FOR THE PURPOSE OF CONVEYING THE BREAD-FRUIT TREE TO THE WEST INDIES IN HIS MAJESTY'S SHIP THE* BOUNTY, 1792

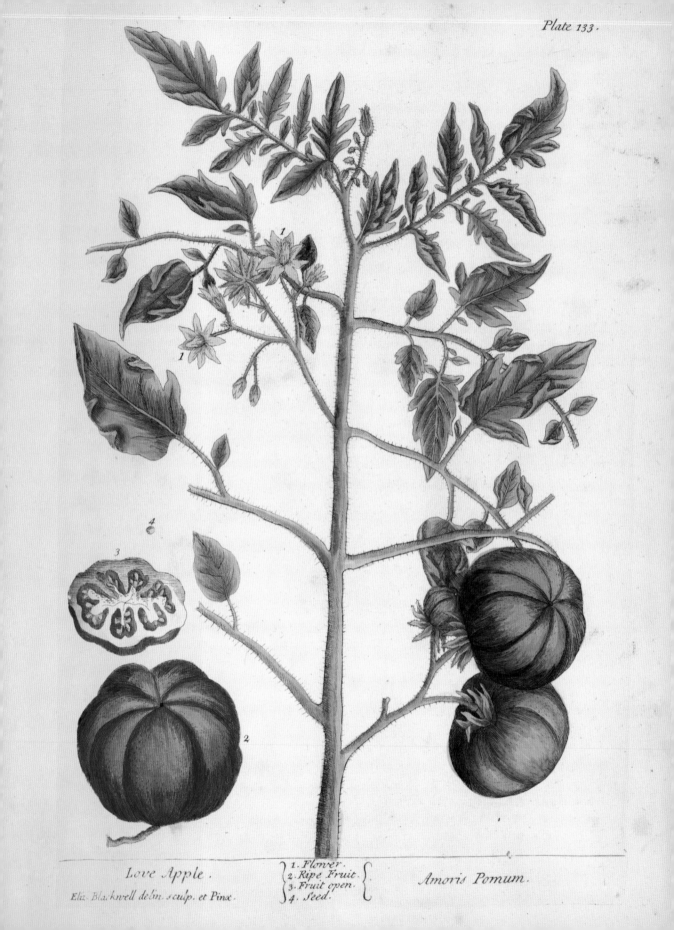

Plate 133.

Love Apple.

Eliz. Blackwell delin. sculp. et Pinx.

1. Flower.
2. Ripe Fruit.
3. Fruit open.
4. Seed.

Amoris Pomum.

TOMATO

Lycopersicon esculentum

Part of the nightshade family, tomatoes in all their colors, shapes, and sizes are consumed around the world—raw, cooked, or processed, for breakfast, lunch, or dinner. The tomato is botanically a fruit: the part of the plant that contains the seeds as they mature. Preceding the tomato fruit, small yellow flowers bloom on stalks that sprout from spreading branches.

The tomato may have originated in the South American Andes. No evidence suggests where it was first cultivated, although that may have occurred farther north. By the time the Spanish reached Mexico in the early 16th century, the markets were full of tomatoes, as chronicled by Bernardino de Sahagún, a Franciscan priest: "The tomato seller sells large tomatoes, small tomatoes, leaf tomatoes, thin tomatoes, sweet tomatoes, large serpent tomatoes, nipple-shaped tomatoes . . . those which are yellow, very yellow, quite yellow, red, very red, quite ruddy, bright red, reddish, rosy dawn colored."

When tomatoes were first introduced in Europe, they were not well received. Perhaps it was because, identified as a nightshade, the tomato was presumed poisonous.

By 1869, when this label was printed in Philadelphia, tomatoes had been accepted as food to be savored.

Tomatoes were also associated with the mandrake, also a nightshade but considered an aphrodisiac, which may explain the old name *pomme d'amour*—apple of love. Scholars believe that the tomato, and horticultural interest in it, slowly spread across Europe. Mediterranean cultures were perhaps more ready to adopt the tomato, since its hot-weather growing season did not interfere with other crops. Called *pomodoro,* golden apple, by the Italians, the first varieties grown there probably bore yellow fruit.

Only after tomatoes had entered European cuisines was the plant carried back across the Atlantic and introduced to the American Colonies. Thomas Jefferson, an advocate of the tomato, cultivated several varieties.

Oddly enough, the plant originally native to the Americas did not become popular in the United States until the early 20th century. It most likely grew in favor thanks to the efforts of Southern farm clubs to grow more healthful foods during World War I. Today, tomatoes are an important agricultural crop worldwide, processed into juice, ketchup, paste, puree, sauce; canned, sun-dried— and savored as fresh whole fruit. ■

TOMATOES THROUGH TIME

before 1500	by 1550	1597	1646	1692	1876	1994
Tomatoes grow wild in South America.	Tomatoes are regular fare in Italy.	Gerard's *Herball* calls tomatoes "of rank and stinking savour."	Spanish painter Murillo includes tomatoes in "The Angel's Kitchen."	First recipe with tomatoes appears in an Italian cookbook.	F & J Heinz Company markets first commercial ketchup.	Genetically modified Flavr Savr tomato is approved by the U.S. FDA.

Botany for the Masses

In the 1780s, as interest in gardens and gardening continued to filter down from the extremely wealthy to the general public, London physician, botanist, and Quaker William Curtis identified a need—and a commercial opportunity. He already had experience, albeit discouraging, with publications. His *Flora Londinensis,* a multi-volume compendium of London plants, failed to excite the locals, whose eyes were trained on the exotic and showy imports. With this firsthand knowledge of consumer preference, Curtis started publishing a periodical, *The Botanical Magazine; or, Flower-Garden Displayed,* which made its debut in 1787. The title page of the magazine promoted an orientation toward its 18th-century targeted demographic: "Intended for the Use of such Ladies, Gentlemen, and Gardeners, as wish to become scientifically acquainted with the Plants they cultivate."

The Botanical Magazine was not an elitist publication, as were many of the botanical publications up to this time as a result of their costly production. It was issued as an octavo, a normal-size volume designed for comfortable perusal. Each issue featured three color plates of novel and interesting species with accompanying descriptions. The magazine's illustrators collaborated with botanists to produce the most accurate illustrations that were drawn from life and colored "as near to nature, as the imperfection of colouring will admit." There was no room for embellishment or artistic idiosyncrasy that would detract from the scientific accuracy.

Many plates contained enlargements, what the English call "exploded details," to add to their usefulness. A cadre of up to 30 colorists applied the color by hand to every copy of every edition. During its first year of publication *The Botanical Magazine* boasted a circulation of 3,000 readers who paid one shilling to learn about the newest and most fascinating ornamental plants to grace the British Isles. Subscribers expected to see the fruits—and flowers and trees—of the efforts of international plant hunters, such as Scottish botanist David Douglas, who scoured the Pacific Northwest for specimens on behalf of the Royal Horticultural Society.

The Botanical Magazine, or Flower-garden Displayed (which came to be called *Curtis's Botanical Magazine*) has published continually since its inception, with a few interruptions, under the stewardship of a series of editors and making use of the talents of a series of artists, including several women. Matilda Smith, the cousin of late 19th-century editor and Kew director Joseph Dalton Hooker, drew more than 2,300 plates between 1878 and 1923. Quite remarkably, hand-colored plates continued to be the standard right up until 1948, when photomechanical reproduction was implemented. Popular protest undid a brief name change to *The Kew Magazine*

To inform horticultural enthusiasts of the mass of new plants coming into Europe from all parts of the world—such as the favored landscaping shrub, Andromeda japonica, *from Asia (opposite)—William Curtis (above) established his* Botanical Magazine *in 1787. It still exists today.*

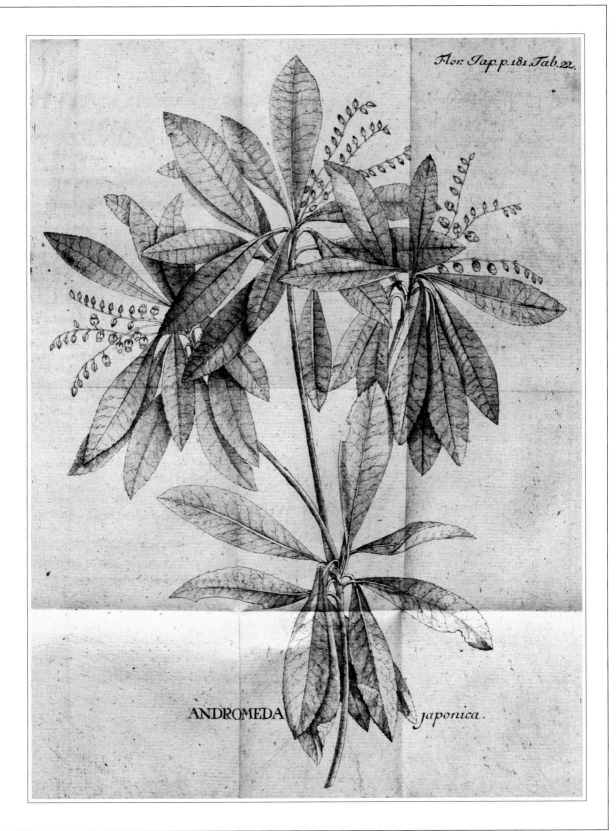

Flor: Jap. p.181. Tab.22.

ANDROMEDA japonica.

for a decade beginning in 1984, and Kew continues to oversee the publication of *Curtis's*—including an online version—to this day.

Worshipping at the Temple

The rise of nationalistic feelings in western Europe in the 18th century fueled cultural rivalries that extended to the world of botanical illustration. In the 1790s Robert John Thornton, a wealthy English physician and avid botanist, conceived of a work that would demonstrate British superiority in botanical publications. It was an ambitious project right from the start, and unlike *The Botanical Magazine,* was targeted toward wealthy subscribers who could bear a fee that covered the high production costs. The overall framework celebrated Linnaeus and his system of taxonomy in illustrated form, in three parts, with the title *A New Illustration of the Sexual System of Carolus von Linnaeus.* The third part, featuring "picturesque botanical plates," was entitled *The Temple of Flora,* and this became the popular name for the whole work.

With *The Temple of Flora* Thornton sought to break the mold of the botanical illustration that preceded it, and bring to bear an English mastery of engraving, printing, and coloring techniques. A middling artist, he produced only one plate for the project, the rose. The rest were assigned to well-known illustrators such as Philip Reinagle, Peter Henderson, and Sydenham Edwards. But Thornton art directed the whole project

Robert Thornton's 1807 Temple of Flora glorified 26 flowers with quotations from classical literature and lush color images of the flowers in landscape contexts. The hyacinth, wrote Thornton, "is one of the most agreeable flowers that Providence has bestowed upon mortals."

himself and oversaw the engravings by English masters including Florence-born Francesco Bartolozzi, who had introduced more advanced Italian engraving techniques to Britain. Thornton also wrote most of the florid text—and chose or commissioned the equally effusive poetry—such as this description of the rose plate: "Nature has given her a vest of purest white, and also imperial robes of the brightest scarlet," which hardly veiled the flower's symbolic representation of England.

Botanically, the illustrations of *The Temple of Flora* do not show the scientific rigor that characterized the work of artists such as Georg Dionysius Ehret or publications such as *The Botanical Magazine.* But that was not their point. Stylized and jaw-dropping exotic blooms appear against evocative historical, allegorical, and fantastic backgrounds that seem to anticipate surrealism. The effect speaks to another driving force of the period, Romanticism and the elevation of Nature. Perhaps the most curious and telling illustration is the one that shows Cupid and the gods of medicine, flowers, and agriculture paying tribute to a bust of Linnaeus with a laurel wreath and flower garland, so sincere in its earnest idealism.

Mounting costs kept Thornton from finishing his project; only some 30 out of the planned 70 plates were completed between 1798 and 1807. To raise money he established a lottery with a smaller octavo version of the publication as the grand prize, but that plan also failed. While facsimile versions of *The Temple of Flora* can today command $12,000, the originals wiped out Thornton, who died destitute in 1837.

Robert Thornton clearly indicated his devotion to Linnaeus in this illustration from The Temple of Flora *of the Swedish scientist's bust being worshipped by Aesculapius, Flora, and Ceres—the Greco-Roman god of medicine and the Roman goddesses of flowers and of grains.*

The Gardener in Chief

As anyone who has ever been to Monticello in the Virginia Piedmont knows, its owner, Thomas Jefferson, took his gardening seriously. In fact, he took an extremely focused and almost obsessive interest in all things horticultural and agricultural, referring to himself as "the most ardent gardener in the state." Jefferson grew cash crops such as tobacco, as well as grains, fruits, vegetables, and flowers on this mountaintop plantation. A thousand acres were allotted to crops, and two full acres on the mountain's southeastern slope were given over to his vegetable garden. He made the vegetable plot his own personal horticultural laboratory where he experimented with more than 350 varieties of plants and kept meticulous records of every action and outcome. With his international connections and other sources such as the

ROSE

Rosa spp.

Beloved of millions over centuries, a blooming rose is the epitome of fragile beauty. No other flower in the world has carried such symbolism and appeared in so many stories, songs, and paintings. Of course, there is not just one rose but many, for there are at least 100 species of rose and approximately 13,000 varieties, hybridized for color, fragrance, or some other combination of delightful traits.

Today the most common roses are known as hybrid tea roses: a cross between the hardy, firm-stemmed hybrid perpetual rose and the delicate but ever blooming tea rose, so named for their somewhat spicy scent, described as reminiscent of "a newly opened sample of the choicest tea."

Rose cultivation as we know it began with the Romans, but they were probably being cultivated in China long before, at least by the time of Confucius in the sixth century B.C. Four seminal Chinese rose forms, arising out of ancient hybrids, were brought to Europe by explorers in the 18th century: Parson's pink China, Slater's crimson China, Hume's blush tea-scented China, and Parks' yellow tea-scented China. What these Chinese roses brought to the rose palette was repeating bloom, a climbing habit, and

Wild and older varieties of rose tend to have a single aureole of petals; cultivation over centuries has resulted in the beloved many-layered bloom.

distinctive fragrance and color, especially a yellow not previously seen in roses known to grow in Europe.

Modern tea roses have five known ancestors: the Apothecary red rose; the Himalayan musk rose, brought through the Middle East; the beloved white rose of the Romans; and two ancient hybrid roses, also from Central Asian origins, the cabbage rose and the particularly fragrant damask rose.

The fruit of the rose, called hips, has long been valued as a medicine to treat illnesses from toothaches to intestinal discomfort. We now know that they contain very high concentrations of vitamin C, most likely the reason rose water was prescribed as a remedy for a number of ailments.

By far the most important use of roses, past and present, is attar of roses. A word that means "fragrant" in Persian, attar is the oil pressed from flower petals, used to make perfume. The first rose attar most likely came from the Himalayan musk rose and appears to have been worth six times its weight in gold.

During the 19th century, the popularity of rose gardens spread across Europe, and eventually to America. Roses gained a place in many a garden, still fragrant and delicate but no longer rarities. ∎

ROSES THROUGH TIME

2800 B.C.	ca 500 B.C.	ca A.D. 50	1455-1485	1608	1799	1939-1945
Roses decorate Minoan wall paintings and pottery.	Greek poet Anacreon calls roses "of all flowers the king."	Pliny the Elder describes Roman rose cultivation.	England's War of the Roses rages.	Samuel de Champlain carries roses to North America.	Empress Joséphine grows roses at Château de Malmaison.	Rose hip syrup provides wartime vitamin C.

exploration of the Northwest Territory led by Lewis and Clark in the early 1800s, Jefferson had no shortage of botanical material for his experiments.

Jefferson's connections at home and his numerous travels to Europe provided him access to the great botanists and nurserymen of his era and also to the endless influx of plants into the continent and Britain. His friends and acquaintances there also obliged him with specimens and seeds from their own gardens, which he then planted at Monticello.

The diplomat and President used his fondness for botany to forge friendships and dissipate political tensions. As he wrote in 1803 to Madame de Tessé, the aunt of the Marquis de Lafayette, "Altho' the times are big with political events, yet I shall say nothing on that or any subject but the innocent ones of botany & friendship." The French countess later sent Jefferson the seeds of the Chinese golden rain tree *(Koelreuteria paniculata),* brought to Europe thanks to the efforts of a Jesuit missionary in the mid-18th century. The showy ornamental had taken the Continent by storm with its clusters of bright yellow blossoms in summer followed by papery bean-filled pods and then a glowing yellow and orange foliage display in the fall. Jefferson's successful planting yielded what is believed to be the first golden rain tree cultivated in North America, and the species now is naturalized at Monticello and the nearby city of Charlottesville.

Jefferson's particular fondness for trees led him to plant some 160 different species on the estate, as ornamentals clumped for visual effect around his self-designed home, as well as in allées that lined the walking paths through the semi-tended section of mountainside he called the Grove. A proud arborist, Jefferson encouraged visitors to inspect what one guest described as his "pet trees."

Jefferson himself was honored by his contemporary, the American physician and botanist Benjamin Smith Barton, with *Jeffersonia,* a spring wildflower in the barberry family. One species, *J. diphylla* or twinleaf, was a native of Jefferson's home territory, central Virginia, and is now the symbol of the Thomas Jefferson Center for Historic Plants at Monticello. From Jefferson's own meticulous records and painstaking modern archaeological methods, vegetable and ornamental gardens as well as orchards again flourish on the "Little Mountain" as they did at their peak during Jefferson's retirement from public office.

The Corps of Discovery

Two years into his Presidency, Thomas Jefferson asked Congress for an appropriation of $2,500—a drop in the bucket today, but the equivalent of more than $400,000 back then—to carry out an exploration of the western lands acquired in the Louisiana Purchase. In a confidential letter he stressed how important it was to

This low-lying rock garden flower, Lewisia, *was named for Meriwether Lewis, the primary botanist of the Corps of Discovery sent westward by Jefferson in 1803.*

W.J.H.del.   Pub. by S.Curtis.Walworth.July 1.1829.

"The prickly pear is now in full blume and forms one of the beauties as well as the greatest pests of the plains. The sunflower is also in blume and is abundant."

— MERIWETHER LEWIS,
THE JOURNALS OF LEWIS &
CLARK, JULY 15, 1805

More than a hundred dried botanical specimens went back to Thomas Jefferson in 1805, and at least another hundred were carried home by members of the Corps. Horticulturists and botanists alike eagerly propagated and studied the new plants, including this annual, named Clarkia after William Clark.

Tab. T.

I.II.ATTALEA funifera.III.COCOS coronata.IV.C. fchizophylla.V.SABAL umbraculifera.

establish an authoritative presence with the Indian nations and cement a commercial position in the new territory. Only at the end of the letter did he add in a roundabout way another beneficial objective: "that it should incidentally advance the geographical knowledge of our own continent, cannot be but an additional gratification."

In Jefferson's own mind, however, the geography and natural science aspects of the expedition ranked much higher. He was, after all, a leader in the American Philosophical Society in Philadelphia, the premier scientific organization in America at the time, and he wholeheartedly espoused the scientific agenda of the Enlightenment. As we already know, he had a particular interest in botany, judging it "among the most useful of the sciences." With the expedition approved and funded, he sent his personal secretary, Meriwether Lewis, who would handle the natural history aspects of the exploration, to Philadelphia for crash courses in various subjects from a number of different experts. These included an astronomer, a physician, an anatomist, and the prominent physician-botanist Benjamin Smith Barton, a professor at the University of Pennsylvania and author of *Elements of Botany.*

Barton taught Lewis the basics of botanical taxonomy and the practical skills of collecting and drying specimens. Lewis brought his quick intelligence and a natural affinity to the task as well. As the son of a well-known herbal healer in central Virginia, he had learned from his mother about the intrinsic usefulness of many different species of plants. Lewis wasted no time putting his learning into practice. Before he and co-leader William Clark even began to lead the Corps of Discovery from its starting point in St. Louis, he described an Osage orange *(Maclura pomifera)* growing in the garden of one of their contacts there and sent cuttings back to Jefferson. This tree had been described by French explorers, who called it *bois d'arc* for its use by Native Americans in making strong, springy bows. Over time this got shortened to bodark, and the tree became an extremely popular planting, as it could be trimmed into dense, impenetrable hedgerows, remaining so until the invention of barbed wire.

The Corps of Discovery proceeded up the Missouri River and then across the northern United States to the Pacific Ocean. No tree, shrub, or flower escaped Lewis's notice, and of the 182 plant species collected over the next two and a half years, half were new to science. Lewis paid particular attention to the horticultural practices of the northern Indian tribes such as the Mandan, whose hardy strains of early ripening corn, beans, and squash were well suited to a short growing season. He brought

*From the far reaches of the globe came new varieties of palm, such as the coconut (opposite), and Malaysian orchid (*Medinilla magnifica, *above), swelling the numbers of plants known and cataloged by botanical science.*

Vitis vinifera

Published by Phillips & Fardon, Dec.ʳ 1ˢᵗ 1806.

GRAPE

Vitis spp.

Grapes are commonly regarded as one of the oldest cultivated fruits in the world. The vine grew wild throughout the Northern Hemisphere, based on the evidence of fossilized leaves and seeds dating back 23 million years. The species *Vitis vinifera,* the most common grape used today for wine, has had perhaps the longest running relationship with humans and still represents the most broadly cultivated species.

The earliest evidence of grape cultivation comes from ancient Egypt where, starting around 2400 B.C., the process of wine production was depicted in tomb paintings. Workers are shown picking grapes and crushing them in vats; hieroglyphics describe antics of drunkenness. By the first millennium B.C., the Phoenicians had transported winemaking across the Mediterranean—later called the Wine-Dark Sea—to Greece. The Greeks reveled in wine, dubbing Dionysus the god of wine, ecstasy, vegetation, and fruitfulness. Festivals in his honor—glorified drinking parties called Bacchanalia—became infamous for their hedonism, and the tradition was eventually banned by the Roman Senate in 186 B.C.

Through many centuries and in many cultures, grapes symbolize abundance sometimes taken to excess, as in this 16th-century German woodcut print.

Grape products other than wine among the ancients included sugar syrups, called *sapa* or *defrutum,* and verjuice, a souring agent. Grapes were so important to the Romans that they transplanted them as they conquered Europe. Viticulture, or grape growing, continued through the Middle Ages, changing little from the time of the Greeks.

The first records of New World viticulture date to the late 15th century. Native grapes already grew in North America, such as the black Concord grape, also known as the fox grape. But the settlers also brought their favorite varieties from Europe, and early growers learned to cross European varieties with the local ones.

In 1860 Europe's grape crop was almost entirely decimated when sap-sucking insects called phylloxeras, closely related to aphids, were accidentally introduced from the United States. American grapes are less vulnerable to the pests, and the harvest-saving solution was to graft European vines onto American rootstock. Today more than 10,000 grape cultivars are grown around the world. They are classified by color—either black or white—and by use—for eating, making wine, or drying to make raisins. ∎

GRAPES THROUGH TIME

2400 B.C.	1000 B.C.	100 B.C.	A.D. 1150	1850	1869	1966
Hieroglyphs and wall paintings show Egyptian winemaking.	Phoenicians bring grapes to Greece and later to France.	Grape cultivation reaches China.	England begins importing French wine.	Grapes now grown in Australia.	Thomas Welch makes unfermented grape juice for communion.	First Napa Valley, California, vineyard opens.

back seeds to President Jefferson and he experimented with them in his Monticello garden, pronouncing a red and white mottled bean named for the Arikara tribe "one of the most excellent we have had." All the botanical specimens were sent back to Jefferson's colleague Benjamin Smith Barton.

Jefferson was so taken with the Pacific coast snowberry bush *(Symphoricarpos albus)*, with its blue-green foliage and pale white berries, that he sent cuttings to friends and acquaintances as souvenirs of the expedition's botanical triumph. As for the intrepid explorers, each ended up with a namesake genus: *Lewisia,* plants in the purslane family, including *L. rediviva,* or bitterroot, the pale pink state flower of Montana; and *Clarkia,* plants in the evening primrose family.

THE REMBRANDT OF ROSES

THE CONCEPT OF ENTOURAGE HAS EXISTED AS LONG AS THERE HAVE BEEN individuals of power who attracted those who needed employment, validation, or protection. The entourages of European royalty have frequently included musicians, artists, and others who sought patronage to eke out a living. Who was considered in and who was out depended on particular royal interests. For Holy Roman Emperor Joseph II in 18th-century Vienna, it was a passion for music, and specifically opera, that brought Mozart into his circle. For his sister, Marie-Antoinette, consort of King Louis XVI of France, it was a love of flowers, no doubt tied in to their of-the-moment fashionableness, that compelled her to bring Pierre-Joseph Redouté into her court as a *dessinateur,* or draftsman. Once the Belgian artist entered the golden circle, he was in for the duration. Redouté managed to thrive (and stay alive) through intrigue, revolution, and restoration, endearing himself to two queens and later to two empresses.

He completed his eight-volume masterpiece, *Les Liliacées,* while in the employ of Napoleon Bonaparte's first wife, the Empress Joséphine, and *Les Roses* under his second, Marie-Louise, who was a double grandniece of Marie-Antoinette's.

The son and grandson of painters, Redouté began his career as an itinerant painter and decorator until he went to Paris to join his older brother, a designer of interiors and theatrical scenery. There he found a mentor in Gerard van Spaendonck, royal professor of painting at the Paris Museum, who taught him stippled engraving. Charles Louis L'Héritier de Brutelle, taught him botanical techniques and dissection and introduced

Asian lilies—Japan's lance-leaved lily (right) and China's tiger lily (opposite), for instance—quickly became gardeners' favorites in Europe and America.

Of all hues, Celestial, Roseate, and gold
And glittering in elegant Splendour, behold
The LILIES, a race to whom Nature has lent
All her Loveliest charms, of Form, Colour, and Scent.
With so many pleasing allurements endued
And by so many light-winged Votaries wooed,
That through all the wide circle of Flora's domain
Where the Loves, & the Graces so constantly reign,
What Tribe can be found so varied, so fair,
Whose forms are so Noble, whose Painting so rare.

LILIUM TIGRINUM.

him at the French court. Marie-Antoinette soon set him to the task of painting the gardens at the Petit Trianon, her private nature palace and playground on the Versailles grounds. After the revolution, Redouté kept busy documenting nationalized gardens—for example, the Jardin du Roi, which became Jardin des Plantes—and did the same later for the Empress Joséphine at her Château de Malmaison south of Paris. The prolific painter contributed to more than 50 volumes on natural history and archaeology.

For *Les Liliacées* (published between 1805 and 1816), Redouté paired graceful watercolor with engraving techniques to create 468 plates not only of lilies but also of daylilies and bromeliads. But it is *Les Roses* (published between 1817 and 1824) for which the artist is best remembered. Redouté's roses are sumptuous and sensual, laid caressingly on the page, thanks to his mastery of stippled engraving. Using fine dots, not lines, on a copper engraving plate, stippling allows for the depiction of finer gradations of tone and makes images appear more luminous. An established art technique when he learned it, Redouté really made it his own. Stippled engraving helped set his botanical illustrations apart from those of his predecessors and contemporaries, earning him the sobriquets "Rembrandt of roses" and "Raphael of flowers"—and ensconcing Redouté in the upper echelons of French society for the rest of his life.

THE INCREDIBLE VOYAGE

FEW PROFESSORS HAVE HAD SUCH AN IMPACT ON THEIR STUDENTS AS DID JOHN Stevens Henslow, the Cambridge University botanist who suggested to a young Charles Darwin that he look into joining an expedition that was mounting to survey the coast of South America. Darwin took the advice and signed on to the H.M.S. *Beagle* as the expedition's naturalist and assistant to its captain, Robert Fitzroy. The *Beagle* sailed from Plymouth, England, in 1831 to begin a voyage that would last five years and would take the ship at first to the eastern coast of South America and from there around the world. The expedition provided Darwin, a meticulous researcher, with enough data to eventually launch his theory of evolution based on natural selection.

Today we often look at Darwin for the bigger picture of his theory of evolution and for the place of the human species within it, and lose sight of the fact that his theories were built up from keen observations of minute details, and that he came to his task with training as a naturalist. From the Galápagos, the isolated volcanic archipelago more than 500 miles off the coast of Ecuador that generated countless epiphanies for the young scientist, we tend to remember the giant tortoises and Darwin's finches, and lose sight of the fact that it was the unique and extremely localized endemic plants as well that pointed him in his theoretical direction.

"From innumerable experiments made through dire necessity by the savages of every land, with the results handed down by tradition, the nutritious, stimulating, and medicinal properties of the most unpromising plants were probably first discovered."

— CHARLES DARWIN,
THE VARIATION OF ANIMALS AND PLANTS UNDER DOMESTICATION, 1868

Charles Darwin pressed live plants for safekeeping and further study during his five-year voyage on the H.M.S. Beagle. *He found this spleenwort fern (Asplenium dareoides Desv.) in December 1834 in southern Chile.*

COTTON

Gossypium

Humans have been wrapping their heads, bodies, and babies in cotton cloth for millennia. Evidence of the plant's use has been found in Asia and in Central America, dating from well before modern exploration connected those regions. Cotton's wild ancestors were domesticated independently in at least two different parts of the world.

In the same family as hibiscus and mallow, cotton grows in warm or tropical regions. It is a shrubby plant that develops seedpods called bolls. Each boll holds several seeds, enveloped by soft fibers, and is the part of the plant that is gathered and processed into fiber and fabric.

While cotton's story is global, the best information about its history comes from the Indus River Valley, where archaeological evidence shows that the spinning, weaving, and dying of cotton date back about 5,000 years. When cotton was introduced to the Mediterranean region is unknown, but scientists think that local cultures easily adopted it, using the techniques they had already developed to produce linen from flax. "No kinds of thread are more brilliantly white or make smoother fabric," wrote the Roman historian Pliny the Elder of cotton, yet cotton cloth did not gain widespread use in

IN THE COTTON FIELD.

Since cotton depletes the soil it grows in, crop rotation alternating cotton with legumes, which fix nitrogen in the soil, was a key innovation.

Europe until the Middle Ages, probably because it does not grow well in the colder European climates and was thus available there only through trade.

Cotton's history in the Americas is even less well documented. It may have been used as early as 3500 B.C. in Peru, most likely spun into fishing line. By the time that Europeans arrived in the New World, cotton was in wide use.

An important industry began when the first cotton seeds were sown in Jamestown, Virginia, in 1607. Over the next centuries, cotton became an essential cash crop in the southeastern United States, but its success depended on the work of slaves. As tension mounted before the Civil War, plantation owners in the South were confident that "King Cotton" would not fail them. Their economic demise came after they misjudged overseas customers who, wanting to avoid wartime politics in the States, turned to India and Egypt for cotton instead.

Today cotton is planted abundantly around the world, its demands on labor answered by machinery and its demands on the soil requiring the use of modern chemical fertilizers in most situations. China leads the world in cotton production today, presiding over a booming industry. ∎

COTTON THROUGH TIME

3000 B.C.	A.D. 712	1492	1793	1842	1873	1936
Cotton is grown in the Indus Valley.	The Moors introduce cotton to Spain.	Columbus finds Caribbean natives wearing cotton clothing.	Eli Whitney invents the cotton gin, which separates fiber from bolls.	The first boll weevil is reported in India.	Levi Strauss & Co. produces the first cotton blue jeans for gold miners.	The first cotton picking machine is invented in the U.S.

Writing in *The Voyage of the Beagle,* Darwin rhapsodizes: "Hence we have the truly wonderful fact, that in James Island, of the thirty-eight Galapageian plants, or those found in no other part of the world, thirty are exclusively confined to this one island; and in Albemarle Island, of the twenty-six aboriginal Galapageian plants, twenty-two are confined to this one island." Other aspects of plant evolution perplexed Darwin. The rise and rapid diversification of flowering plants as in the fossil record were regarded as "an abominable mystery."

Darwin also drew on his lifelong study of orchids. As the Victorian age wore on, he had more and more examples—in addition to the indigenous orchids of the British Isles—to cite, as orchid hunters supplied plants to obsessed British orchid growers, who passed on specimens to Darwin. He made note of all the different strategies that orchids have evolved to guide specialized pollinating insects to their blossoms. He hypothesized, rightly, that cross-pollination between different flowers produces fitter offspring than those that have to rely on self-pollination. Darwin published his findings on the subject in an 1862 book, *On the Various Contrivances by Which British and Foreign Orchids Are Fertilised by Insects,* a work totally eclipsed by *On the Origin of Species* but a fond undertaking for the man who at heart was always a botanist.

American Giants

As knowledge of the American West filtered into Europe's botanical circles, attention focused on the giant conifers that rise along its Pacific shores. Tall, stately

Scottish botanist David Douglas, an explorer of the American West, brought California annuals like Calochortus *(near right) and penstemon (far right) to the world's attention, but he is best known for chronicling the fir tree that now bears his name:* Pseudotsuga, *or the Douglas fir (opposite).*

PSEUDOTSUGA DOUGLASII. CARRIÈRE.

Avid horticulturists came to value oddity as much as traditional beauty in their plant collections, as cactus varieties from around the world, and especially from the American West, became available for planting.

pines, firs, and redwoods captured their imagination, as always curious about the possibilities of new species in northern European lands for purposes of both ornament and timber. Parts of Scotland, especially, share a climate with the Pacific Northwest, and a young but experienced botanist there named David Douglas was beginning to attract a considerable amount of attention.

In 1824 Douglas's mentor at the Royal Botanic Institution of Glasgow, William Hooker—later to become the first director of the Royal Botanic Gardens at Kew—arranged for Douglas to undertake a plant expedition that ranks among the great botanical explorations of a heroic generation. A year later, Douglas shipped specimens to Britain, effectively introducing more than a dozen conifers, including the fir that came to bear his name—a fitting way to honor his contribution, since Douglas was the first European botanist to recognize the iconic conifers of the Pacific Northwest.

The western or Idaho white pine is credited to Douglas, and his collections also underpinned the world's first botanical knowledge of the ponderosa, lodgepole, and sugar pines as well as the noble fir. Writing back to Hooker in Scotland, Douglas mused on the number of species his explorations were uncovering: "You will begin to think I manufacture pines at my pleasure." His contributions did not end with conifers, however; Douglas was responsible for introducing more than 200 plant species to Britain, including the lupine, gooseberry, penstemon, and California poppy. He died an untimely death at the age of 35, gored by a bull in Hawaii. His name graces the genus *Douglasia,* members of the primrose family, so named by the English botanist John Lindley in 1827.

A Transparent Solution

Like many Londoners today, physician Nathaniel Bagshaw Ward enjoyed the pleasures of his garden, located at his residence on a square in East London. It formed part of his passionate pursuit of botany; during his lifetime he amassed some 25,000 specimens in an herbarium, the assemblage of dried, pressed, and mounted plants forming the heart of any serious botanical collection, amateur or professional. But dead and dried specimens do not have the same requirements as live plants, and the ferns in Dr. Ward's garden were in a bad way because of the heavy pollution of 19th-century London.

One day while inspecting a moth pupa he was incubating in a sealed jar—entomology being another one of his hobbies—Ward noticed that some fern spores had taken hold in soil in the bottom of the jar and were thriving. This led him to experiment deliberately with growing plants in a sealed, protected environment. He hired a carpenter to construct a tightly fitted wooden case with glass panels and successfully raised ferns in it.

The big test came when in 1833 Ward sent two glazed cases filled with ferns and grasses all the way to Sydney, Australia. With the benefit of sunlight and moisture from condensation and protected from the elements and salty spray, the plants

> *"In ordinary horticulture much is effected by closely imitating the natural conditions of plants."*
>
> — N. B. Ward, *On the Growth of Plants in Closely Glazed Cases,* 1842

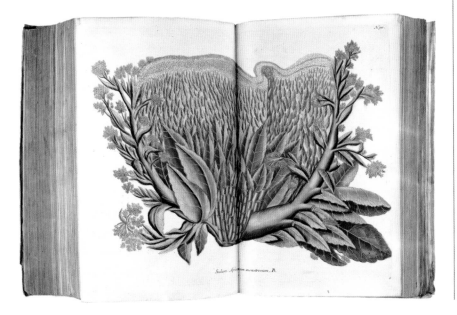

As glass cases and greenhouses allowed 19th-century plant lovers in temperate zones to replicate tropical and desert conditions, they began growing their own exotic heat lovers, such as this African sedum.

Plate 141.

The Apple Tree or Pearmain {
1. Blossome.
2. Fruit.
3. Fruit open.
4. Seed.
}
Malus sativa.

Eliz. Blackwell delin. sculp. et Pinx.

APPLE

Malus spp.

All began with an apple, if we are to believe the Book of Genesis—and yet botanical science suggests that if Eve really did give Adam a primitive apple, it was a small, hard, sour fruit—nothing like the big, fleshy, sweet globes we enjoy today. But whether it's an ancestor of today's apples, still growing in the Caucasus, or the most popular varieties for sale in the grocery store, every apple seed is genetically different and would grow into a tree bearing fruit different from that in which it matured.

This variability, or genetic heterozygosity, is found in plants and animals but is particularly significant to the culture of apples. Because each seed is genetically different, every apple tree would be different from every other apple tree were it not for the ancient technique of grafting.

Grafting is the process whereby a shoot from one plant is connected carefully to the growing portion of another plant so that their tissues form a living bond. Grafting was invented by both the Chinese and the ancient Romans independently.

Apples appear in myths and stories from many different cultures. Often ancient languages used the same word to name any fruit that grew on a tree, so mythic references to apples might be referring to oranges, peaches, pears, or plums instead.

Apple growing slowed with the fall of the Roman Empire, and grafting techniques were nearly forgotten until the 16th century, when production began again.

The earliest of New World settlers carried apple seedlings across the Atlantic, and from those starts grew a new industry. The only native trees on which they could graft were crab apples, small and tart, so New World apple horticulture had to make its own start. Soon it became important to westward expansion.

Though surrounded by myth, John Chapman—known as Johnny Appleseed—traveled up and down the major waterways of the American East and Midwest, planting small orchards along the way. From those orchards the United States' apple industry has grown, developing varieties such as Red Delicious, Golden Delicious, Winesap, and McIntosh. Recently new varieties developed on other continents—Granny Smith from Australia and Fuji from Japan, for example—have helped the apple industry reach global proportions. ∎

The apple—which may be a linguistic stand-in for other fruits—has found its way into myths and legends the world around.

APPLES THROUGH TIME

ca 200 B.C.	A.D. 400	1000	1618	1790	1904	2000
Cato the Elder describes grafting in *De agricultura*.	St. Jerome practices fruit tree grafting "to escape sloth and the devil."	Apples are under cultivation in China.	Lawson's *New Orchard and Garden* is the first English book on apples.	Thomas Andrew Knight systematically develops hybrid apples.	A Missouri fruit expert states, "An apple a day keeps the doctor away."	California scientists identify new antioxidants in apples.

arrived there in mint condition. Ward had also ordered a plant exchange, and so a number of fragile Australian plants were transported in the cases back to England, with the same results.

The Wardian case, ancestor to the modern terrarium, soon became standard botanical equipment, used in Victorian homes to protect plants from the fumes of gas lamps, and on a much larger scale to transport and transfer delicate and finicky plants from one end of the Earth to another.

LEGENDARY POMOLOGIST

IN THE LATE 18TH CENTURY, A LONE FIGURE TOOK TO THE ROAD FROM PENNSYLVANIA, heading west. He carried with him a huge quantity of apple seeds obtained from the pomace, or solid remains left after pressing, that piled up around cider mills. Stopping at scantly populated areas in Ohio, he planted apple tree nurseries, which he usually left in the care of a local resident. Within a few years the trees were sold to new arrivals, and the money was given to the planter when he returned every other year or so to check on his nurseries.

Proceeding westward into Indiana and Illinois and becoming more eccentric and tattered in appearance as the years wore on, this lone figure grew into a living legend: an itinerant nurseryman and singing preacher who eschewed creature comforts to gain a better situation in heaven, a tenet of the Swedenborgian Christianity he practiced. The man's name was John Chapman, but he was known universally by his nickname, Johnny Appleseed.

With probable origins around Kazakhstan in Central Asia, the apple most likely traveled the route of the Silk Road, gaining a welcome wherever it went. Early on, British settlers brought with them cuttings of their favorite varieties to plant in North America, where they frequently crossbred with the native crab apple. For apples to breed true generation after generation, trees must be propagated by grafting. Sowing apples by seed yields trees that may differ tremendously from the parent plants. Apples from seed trees also tend to be smaller and less sweet than grafted apples.

These properties did not matter much in the pioneer days, when apples were grown mainly for the manufacture of cider—hard cider, to be specific, since before the advent of refrigeration, nearly all freshly pressed cider soon fermented. Cider's alcoholic content gives it a potency about half that of wine, and people of all ages enjoyed it. Besides, it was often the only available and safe liquid to drink. Seen almost as a naturally occurring beverage since its manufacture involved only the simple process of pressing the fruit, cider managed to escape condemnation by temperance advocates for a time.

But by the 20th century cider, too, came under attack, and desperate apple growers started to talk up the health benefits of regularly eating apples to save their industry.

"He would describe the growing and ripening fruit as such a rare and beautiful gift of the Almighty with words that became pictures, until his hearers could almost see its manifold forms of beauty present before them."

— "JOHNNY APPLESEED: A PIONEER HERO," *HARPER'S NEW MONTHLY MAGAZINE,* 1871

Chrysanthemum: "A large and, from a garden standpoint, important genus," reads The Illustrated Dictionary of Gardening, *published in London in the 1880s. This illustration pictures three of its many variants.*

One of the most widespread and popular fruits of the present day, apples (*Malus* spp.) are represented by some 20,000 named varieties and countless unnamed ones. As for Johnny Appleseed, even before his death in 1845 he had passed into the pantheon of American folk icons, which came to include the likes of Davy Crockett, John Henry, and Casey Jones.

THE END OF ISOLATION

AS THE UNITED STATES CELEBRATED ITS 50TH ANNIVERSARY, THE COUNTRY HAD NOT yet made its mark in what was becoming a very competitive world of international expeditions. Concerned American scientists pushed for Congress to address this deficiency by approving a mammoth expedition known as the United States South Seas Exploring Expedition, or the Wilkes Expedition, named for its commander, Captain Charles Wilkes.

In 1838 the expedition set sail with Wilkes in the flagship *Vincennes* along with a fleet of six additional vessels. The nine expedition scientists included William Dunlop Brackenridge and William Rich, both botanists. America's premier botanist at the time, Asa Gray, originally agreed to go but instead accepted a position at the University of Michigan. The expedition lasted four years and logged nearly 87,000 miles, proving definitively that Antarctica was a continent and visiting most other continents. It returned in 1842 absolutely laden with specimens covering all aspects of natural history as well as geology and anthropology.

But there was no place to deposit the collections for study and preservation. Many were farmed out to different institutions and individuals. Nearly 10,000 botanical specimens were sent to Asa Gray, who made valiant efforts to organize and identify them. Against the wishes of Captain Wilkes, who wanted to keep the expedition a totally American enterprise, Gray opened up channels of communication with European botanists and sent duplicate specimens from the Wilkes Expedition for their examination and assistance in developing proper taxonomy.

Gray's good sense heightened the importance of the United States and its flora within the international botanical community. In the long run, the plight of the Wilkes Expedition and its collections made clear to many the pressing need for a national facility in the U.S. to receive and store specimens. In fact, the expedition and its plentiful collections provided the impetus for establishing both the Smithsonian Institution (made possible, ironically and controversially, by the bequest of English scientist James Smithson) and the United States Botanic Garden. ⁓

English gardener William Thompson cultivated wild violas, or heartsease (below), and in 1839 happened on a variant that looked like a face. He called it Thompson's Medora and started a pansy fad across Europe. Just as much as householders, botanical illustrators like the renowned Redouté enjoyed creating bouquets of spring flowers (opposite).

Bouquet de Camélias Narcisses et Pensées.

Redouté

Victor

"How fair is a garden amid the trials and passions of existence."
—BENJAMIN DISRAELI, *SYBIL, OR THE TWO NATIONS*, 1845

EMPIRE
1840–1900

R ising nationalistic identities combined with the business of empire enhanced competition among nations of the 19th century, and botany often sat in the center of the mix. A number of colonial powers established local botanical gardens in places such as Calcutta and Singapore to manage the cultivation of indigenous plants for commercial cultivation and export, and provide familiar venues for growing numbers of expatriates. As titular head of the world's most sprawling empire, Queen Victoria put her distinctive mark on the era both in and out of Britain, which contributed Victorian fashions in all things botanical. On the way to its centennial the United States sought to establish a greater presence in botany, as it did in other sciences, to create the national institutions it needed for scientific credibility. North America itself continued to remain a prized destination for plant hunters. So did East Asia, and various methods were used—both nefarious and straightforward—to obtain access to the flora of China and Japan. Industrial age innovation and technology benefited the botanical world as well, allowing a wider range of plants to be propagated in a wider range of climates outside of their indigenous areas. ⌇

As European-based empires stretched to the far reaches of the globe, so did the quest for new and exotic plants, bringing exquisite Asian azaleas into the gardens of Europe and the eastern United States. PRECEDING PAGES: Botanical exploration of the American West brought to the world's attention new species of fir trees with their remarkable cones.

	KNOWLEDGE & SCIENCE	POWER & WEALTH	HEALTH & MEDICINALS
AFRICA & MIDDLE EAST	**1859** Austrian Friedrich Welwitsch reports on huge two-leaved African desert plant, later named for him: *Welwitschia mirabilis*, called by Joseph Hooker the century's "most wonderful" botanical discovery.	*"A traveller should be a botanist, for in all views plants form the chief embellishment."* — CHARLES DARWIN, *JOURNAL OF RESEARCHES . . . DURING THE VOYAGE OF THE H.M.S. BEAGLE, 1839*	
ASIA & OCEANIA	**1851** Hugh Low discovers the giant pitcher plant *(Nepenthes rajah)* on Kinabalu, a mountain in Borneo. **1883** Richard Henry Beddome publishes *Handbook to the Ferns of British India, Ceylon and the Malay Peninsula.*	**1842** The Opium Wars end, opening up China to plant explorers. **1843-1860** Robert Fortune introduces such Chinese plants into England as balloon flower, bleeding heart, golden larch, Chinese fringe tree, hardy orange, abelia, weigela, and winter honeysuckle. **1858** Treaty of Amity and Commerce opens up foreign trade, including botanical exchange, between Japan and the Western world.	**1867** Indian scientist K. L. Dey publishes *Indigenous Drugs of India.* **1868** British doctor E. J. Waring publishes *Pharmacopoeia of India.*
EUROPE	**1842** First chemical fertilizer is manufactured, in Deptford, England. **1842** N. B. Ward publishes *On the Growth of Plants in Closely Glazed Cases,* popularizing greenhouses, terraria, and collecting cases. **1870** William Robinson publishes *The Wild Garden,* introducing naturalized wild plants and self-maintaining gardens. **1875** Charles Darwin publishes on habits of climbing plants. **1888** John Boyd Dunlop invents the rubber tire, a major use of natural rubber.	**1899** John Veitch's nursery sends botanical expeditions from England to western China in search of rhododendrons. *Luna moth*	**1859** German chemist Albert Niemann develops a method to extract the active ingredient from coca leaves; he calls the resulting anesthetic cocaine. **1897** Germany's Bayer Company develops method for producing acetylsalicylic acid, derived from willow bark and soon named aspirin. **1898** Germany's Bayer Company introduces heroin as a painkiller, discontinuing it by 1917 once it is found to be highly addictive.
THE AMERICAS	**1841** Andrew Jackson Downing's influential *Treatise on the Theory and Practice of Landscape Gardening, Adapted to North America* is published. **1869** Gypsy moths are brought to the U.S. for study. A few insects escape, ultimately devastating forests of the American Northeast. **1877** Michigan Agricultural College's W. J. Beal creates the first controlled crossbred corn variety, designed to increase yield.	**1854** Alfalfa seed, ultimately an important forage and field crop, is first brought from Chile to the United States. **1862** The U.S. Department of Agriculture is created. **1893** The U.S. Supreme Court declares the tomato a vegetable; thus importer John Nix must pay a 10 percent vegetable tariff on tomatoes shipped from the West Indies.	**1867** East India Company clerk transports cinchona from Peru to grow it in India as an antimalarial.

SUSTENANCE & FLAVOR	CLOTHING & SHELTER	BEAUTY & SYMBOLISM

1800s Impatiens species native to Africa first grown as a bedding flower in England.

1892 Baron Walter von St. Paul-Illaire sends first specimens of African violet to Germany.

1896 The most common impatiens species comes to America from the territory of the Sultan of Zanzibar, hence its early name, *Impatiens sultani*.

1870 Japanese plum, *Prunus salicina*, arrives in the United States.

London's 1851 Crystal Palace, containing trees and water lilies

1856 Lal Bagh in Bangalore, India, established in 1760, is recognized as a Government Botanical Garden.

1878 The Lloyd Botanical Garden is established in Darjeeling, India.

1883 Viscount Itsujin Fukuba builds Japan's first greenhouse and imports tropical orchids from England and France.

1840 The Duchess of Bedford introduces the practice of afternoon tea.

1845 Potato blight, imported to Europe from the Americas, causes the Irish Potato Famine; a million die and more than a million emigrate from Ireland.

1875 Daniel Peter adds dried milk to chocolate to create milk chocolate.

1844 Englishman John Mercer invents a cotton treatment called mercerization that increases sheen and durability and promotes dying.

1880 German Adolf von Baeyer and his laboratory successfully synthesize indigo.

1840s European gardeners prefer beds with solid masses of color, prompting horticulturists to develop larger flowers.

1900 Joseph Pernet-Ducher introduces what is thought to be the first yellow hybrid rose, called Soleil d'Or.

Caladium, a tamed tropical

1848 John Curtis produces the first chewing gum from spruce resin in Bangor, Maine.

1857 Export of grain through Chicago totals nearly 18 million bushels annually, up from 100 bushels 20 years earlier.

1864 Jabez Burns devises a machine that roasts coffee beans and ejects the ground coffee.

1886 John S. Pemberton invents Coca-Cola, very likely made of water, caramel, kola nut, sugar, vanilla, cinnamon, lime, and coca leaf extract.

1840 John Dresser of Stockbridge, Massachusetts, patents a hand-powered veneer lathe, essential for making plywood.

1873 Levi Strauss & Co. patents pocket stitching and rivets for their cotton denim blue jeans.

1841 Physician and botanist William Darlington proposes to add botanic gardens to the Smithsonian Institution.

1896 The New York Botanical Garden is established.

"*The great plan of natural affinities, sublime and extensive, eludes the arrogance of solitary individuals, and requires the concert of every Botanist and the exploration of every country towards its completion.*"

— THOMAS NUTTALL,
THE GENERA OF NORTH AMERICAN PLANTS, 1818

AMERICAN FLORA CONTINUED TO TANTALIZE THE INTERNATIONAL botanical community—the demand exceeded the supply for plants from all regions, although the less familiar and often more spectacular Western species held the greatest attraction. The competition to meet this demand was fierce, with the Americans laboring to establish their own botanical credentials and scientific command of American flora—as well as the profits to be made from it—while feeling the pressure from British and European botanists, horticulturists, and plant hunters. The challenge also included the desire to get into print as much information as possible about North American flora. The continent's natural history was getting full coverage on all fronts, with birds and mammals, especially, receiving coverage and attention nearly equal to that of plants.

Botanist, zoologist, and sometime printer Thomas Nuttall had been working more or less simultaneously in the areas of North American botany and ornithology for more than three decades, beginning in 1808. Upon arrival from England, he had immediately sought out eminent professor of botany Benjamin Smith Barton in Philadelphia and took his counsel, as well as that of an aging William Bartram, the younger member of the famous Quaker horticultural team.

Barton sent Nuttall out on several expeditions—to the Delaware and Chesapeake Bays, the Great Lakes, and up the Missouri, where he collected some species that Meriwether Lewis and William Clark had gathered and lost. After riding out the War of 1812 in England, Nuttall returned to America and resumed collecting, rounding out his accumulated knowledge and publishing in 1818 *The Genera of North American Plants,* of great interest in North America because it was published in English, not Latin. He continued to botanize, took a professorship in natural history at Harvard, and worked on his ornithological contribution, *Manual of the Ornithology of the United States and of Canada,* in volumes published in 1832 and 1834. Nuttall then headed west, botanizing by land and then sailing on to Hawaii and back to the Pacific Northwest. In 1841, just before he had to return to England to fulfill residency requirements imposed by an inheritance, Nuttall finished *The North American Sylva,* a work that completed the task undertaken by French botanist François-André Michaux. Their works combined represented the first comprehensive treatment of North America's forest trees.

AMERICA GETS A BOTANIC GARDEN

WITH THE ERA OF GOVERNMENT-SPONSORED SCIENTIFIC EXPEDITIONS IN FULL SWING BY the 1840s, creating a continuous stream of botanical specimens, the need to find a place to house them, organize them, and make them available for research continued to press. The four-year-long Wilkes Expedition to the South Seas (described in Chapter 4) had brought back both dried and living plants when it returned in 1842. The herbarium

Gloxinia Princesse de Prusse.

Semis Erfurt. — (Serre chaude.)

From Brazil came the parent plants of all hybrid gloxinias including this one, named after Maria Luise Augusta Katharina, daughter of the grand duke of Saxe-Weimar-Eisenach, who was princess of Prussia when the plant was named but ultimately became empress.

specimens passed to the custody of Asa Gray, regent of the newly formed Smithsonian Institution, at Harvard University, and to John Torrey, a professor of botany at Columbia College in New York City. Physically, however, the collections resided at Columbia.

It was not a good situation. The live plants hardly fared better; they lived for eight years in a temporary greenhouse behind the Old Patent Office Building in Washington, D.C., then were moved in 1850 to what would become the first U.S. Botanic Garden location in front of the U.S. Capitol, where the Reflecting Pool now stands. It was not until 1933 that the facility moved to its present permanent location southwest of the Capitol. Botanists there today think that three of the plants the USBG houses—a cycad and also male and female sago palms—may be the actual specimens brought back by Wilkes. The expedition's herbarium specimens eventually were transferred to the Smithsonian and now form part of the extensive research collections of the botany department of the National Museum of Natural History.

THE BOTANIST OF WALDEN

WHILE SOME AMERICANS BOTANIZED AMONG THE GIANT TREES OF THE FAR WEST, A DOUR New Englander stuck very close to home and trained his considerable powers of observation on the flora of his Concord, Massachusetts, birthplace. Both before and after his Walden period—the years 1845 to 1849, which he spent living in a simple cabin on the shore of Walden Pond—Henry David Thoreau took a very serious interest in botany.

He walked the forest paths of Concord so often and so long with his gaze fixed on the ground that he developed headaches. Of some 3,000 species of vascular plants that grow in New England, Thoreau collected 900, and he dried and pressed them to create his own herbarium. His copious botanical notes were assembled into the volume *Wild Fruits*, which was published very much posthumously in 1999. As the book demonstrates, Thoreau knew the intimate details of each species and also had a good grasp of botanical exploration and scholarship. Still, he connected to the flora in a very personal way, writing a 20-page essay on the huckleberry and waxing rhapsodic in his assessment of the blackberry *(Rubus):* "Surely the high blackberry is the finest berry that we have—whether we find their great masses of shining black fruit, mixed with red and green, bent over amid the sweet fern and sumac on sunny hillsides, or growing more rankly and with larger fruit in low ground and by rich roadsides."

Though he dearly loved Concord, Thoreau did realize that a town 15 miles from Boston did not represent the forest primeval. To get a taste of more pristine forest ecology, he made several extended trips to Maine. "It is all mossy and moosey," was Thoreau's assessment of his destination. But even Maine had become inexorably transformed by the time Thoreau visited. Many of the tall and straight white pines *(Pinus strobus)* of the original forests that early settlers would have encountered had been cut. In colonial times, white pines—especially those that grew near water—were often marked with the "king's arrow," reserving the trunks,

"It takes a savage or wild taste to appreciate a wild fruit."

— HENRY DAVID THOREAU, *WILD APPLES,* 1862

American wildings ranged from the rustic blackberry (above) to the giant sequoia tree (opposite), first reported to the botanical community in 1852 and by 1864 protected from harvest for lumber.

Plate XV.

1.

2.

3.

4.

5.

6.

CANNABIS

Cannabis sativa

The cannabis plant dwells in controversy—botanical, legal, and ethical: Botanists do not agree on what family it belongs to—Urticaceae (nettle), Moraceae (mulberry), or a family all its own, Cannabaceae—and, more important, they have not resolved whether its different forms represent separate species, subspecies, or varieties.

Originating in Central Asia, cannabis has long been cultivated, more for its useful fiber than for any other reason. Somehow, whether by human selection, geographic spread, or both, its evolution split into at least two forms, distinguished by growing habits and by the level of tetrahydrocannabinols, psychoactive compounds specific to cannabis. The plant grown to harvest that chemical is called marijuana. The plant grown to harvest the fiber is called hemp.

One of the oldest known plant sources of fiber, hemp was greatly valued in the ancient cultures that grew it. Its strands are longer, stronger, more absorbent, and more resistant to mildew than cotton. Though spun into cloth for clothing and pressed into paper, hemp found its special usefulness on the sea, in sails and line. Thus, during the eras of exploration and ocean trade, hemp became very important and was grown around the world. It was an abundant crop during the early years of the American Republic. George Washington, Thomas Jefferson, and Benjamin Franklin all raised hemp. The Declaration of Independence was penned on paper made of hemp.

Hemp has recently made a comeback. Naturally pest resistant, it requires virtually no pesticides, unlike cotton. It also offers a sustainable alternative to wood pulp for paper production, yielding four times as much fiber per acre as forest. Hemp paper lasts longer than wood-pulp paper without yellowing. Many Bibles have been printed on hemp paper.

"Medical men" entertained "varied views" of hemp, according to an 1852 homeopathic manual, while children labored in hemp twine factories in New York.

But cannabis's other identity has kept hemp from reaching its modern commercial potential. During the 20th century, more than a hundred countries around the world established laws against possessing marijuana, linking it to escalating drug use.

Meanwhile, medical professionals have found compounds in the plant helpful in treating some diseases, including glaucoma and the aftereffects of chemotherapy in the treatment of cancer. The debate still rages—and cannabis still grows amid controversy. ∎

CANNABIS THROUGH TIME

4000 B.C.	by 1000 B.C.	A.D. 500	1840-1860	1937	1942	1957
Cannabis sativa is first cultivated in Central Asia for fiber.	Hemp cloth making reaches western Asia and Egypt.	Cannabis is grown widely throughout Europe.	The U.S. hemp industry flourishes.	Tax Act bans marijuana and virtually halts U.S. hemp agriculture.	U.S. citizens are asked to grow "Hemp for Victory" in WWII.	Cannabis is again declared illegal to grow in the U.S.

6370

H.T.D.del

Vincent.Brooks Day & Son.Lith.

which can grow to 230 feet tall, for royal use, mostly as masts for Royal Navy ships. The appropriation of one of their main resources had created yet another grievance for New England colonists, who favored the soft wood of the white pine for use especially in decorative millwork for their homes as well as for making furniture (and coffins). Nevertheless, Thoreau cast the same kind of focused gaze at Maine's natural wonders as he did at those of his home turf. He reported that blueberry patches often acted as an incentive to the weary hikers in his party. They "afforded a grateful repast, and served to bait the tired party forward. When any lagged behind, the cry of 'blue-berries' was most effectual to bring them up."

Thoreau botanized throughout his life and left meticulous records of the first appearance of blooms for some 500 plant species around Concord. When compared with modern records for the same area, they show which species have been lost over time and which are blooming at a much earlier date—a great boon to our understanding climate change. Thoreau died at age 44 in 1862 from tuberculosis, and his botanical specimens passed to his alma mater, Harvard, where they added to the growing collections that were being amassed by his friend, the botanist Asa Gray.

Hooked on Asia

THE 19TH CENTURY'S AGE OF EMPIRE BROUGHT GREATER NOTICE OF BOTANICAL treasures from all parts of Asia, especially China, Japan, and India. For centuries, Western contact with China and Japan had been suppressed by xenophobic isolationism on the Eastern end. Traders and travelers to China basically were restricted to two ports, Canton and Macao. One of the few groups with access to the inner workings of China and Japan was the Jesuits, who became conduits for culture and knowledge and out of scholarly interest as well as necessity, experts in botanical matters in these countries.

It wasn't just foreign ideas that the Chinese shunned. The British, like other Europeans, had grown alarmed at the uneven balance of trade between China and the West. European demand for exports such as tea, porcelain, cotton, and silks, which by Chinese insistence had to be paid for only in silver, went mostly unanswered by Chinese imports, and so the British imported opium from India in huge quantities, creating an outward flow of silver and a widespread culture of addiction in China.

In 1839, with their society and economic activity hobbled by the opium imports, the Chinese government responded by confiscating the warehoused opium in Canton, which led to a series of military confrontations between the British and Chinese, and later the British and French against the Chinese, over the course of the next 21 years. The defeated Chinese were forced to sign and

Japanese beauties emigrated in the 1860s: the star magnolia, soon a favored landscape shrub with early spring blossoms (opposite), and the kakitsubata *or rabbit-ear iris, a water dweller highly honored in its homeland (below).*

honor several treaties that increased the number of ports open to trade and allowed for travel in the interior of China. Thus, as the Opium Wars were settled, the doors opened to Westerners eager to conduct full-scale botanizing in China.

Before all this was ironed out, the Scottish botanist Robert Fortune set out for China on an exploratory mission sponsored by the Royal Horticultural Society in London. To avoid drawing attention to himself, he adopted local dress and learned Mandarin Chinese sufficiently well to pass unnoticed. This allowed him to send many filled Wardian cases (described in Chapter 4) back to England from his first expedition. On his second mission he worked for the British East India Company with an assignment to obtain tea plants and learn as much as possible about the tea trade so that it could be established on a wide scale in India. Adopting the methods that had worked for him on his first expedition, Fortune amassed more than 20,000 tea seedlings in his Wardian cases, which were sent to the Himalayan foothills in India to establish the tea industry there, along with Chinese tea workers to help get them started.

The policy of greater access brought plant hunters to China in great numbers, although some of the earliest, most comprehensive botanizing was accomplished by French missionaries. The most notable was Père Armand David, who worked in western China and was responsible for collecting thousands of seeds and plants, which he preserved in herbaria.

European nurseries did not hesitate to dispatch plant hunters to China and also to Japan, which in the interim had opened up to trade and foreign visitors as well, as a result of the successful negotiations of Commodore Matthew Perry in 1854. Perhaps the most ubiquitous of these firms was the Veitch nurseries in Exeter, England, established in the early 19th century by Scottish horticulturist John Veitch, who was succeeded by his son and grandson. The Veitches created a nursery empire, sending plant hunters all over the world to obtain specimens for cultivation and sale to public gardens and private individuals and winning awards left and right for their successful propagation of exotic plants. With the East again open, curiosity and the demands of horticulturists worldwide would assure a steady stream of plant explorers traveling well beyond Europe.

IN AND OUT OF INDIA

ENSCONCED FOR THE LONG HAUL IN THE INDIAN OUTPOST OF THEIR EMPIRE, the British turned their bent for scholarship and attention to detail on the natural and cultural phenomena of the South Asian subcontinent. They covered many topics, including religion, folklore, languages and linguistics—and botany. Many of the data were collected by local administrators, military officers, and missionaries, some by qualified academics, and some as a result of expeditions planned from home.

"Much as I had heard and read of the magnificence and beauty of Himalayan scenery, my highest expectations have been surpassed!"

— JOSEPH DALTON HOOKER, QUOTED IN THE PREFACE TO *THE RHODODENDRONS OF SIKKIM-HIMALAYA*, 1849

Intrepid flower hunters such as Joseph Dalton Hooker scaled Himalayan heights in China and India (opposite) to find new varieties, such as the delicate Rhododendron virgatum *(below).*

Tab. I.

Hevea brasiliensis Müll. Arg.

RUBBER

Hevea brasiliensis

Life without rubber is hard to imagine. Tires, gaskets, gloves, boots, toys, tools, flooring—this is just the beginning of a long list of modern-day essentials made from rubber. It is such a common material, it is easy to forget that it originally came from a plant.

Natural rubber begins as the sap of a tree, a milky emulsion called latex. It is harvested by tapping into the tree trunk and redirecting the sap as it flows. Once the tree is tapped, the latex runs out to be collected and then treated, chemically and by heating. Several different kinds of plant are able to produce rubber, but most of today's rubber comes from the tree called *Hevea brasiliensis*.

Originally from South America, as its scientific name suggests, rubber has a long history. Several pre-Columbian sources mention natives who coated their clothing with a waterproof liquid that they called *cahuchu*—crying wood. It came to the broader attention of Europeans around 1735, after two French scientists returned from an expedition in South America and described it to fellow botanists. English chemist Joseph Priestley found a new use for it: He could remove pencil marks on a paper by rubbing it against them; hence he called it rubber.

Not long after their usefulness was recognized by Europeans, rubber trees were propagated and grown in commercial plantations yet still tapped by hand.

Rubber use grew in Europe and North America, and demand spiked in 1839 after the invention of vulcanization, a chemical process that makes natural rubber tougher and longer lasting. Soon vulcanized rubber became a common industrial material.

Companies around the world jumped at the opportunity to harvest latex, and growing demand forced the search for sources beyond South America. In particular the British, who had grown dependent on it, realized it would be more economical to produce it themselves. In 1872 a large shipment of seeds went from South America to England and from there on to British colonies in suitably tropical regions in South and Southeast Asia. By 1910 nearly one million acres of Asian *H. brasiliensis* plantations had been established, nearly overwhelming the South American rubber industry.

Rubber was so precious during both world wars, its use by the general public was rationed. High demand and Japanese control of the Asian plantations sped the development of synthetic rubber, yet natural rubber remains important, since not all of its valuable properties are found in synthetic rubber. In fact, the demand for natural rubber will probably never disappear. ∎

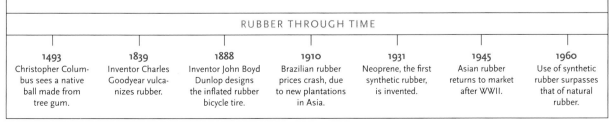

RUBBER THROUGH TIME

1493	1839	1888	1910	1931	1945	1960
Christopher Columbus sees a native ball made from tree gum.	Inventor Charles Goodyear vulcanizes rubber.	Inventor John Boyd Dunlop designs the inflated rubber bicycle tire.	Brazilian rubber prices crash, due to new plantations in Asia.	Neoprene, the first synthetic rubber, is invented.	Asian rubber returns to market after WWII.	Use of synthetic rubber surpasses that of natural rubber.

RANUNCULACEÆ

$\frac{1}{3 \times 4}$

CLEMATIS MUNROIANA. R.W.

Rungia del.

R.W. lith.

On-site botanists created comprehensive herbaria for study and collected live plants for establishment in botanical gardens in places such as Calcutta (today's Kolkata), Bombay (Mumbai), Madras (Chennai), and Bangalore (Bengaluru), often with an eye to exporting them to Britain. Plants also were studied and collected for their commercial potential, and some, such as tea from China, were brought in from other tropical regions to determine if India's environment supported commercial cultivation. (It did.)

The Royal Botanic Garden in Calcutta, for example, was established in 1787 by an army officer of the British East India Company to test potential commercial species and grow spices for trade. When a botanist, William Roxburgh, took the reins in 1793, the garden's mission became more scientific: A representative sample of plants was brought in from different parts of India and an herbarium was created. After the next change of leadership, the Calcutta Botanic Garden became a major international player in the private and public market for both commercial and ornamental plants all over the world. The garden's herbarium eventually became the core of the collection of the Botanical Survey of India, which now holds some 2.5 million specimens.

Not all of India's botanical gardens were introduced by the British, however. The sumptuous Lal Bagh (Red Garden) in Bangalore was commissioned in 1760 by the local ruler Hyder Ali and completed by his son, Tipu Sultan. The Mughal-style gardens have evolved over time and now have a magnificent glasshouse, originally designed after London's Crystal Palace.

In 1847 Joseph Dalton Hooker, who would serve as director of the Royal Botanic Gardens at Kew later in the century, was sent out to India on commission from Kew to explore northern India and collect plants for that institution. The son of botanist and Kew director William Jackson Hooker, the younger Hooker already had an impressive résumé before he set out to traverse the Himalaya. After obtaining a medical degree in Glasgow, he was invited in 1839 to sail to Antarctica on an expedition headed by James Clark Ross, a friend of his father's. Soon after returning from that adventure, Hooker started to think about his next expedition, looking to the tropics for a climate that would contrast with his Antarctic experience.

Arriving in 1848 in Calcutta, he made his way to Darjeeling, stopping along the way at Patna in Bihar to observe the manufacture of opium. His hosts gave him samples and drawings to take with him, which he planned to give to his father's Museum of Economic Botany. In the hill station of Darjeeling, Hooker had to cool his heels

SALICARIEÆ LAGERSTRŒMIEÆ

LAGERSTRŒMIA INDICA .(LINN.)

It interested European botanists that explorations in India revealed not only new plant species, like the crape myrtle (above) but also new species of garden flowers already known and beloved, like the clematis (opposite).

for some time while waiting for permission from the local ruler to travel in Sikkim, but eventually—after some bullying from the area's British agent—he was given the green light.

Hooker traveled with a huge entourage to handle all the practical matters and kept his focus on his mission, fascinated with the plants of the forested foothills, such as the silvery rhododendron *(Rhododendron grande)* and the epiphytic Dalhousie rhododendron *(R. dalhousiae),* which produces fragrant white blossoms while attached by its roots to a host tree. He would also visit Nepal and Assam, and his detailed sketches from the expedition were turned into beautiful lithographs by Walter Hood Fitch for Hooker's *The Rhododendrons of Sikkim-Himalaya,* published from 1849 to1851.

DARWIN AND GRAY

THE YEAR 1859 SAW THE PUBLICATION OF CHARLES DARWIN'S *ON THE ORIGIN OF SPECIES,* the startling work that explained his theory of evolution based on a principle he called natural selection. As the world now knows, Darwin was not the only 19th-century naturalist to be thinking along these lines. Alfred Russel Wallace had come to a similar understanding around the same time, but it is Darwin's exposition in *Origin* that caught the public attention. To be expected, Darwin's theories created an international stir among the scientific and religious communities. One of his staunch defenders and close friends was Harvard botanist Asa Gray.

From the start of his botanical career in 1831, Asa Gray took a path that would put him at the center of some of the most important developments in botanical science, but in an altruistic, not a self-serving, way. Trained as a physician in Fairfield, New York, he nonetheless felt the pull of botany, studying under John Torrey and botanizing extensively in the United States. By the age of 26, he had published a textbook, *Elements of Botany,* and had become librarian of the New York Lyceum of Natural History.

Although tapped to join the Wilkes Expedition to the South Pacific, Gray instead took a teaching position at the fledgling University of Michigan, where he helped establish a botanical library by buying books and visiting herbaria in Europe. Gray landed at Harvard in 1842 and stayed there until his retirement, building its botany department nearly from scratch and creating an enviable herbarium that now bears his name. He published extensively, becoming best known for his *Manual of the Botany of the Northern United States, from New England to Wisconsin and South to Ohio and Pennsylvania Inclusive* (1848), now widely referred to as *Gray's Manual* and still a respected reference in the field.

The houseplant known as African violet was a wildflower discovered in northern Tanzania in 1892 by the Baron Walter von St. Paul-Illaire, stationed there during Germany's occupation of East Africa. The plant's genus name honors its discoverer: Saintpaulia.

6643

M.S.del, J.N.Fitch Lith

Vincent Brooks Day & Son Imp

*"As I am no
Botanist, it will
seem so absurd
to you my asking
botanical questions,
that I may premise
that I have for
several years been
collecting facts
on 'Variation,' &
when I find that
any general remark
seems to hold good
amongst animals,
I try to test it
in Plants."*

— CHARLES DARWIN,
LETTER TO ASA GRAY,
APRIL 25, 1855

*First brought to Europe
and the United States from
Zanzibar in the 1890s, the
impatiens thrives in summer
gardens that mirror the
steamy yet shady conditions
of the rain forest floor where
it originally grew.*

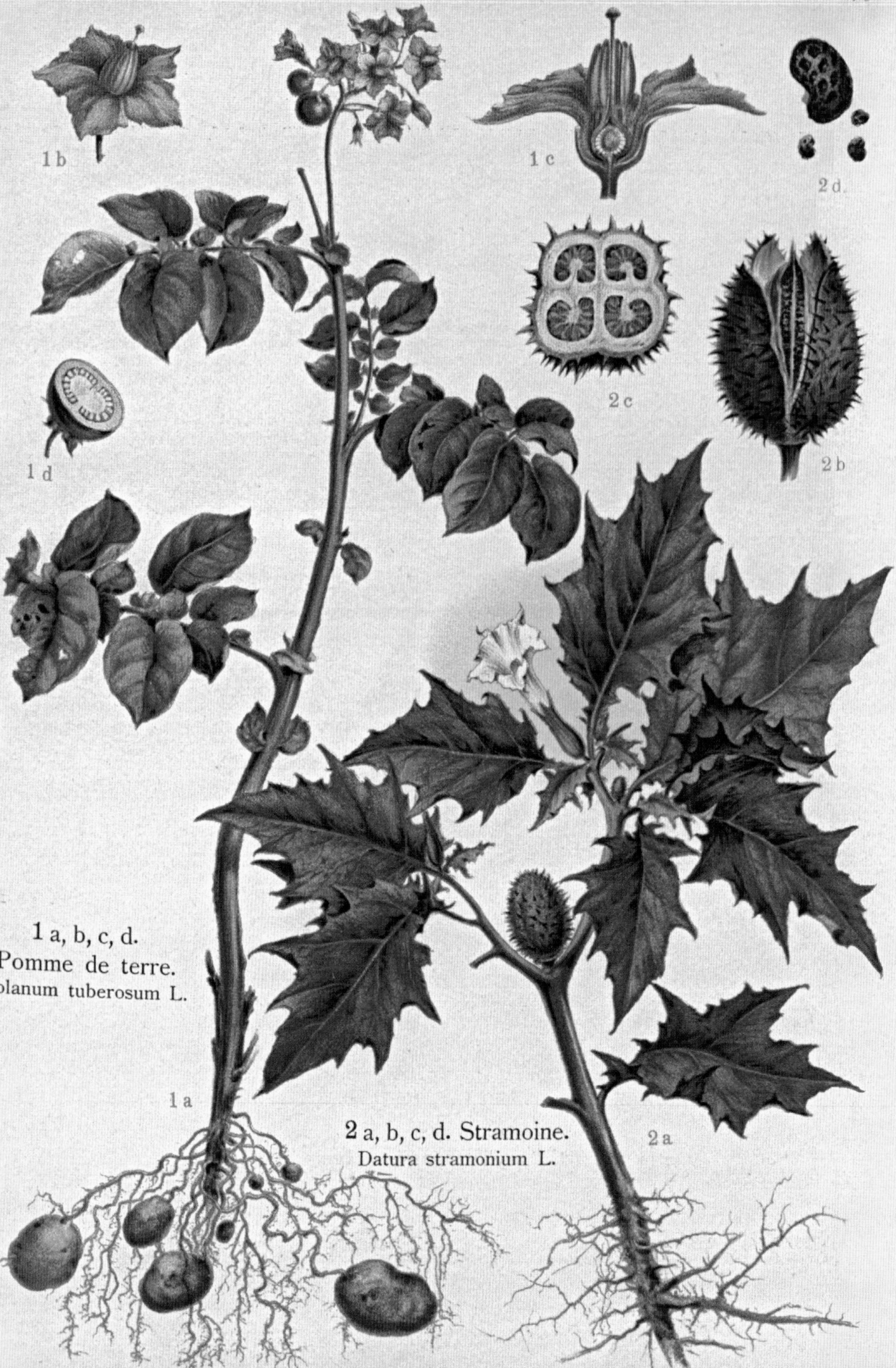

1 b

1 c

2 d

2 c

2 b

1 d

1 a, b, c, d.
Pomme de terre.
Solanum tuberosum L.

1 a

2 a, b, c, d. Stramoine.
Datura stramonium L.

2 a

POTATO

Solanum spp.

Although the potato played a central role in the calamity of Ireland in the 1840s, its history starts much earlier, in South America, where these tubers had been growing naturally for thousands of years. Most sources agree that by 5000 B.C. this starch-rich food plant was under cultivation. A naturally hardy plant, the potato grows well in poor soil, needs little sunshine, and is unaffected by extreme temperature changes. And the rewards for cultivating it are significant: A single potato provides many essential nutrients, all that humans need except calcium and vitamins A and D. Add a dairy product, such as milk, to potatoes, and the result is a nutritionally complete diet. Potatoes formed the staple food for the cultures of the Andes Mountains, where the altitudes and landscape inhibited almost all prospects of animal husbandry and agriculture.

The Spanish conquistadores probably became acquainted with the potato as early as the mid-1530s, but the plant did not take root in Europe right away. Western Europeans gave the potato a cold reception: The plant was not mentioned in the Bible; it belonged to the nightshade family, known to be poisonous; and the tuber's strange root sprouts, which looked like eyes, led many to think

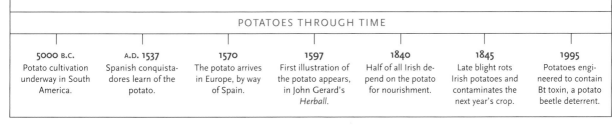

Europeans first dismissed the potato as inedible, in part because of its botanical relation to deadly nightshades such as Datura (opposite, lower right).

it was evil. Some even accused the potato of causing leprosy or immoral behavior. This bundle of stigmas meant that the potato most likely entered Europe as a botanical curiosity, not a food. That changed once the potato reached Ireland.

Distressed and starving, the Irish ignored all fears about potatoes, which soon became a dietary mainstay for them. Unlike most cereals, the potato thrived in the cool, wet Irish weather. A small plot of land could produce enough potatoes to feed a family and their livestock.

By the 1840s the Irish diet had evolved to near-total dependence on a single variety of potato, called the lumper. Late blight, a fungus that causes potatoes to rot, was accidentally introduced from America in 1845. Both growing and harvested tubers developed black spots of rot that made them inedible. In five years, Ireland's population fell from around 8.4 million to 6.6 million, with more than a million people dying of starvation and disease and nearly as many immigrating to Britain and America.

Today a single species of potato, *Solanum tuberosum*, is the fourth most widely cultivated food in the world, exceeded only by corn, wheat, and rice. ■

POTATOES THROUGH TIME

5000 B.C.	A.D. 1537	1570	1597	1840	1845	1995
Potato cultivation underway in South America.	Spanish conquistadores learn of the potato.	The potato arrives in Europe, by way of Spain.	First illustration of the potato appears, in John Gerard's *Herball*.	Half of all Irish depend on the potato for nourishment.	Late blight rots Irish potatoes and contaminates the next year's crop.	Potatoes engineered to contain Bt toxin, a potato beetle deterrent.

in larger sheets so that greater areas could be spanned by glass alone. By mid-century, these combined inventions and innovations allowed the design and construction of bigger and lighter glasshouses and conservatories. They met a great demand because of the growing popularity of large tropical plants such as palm trees. They also satisfied the fascination bordering on obsession for imported giant water lilies, especially the largest South American water lily *(Victoria amazonica),* boasting leaves with six-foot diameters that required a lot of space and light.

PAXTON'S LEGACY

In 1826 a young Bedfordshire man working for the Royal Horticultural Society at Chiswick House gardens met a patron and soon-to-be employer who would change the course of his life, allowing him to revolutionize the design of glasshouses in Britain and, by extension, the rest of the world. Twenty-three-year-old Joseph Paxton accepted the Duke of Devonshire's offer to take the position of head gardener at the duke's palatial estate Chatsworth in the High Peak District, considered to have some of the finest gardens of the era.

The young Paxton worked wonders at Chatsworth, altering the landscape in ambitious ways and making dramatic botanical statements. He established a specialized grove dedicated to conifers, known as a pinetum, part of a 40-acre arboretum that boasted more than 1,600 species. He also proved himself adept at moving very large trees—weighing up to eight tons—over long distances.

Reports of huge Amazonian water lilies, with floating pads six feet across, began arriving in England around 1800, but it took decades of trying to keep them alive there. Joseph Paxton, gardener to the Duke of Devonshire, devised ways to warm and circulate the water in the greenhouse he tended. The first bloom opened on November 9, 1849.

Undoing some of the natural effects designed by the 18th-century landscape gardener Capability Brown, Paxton reintroduced some of the features of more formal gardens such as parterres and fountains. In the next decade he tackled the dilapidated greenhouses on the estate and made his biggest statement in constructing the Great Conservatory, a glasshouse more than 275 feet long, 120 feet wide, and 60 feet high. Working with architect Decimus Burton, who was also responsible for the magnificent Palm House at Kew, Paxton created a huge interior space using a combination of iron, wood, and glass, with parts mass-produced by the latest fabrication methods. The conservatory's glazing technique maximized the capture of both morning and evening light.

As a recipient of a single Victoria lily seed from Kew, Paxton was challenged to bring the lily into cultivation, and he succeeded where others had not. He built a big aquatic tank in a special greenhouse of glass panes interspersed with lightweight girders that let in an optimum amount of light. He also repeatedly changed and aerated the water of the tank, which proved key to successful propagation. Intrigued by the lily leaf's size and apparent strength, Paxton had his young daughter stand on a board atop one of the leaves to test it. He later made a claim that the pattern of radiating ribs on the leaf's underside inspired his greatest accomplishment, the design of the Crystal Palace for the Great Exhibition of 1851, but in fact that structure also owes much to his two previous modern and innovative glasshouses.

Erected in London's Hyde Park, the Crystal Palace had dimensions that were mind-boggling—more than 1,800 feet long, 400 feet wide, and 108 feet high. It was tall enough to shelter full-size living elm trees as well as two-story fountains. It did such a convincing job of bringing nature indoors that legions of sparrows moved in, as they often do now in the rafters of warehouse-style stores, prompting the Duke of

"All calamities were forgotten; I was a botanist, and felt myself rewarded! There were gigantic leaves, five to six feet across, . . . [and] luxuriant flowers, each consisting of numerous petals, passing, in alternate tints, from pure white to rose and pink. . . . As I rowed from one to the other, I always found something new to admire."

—Sir Robert Schomburgk, of his January 1837 expedition in British Guiana

Papaveraceae.

W.Müller n.d.Nat.

Papaver somniferum L.

OPIUM POPPY

Papaver somniferum

The paper-thin red petals of the poppy flower evoke thoughts of rolling countrysides and lazy afternoons, moody paintings by Impressionists Claude Monet or Mary Cassatt, luxurious scenes of summertime splendor. Yet one variety of poppy, despite blossoms so beautiful, has caused wars, addiction, and misery for centuries.

Seedpods more than 4,000 years old found in archaeological sites in southern France, Spain, and North Africa suggest that the poppy first grew native around the Mediterranean. Ancient peoples may already have discovered some of the plant's powerful properties, in particular its ability to relieve pain and induce sleep. The Greeks fully understood these qualities—Hippocrates considered opium a medicinal—and the trade in poppies began.

All poppies develop a globelike seedpod, held on tall stalks after the flower blooms, but only one species contains opium (from the Greek *opos,* juice). This milky sap is collected from unripe seedpods and processed into several different narcotics. It is a natural painkiller, sometimes to the point of being a sedative, and it is highly addictive. For centuries the medicinal value of opium and its derivatives clouded any concern over the dangers of addiction, and until modern medical research developed other painkillers, opium-derived drugs such as laudanum were regularly dispensed as medicine. A case like the English poet Samuel Taylor Coleridge's was not unusual: Prescribed laudanum, a tincture of opium, for digestive problems, Coleridge became so addicted that he suffered more from his addiction than from the symptoms that the drug was meant to relieve.

Opium from the immature seedpods of Papaver somniferum *was a dispensary medicine as recently as the early 20th century.*

From the 18th century on, the English imported Bengali opium to China, finding it one of the few commodities that they had to offer in trade to the Chinese. From 1729 China's emperors attempted to outlaw opium smoking, believing that it made their citizenry lazy and unproductive, but British and Portuguese mercenaries continued to sell it. Tensions escalated into the Opium Wars, involving Britain, France, and China.

Many have tried to produce an opium derivative that treats pain without addiction. Morphine, codeine, and even the "heroic drug," heroin, were isolated, yet none fit the description. The hypodermic needle, invented in the 19th century, worsened the situation, by presenting a way to introduce the drug directly into the bloodstream. By 1900 a million Americans suffered from addiction to morphine, which they could even buy from the Sears, Roebuck catalog. ∎

OPIUM POPPY THROUGH TIME

ca A.D. 65	1604	1804	1832	1898	1912	1960s
Dioscorides records how to extract opium from pods.	Iago, in Shakespeare's *Othello,* calls poppy a "drowsy syrup."	German chemist Friedrich Wilhelm Sertürner isolates morphine.	French chemist Pierre-Jean Robiquet isolates codeine.	German pharmaceutical company Bayer introduces the "heroic drug."	Prohibition is proposed at first international Opium Convention.	Methadone, synthetic heroin, is first used with addicts in the U.K.

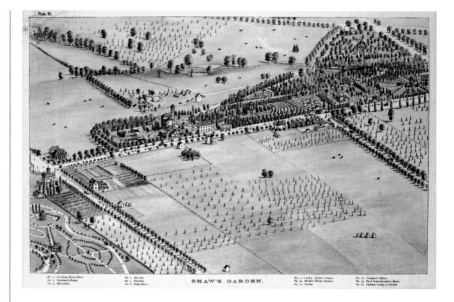

Henry Shaw (opposite), an Englishman who made his fortune as a merchant in frontier-era St. Louis, Missouri, took inspiration from Kew Gardens and Joseph Paxton's gardens at Chatsworth. On a 760-acre tract covered in prairie grass and wild strawberries, he founded the Missouri Botanical Garden (right).

A modest drinker but passionate wine collector, Shaw wrote The Vine and Civilisation *in 1884.*

Wellington to offer the suggestion "Sparrow hawks, Ma'am" when queried by Queen Victoria for a solution to the problem. The Crystal Palace, which was moved to a site in South London in 1854 after the Exhibition closed and then burned down in 1936, made a dramatic statement of British engineering know-how in iron and glass and has had a lasting influence on glasshouse construction.

The Botanical Spirit of St. Louis

The Great Exhibition of 1851 drew the interest of a wealthy Missouri merchant who was completing his grand tour, the pilgrimage through Europe that had been an upper-class male tradition for centuries in Britain and northern Europe. English-born Henry Shaw started his rise to the top in the United States by providing iron and steel goods to settlers in or passing through the former French village of St. Louis on the Mississippi River. In the proverbial right place at the right time, he quickly amassed a fortune, and became wealthy enough to retire in his 40s. A keen interest in botany took him to the beauty spots of Britain, including Joseph Paxton's showcase garden at Chatsworth and the Royal Botanic Gardens at Kew, and of course to the spectacle of London's Crystal Palace.

Shaw returned to St. Louis brimming with ideas and directed the planting of thousands of trees and shrubs near his villa outside of town, with the idea of creating a public garden like those he had seen in Britain, especially the gorgeous garden and greenhouses of Chatsworth. He sought advice from the leading botanists of his day, including Asa Gray at Harvard and William Jackson Hooker at Kew, and also relied heavily on the counsel and logistical support of the German-born physician-botanist George Engelmann. Hooker provided guidelines that Shaw took to heart, suggesting

Vue d'une partie de l'Établissement horticole d'Amb. Verschaffelt.

The Verschaffelt nursery in Brussels, Belgium, supplied exotic species to the growing number of amateur gardeners throughout northern Europe in the 19th century. Camellias were one of the Verschaffelt specialties.

he include a strong educational component in the form of a library and museum, and Engelmann helped Shaw acquire both botanical specimens for the garden and research collections for the library. Engelmann also spent time botanizing on his own in the southwestern United States and Mexico and had his name attached to newly cataloged species, among them the Engelmann spruce *(Picea engelmannii).*

The Missouri Botanical Garden opened to the public in 1859, featuring a large conservatory and a number of greenhouses to support it. Shaw hired James Gurney, a head gardener trained in Britain, to oversee the operation. In the international fashion of the day, the garden acquired a number of water lily species—Gurney's pet project—including the spectacularly popular and enormous Victoria water lily, which had been Paxton's inspiration for the Crystal Palace structure. Shaw continued to pour his treasure and talent into the botanical garden, living to the ripe old age of 89. Toward the end he enjoyed posing for the life-size recumbent figure that would grace his tomb, and at his death he was laid to rest in the second of two very Victorian mausoleums he had built on the garden grounds—the first, of limestone, being deemed too vulnerable to the elements. The effigy's serene countenance shows a man satisfied with his life and philanthropic efforts, especially his gift to the nation of its oldest botanical garden in continual operation.

Defining an Era

QUEEN VICTORIA'S REIGN FROM 1837 TO 1901, THE LONGEST OF ANY ENGLISH MONARCH, conveniently lent a name to a span of six decades that witnessed a great deal of change and affected not only Britain and its empire but the European continent and North America as well. The plain and proper queen, who spent almost half her life in mourning after the death in 1861 of her husband, Prince Albert, exerted a great deal of influence on social and cultural matters. She had definite likes and dislikes—that attitude best represented, perhaps, by the apocryphal "We are not amused"—and flora definitely ranked among the former. One of her earliest actions as queen was to present to the nation the beautiful gardens at Kew, up to this time a private royal botanical treasure. But whether or not she liked plants, she was destined to have many named for her, from the giant water lily *(Victoria amazonica)* to a showy orchid *(Dendrobium victoriae-reginae)*.

Victorian interior decoration favored dark, heavy furniture and fabrics and elaborately patterned wall coverings and ornamentation. Plants figured prominently in the scheme. Wealthy Victorians built their own conservatories on the south-facing sides of their homes—often the only substantial light in their otherwise dark interiors—and also amassed plants in their other rooms, forcing one English designer to remark, "I have seen many a drawing room where it appeared to me less a room than a thicket." Among Victorian favorites were the ferns and small palms, perhaps because they tolerate low light. Favorite, actually, is a gross understatement. Charles Kingsley, a contemporary writer, coined a name for the craze that swept through the British Isles—pteridomania, or fern mania—and described its symptoms in his book *Glaucus, or the Wonders of the Shore:*

In their gardens, Victorian ladies and gentlemen sought to re-create a wilderness—all well within their control and in fact very demanding of their attention.

> Your daughters, perhaps, have been seized with the prevailing "Pteridomania," and are collecting and buying ferns, with Ward's cases wherein to keep them (for which you have to pay), and wrangling over unpronounceable names of species (which seem to he different in each new Fern-book that they buy), till the Pteridomania seems to you somewhat of a bore: and yet you cannot deny that they find an enjoyment in it, and are more active, more cheerful, more self-forgetful over it, than they would have been over novels and gossip, crochet and Berlin-wool.

Kingsley makes mention of Wardian cases, the prototerraria developed by Nathaniel Bagshaw Ward that allowed Victorian plant lovers to shield their precious ferns and other flora from industrial age pollution—and had made for successful shipments from plant

Cypripedium venustum.

ORCHIDS

Orchidaceae family

Orchids have long been admired for their fascinating shapes, which draw people—and other creatures—to them. Thousands of varieties grow in tropical and temperate regions around the world, and their diversity is almost unimaginable. Orchid flowers can range from one-tenth of an inch to 15 inches across; they can grow in soil, in air, or on host plants; their flowers bloom in every color of the rainbow.

Many orchids have coevolved with a specific insect partner needed for pollination. The flower of Europe's *Ophrys apifera,* or bee orchid, for example, looks like a wasp, its lower petal having the shape and hue of an insect abdomen, and it exudes an odor like that of a female wasp. Male wasps light on the orchid and peer into the flower, along the way brushing up against its pollen supply and carrying a few grains inadvertently to the next flower.

In another example, the Peruvian bucket orchid *(Coryanthes mastersiana)* entices bees with its fragrance. A male bee lands on the flower and slips into a cuplike petal—the "bucket"—full of water. Its wings too wet to fly, the bee climbs through a snug escape hatch, struggling enough to shake loose pollen grains onto

Few botanical imports were as exotic as the orchids, such as this handsome lady's slipper from India (opposite). Some growers built special greenhouses for them.

its back. As it exits, it touches the receptive and sticky stigma, and pollen is transferred to the female portion of the flower. These complex partnerships made orchids particularly interesting to Charles Darwin.

Despite these remarkable reproductive strategies, orchid pollination occurs infrequently, but orchids still flourish because they occupy specialized niches in tropical forests and other habitats. Many grow high up in the rain forest, depending on air rather than soil to survive. Few creatures graze on such orchids, and so long as the climate cooperates, orchids seem to live virtually forever.

General fascination with these flowers first began in the 1730s, when large numbers of orchids were imported to England from the Caribbean. These tropical specimens were kept in hot rooms with low ventilation. In fact, they required much more moisture and circulating air, so most of the plants died—which only increased the demand for orchids.

Today more than 25,000 orchid species are known. Orchid enthusiasts have created hybrids as well and easily twice that number of those exist. Nevertheless orchid conservatists estimate that hundreds, perhaps thousands, of orchids are lost each year. ■

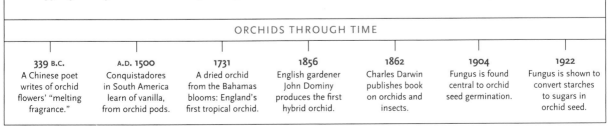

ORCHIDS THROUGH TIME

339 B.C.	A.D. 1500	1731	1856	1862	1904	1922
A Chinese poet writes of orchid flowers' "melting fragrance."	Conquistadores in South America learn of vanilla, from orchid pods.	A dried orchid from the Bahamas blooms: England's first tropical orchid.	English gardener John Dominy produces the first hybrid orchid.	Charles Darwin publishes book on orchids and insects.	Fungus is found central to orchid seed germination.	Fungus is shown to convert starches to sugars in orchid seed.

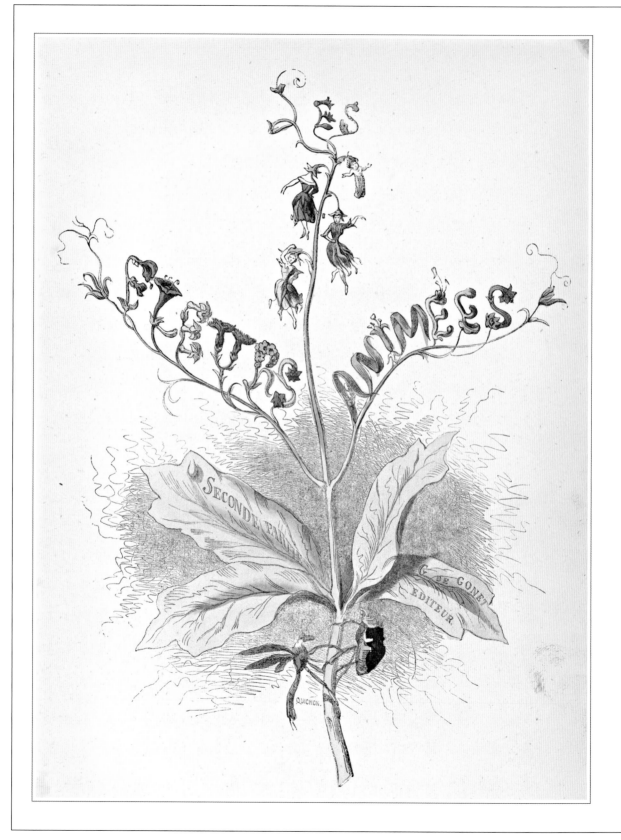

DAHLIA

French artist J. J. Grandville (a pseudonym for Jean-Ignace-Isidore Gérard) first created social commentaries in the form of cartoons by combining human and animal characteristics. He then migrated into the plant world and illustrated the sentimental Les Fleurs Animées (Flowers Personified) *in 1847. Many consider Grandville to have inspired the early 20th-century surrealists.*

hunters all over the world. Highly ornamental Wardian cases figured into the decor of many Victorian parlors and helped sustain the fern trend.

Thomas Moore, the curator of the Chelsea Physic Garden in London, contributed to the fern frenzy with his comprehensive 1855 work, *The Ferns of Great Britain and Ireland.* Moore's book featured the new and very expensive technique of nature printing. Ferns were especially suited to this process, which involves laying a plant specimen between a steel plate and a lead one. With pressure applied, the plant creates an impression in the lead plate, which is then galvanized with copper for strength. Color is applied directly to the copper and a print is pulled from the plate. Botanists appreciated the precision of nature printing, but it did not become commonplace because of the expense. During Moore's tenure at Chelsea, not surprisingly, the number of fern cultivars there increased by some 50 percent.

Fern mania took a heavy toll on endemic species, of which there were many in the suitably wetter and cooler climates in the western and northern reaches of the British Isles. Overcollecting by zealous amateurs and professionals became a problem, and some species were collected nearly out of existence. The ferns sometimes got the chance to exact their revenge. Over the years, a number of collectors lost their lives while scrambling over high cliffs in search of the prized fronds.

Say It With Flowers

Victorian manners prescribed polite and reserved communication, particularly between the sexes, and strongly defined gender roles, with women, the "fair sex," often compared to flowers. Straightforward speech and declarations of feeling and emotion

"For thousands of years we have supplied mankind with their themes of comparison; we alone have given them all their metaphors; indeed, without us poetry could not exist."

— Hellebore, speaking on behalf of the Flowers to the Flower Fairy in *Les Fleurs Animées,* 1847

were deemed unseemly, and so individuals, particularly suitors and their objects of desire, communicated through a well-defined language of flowers.

The vehicle for this communication was often the tussie mussie, a nosegay or hand-held bouquet of flowers and herbs. Floral messages could be tailored with the inclusion of specific species and varieties such as the red rose for passionate love, the daffodil for regard, or a sprig of ivy for fidelity. There was no room for guessing in a tussie mussie, as dictionaries listing the meanings of hundreds of plants were widely available, although it was possible to send a mixed or otherwise confusing message by the choice of species for inclusion.

Fin de Siècle

PLANTS ALSO FIGURED INTO VICTORIAN LIFE IN WAYS THAT WOULD SEEM TO BELIE THE era's otherwise staid and seemly demeanor. Many plant-based substances that have now been deemed illegal for casual and most medical uses, such as cannabis, morphine, and cocaine, were in the 19th century routinely used for both medicinal and recreational purposes. Queen Victoria's own physician prescribed cannabis as an antidote to menstrual cramps; it was also recommended for insomnia, depression, and migraine and used as a local anesthetic in dentistry.

Cocaine, the active ingredient in the leaves of the coca shrub (*Erythroxylum coca*), was recommended as a tonic and included in cough drops and other patent medicines. Coca also was an original ingredient in the soft drink Coca-Cola, developed in Georgia in 1886. Queen Victoria, along with several popes of the era and legions of ordinary folk, enjoyed a concoction known as Vin Mariana, a mixture of Bordeaux wine and coca leaves, the alcohol in the wine acting to liberate the cocaine in the leaves. Although the cocaine was removed from Coca-Cola in 1902, the beverage still obtains flavor from cocaine-free coca leaves, which are processed with special government approval by a laboratory in New Jersey.

As the addictive nature of opium poppy derivatives such as morphine and codeine came to be understood, routine and unregulated use was discontinued, although not before heroin, another strong opioid derived from *Papaver somniferum,* was distributed by the Bayer company as a cough suppressant and promoted along with another of its recently developed drugs—aspirin. When heroin was discovered to quickly metabolize into morphine in the body, it was dropped by Bayer as an advertised cure for morphine addiction.

Victoria's era would end soon after the turn of the century, and there would never again be a sovereign as influential on so many different matters, as before long world wars would drive aside many of the Victorian preoccupations. But botanical pursuits survived the new international order and priorities, and would take on new and urgent dimensions in the 20th century. ⌒

"The Bracken is the most abundant of our wild Ferns . . . and certainly none of our British species, except this, are capable of producing the scenic grandeur which we have witnessed in its expansive fronds, eight to ten feet high, gracefully arching out from among the brushwood which skirted a deep shady land in the west of Surrey."

—THOMAS MOORE,
THE FERNS OF GREAT BRITAIN AND IRELAND, 1855

To illustrate Thomas Moore's Ferns of Great Britain and Ireland, *Henry Bradbury created nature prints, using the plant itself to make an impression on a lead plate, first step toward a copper printing plate. Prints were then hand-colored for the grandiose folio edition, published in 1855.*

SCIENCE
1900—Present

Botany was well on the path to becoming a distinctly different kind of pursuit at the start of the 20th century than it had been in the past. There were still some far-flung botanical strongholds for explorers to seek out and investigate, such as the remote inner areas of China, but these were approached in a manner different from that of previous centuries. Botanical exploration left the realm of the adventurous amateur to become the domain of the trained expert and educated professional—the scientist with often very specialized knowledge and research interests. In the 20th century, the discipline of botany became more strongly aligned with the hard sciences and with newer frontiers within the biological sciences, represented by such fields as molecular biology, genetics, and biochemistry. Advances in technology meant that agriculture turned corporate on a gargantuan scale, changing the entire relationship between human knowledge and the plants that human beings grow to eat—a situation that many are now trying to reverse. Recent decades have revealed that nature's pharmacopoeia is more generous than medieval monks could ever fathom, but by our environmental missteps in the tropics, we may lose cures before they are ever known. ∾

This hand-colored engraving of a detail of a thistle comes from one of 3,240 plates in Flora Danica, *a compendium of the plants native to Denmark published from 1761 to 1833. PRECEDING PAGES: The Iranian or great red poppy* (Papaver bracteatum), *marked with a black spot near the base of its petals, is the largest of the world's red poppies.*

	KNOWLEDGE & SCIENCE	POWER & WEALTH	HEALTH & MEDICINALS
AFRICA & MIDDLE EAST	*Mushrooms from Hungarian mycology codex, 1900*	**1904** Benjamin Ginsberg begins experimenting with techniques of curing rooibos (red bush) tea in South Africa.	**1942** H. Roques and P. Fourment publish *Répertoire des plantes médicinales et aromatiques d'Algérie*, detailing 200 useful plants of Algeria. **1957** Alkaloids in Madagascar periwinkle are found effective against childhood leukemia.
ASIA & OCEANIA	**1944** A living specimen of dawn redwood, a Chinese tree known from 20-million-year-old fossils and thought extinct, is found. **1994** A living specimen of *Wollemia nobilis*, a tree thought extinct, is discovered near Sydney, Australia.	**1949** New information on the life cycle of *Porphyra* seaweed advances Japan's nori industry. **2007** Global Botanic Gardens Congress takes place in Wuhan, China.	**1952** Reserpine is first extracted from *Rauwolfia* species native to Africa and India; it soon becomes used to treat mental disease and hypertension. **1990s** A major planting program in Thailand, Malaysia, and the Philippines significantly increases commercial production of the mangosteen.
EUROPE	**1900** Gregor Mendel's paper on genetics in peas comes to world attention, reprinted by Royal Horticultural Society. **1915** Richard Martin Willstätter receives the Nobel Prize for his work with chlorophyll and other plant pigments.	*Seed and plant guide, 1899*	**1937** Albert Szent-Györgyi receives the Nobel Prize for extracting vitamin C from paprika. **1970** A study finds low heart disease among those with a Mediterranean diet, rich in olive oil. **1993** Garden of World Medicine opens at Chelsea Physic Garden, making it Britain's first garden of ethnobotany.
THE AMERICAS	**1922** Lewis Knudson revolutionizes orchid propagation. **1940** American Association of Botanical Gardens and Arboreta is founded. In 2006 the name is changed to the American Public Gardens Association. **1962** Rachel Carson's *Silent Spring* is published, raising awareness of environmental issues. **1987** First field trial of recombinant DNA on food crop: Genetically modified bacteria is sprayed on strawberries to minimize frost damage.	**1921** George Washington Carver argues for a peanut tariff before the U.S. Congress. **1934** Henry Ford sponsors an "Industrialized American Barn" at the Chicago World's Fair, promoting soybeans. **1958** The U.S. establishes its National Seed Storage Laboratory in Colorado. **1973** A U.S. ban on whaling prompts commercial cultivation of jojoba, a North American desert plant, for cosmetics. **2007** U.S. production of maize-based biofuel affects prices of corn worldwide.	**1940** Russell Marker discovers a way to manufacture progesterone from steroids in yam, leading to the birth control pill. **1945** Commercial plantations in Puerto Rico begin to grow acerola, or Barbados cherry, for its vitamin C. **1962** Rachel Carson's *Silent Spring* is published, a harbinger of environmental activism and concern over pesticides.

1925 California nursery obtains seeds of African violet *(Saintpaulia)*, from which the popular houseplant is cultivated.

"When you have seen one ant, one bird, one tree, you have not seen them all."

— EDWARD O. WILSON,
QUOTED IN *TIME* MAGAZINE, 1986

1904 Kiwifruit is introduced to New Zealand; by the 1930s it has become a commercial crop.

1947 Seeking to explain the prevalence of South American sweet potatoes in the South Pacific, Thor Heyerdahl sails by raft from Peru to Polynesia.

2001 China leads the world in cotton production.

2006 Since 2000 world hemp fiber production has doubled, nearly half of it grown in China.

1911 The first Hibiscus Society is founded, in Hawaii.

1912 Washington, D.C., receives cherry trees as a gift from Tokyo, Japan.

1924 Frank Kingdon-Ward collects blue poppy seed in Tibet.

1990s Cultivars of New Guinea species of impatiens come onto the market in Europe and Asia.

1990 Spain and Italy lead the world in the production of olive oil.

1998 In the U.K., Prince Charles publicly decries genetically modified food including agricultural products.

2007 A 3.3-pound Italian white truffle sells at auction for a record price of $330,000.

1948 George de Mestral invents Velcro, inspired by burdock seeds and their ability to attach to cloth.

1901 Silas Cole, head gardener at Althorp House, Northamptonshire, U.K., develops the Lady Spencer sweet pea with wavy-edged petals.

1960s Graham Stuart Thomas revives old rose varieties at Sunningdale Nurseries in Berkshire, U.K.

1904 Iced tea is invented at the St. Louis World's Fair.

1904 Chestnut blight, probably brought accidentally from Asia, first appears in chestnut trees in the Bronx.

1970 Norman Borlaug receives the Nobel Peace Prize for scientific improvements to wheat, key part of the "Green Revolution."

1978 Living stand of corn similar to ancient teosinte found in Mexico.

1983 The U.S. grants the first patents to producers of genetically modified food plants.

1945 The Peace rose is introduced in California, coinciding with the end of World War II.

Ivory-billed woodpecker, thought extinct, painted from life by Mark Catesby circa 1730

DESPITE IMPROVED RELATIONS BETWEEN THE WESTERN WORLD AND China, the quest of the plant hunter there in the early 20th century remained a perilous one—especially in the remote inner regions at a remove far from the Imperial City of Peking (Beijing). The rugged terrain and freewheeling atmosphere of China's western interior and boundary provinces in Central Asia turned nearly every plant-collecting expedition into an Indiana Jones adventure, and botanical explorers accrued as many wild and woolly tales about the perils faced and survived (until, as it often happened, one day they didn't) as they did plant specimens, which numbered in the thousands.

The new breed of more professional plant seekers in China included three men who characterized all the talents necessary to retrieve some of the world's now most popular plant species from botany's last frontier: the Scot George Forrest, the Englishman Ernest Henry Wilson, and the Austrian American Joseph Rock. All three risked life and limb—one quite literally—to make some of the most significant botanical expeditions of the century.

INTO THE HEART OF CHINA

GEORGE FORREST CAME TO BOTANY AS AN APPRENTICE CHEMIST, LEARNING THE MEDICINAL uses of plants as well as specimen preparation before striking off to try his luck during Australia's gold rush. When he returned to Scotland at the age of 30 in 1903, he worked

Blooming cherry trees given to the people of the United States by the people of Japan in 1912 dapple Washington, D.C., with vernal pink every year.

as a clerk in the Royal Botanic Garden in Edinburgh, brimming with resourcefulness and making a favorable impression. Before long he was making the first of seven expeditions to China. Yet this first, to Yunnan in southwestern China, nearly proved his last, as he and his team of 17 local collectors, after a very successful time in the rhododendron forests of northwestern Yunnan near the Tibetan border, were set upon by xenophobic warrior Tibetan lamas. Only Forrest escaped and was smuggled out by locals.

He regrouped and persisted in his collection, returning to Britain in 1906 with a huge haul of plants, seeds, roots, tubers, and dried specimens from the Far East. Over the course of six more expeditions, George Forrest discovered more than 1,200 new species of plants, including 6 species of rhododendron and more than 50 types of primrose. A number of plants bear his name, including an orchid, a rhododendron, a fir, and a maple also called snake-bark maple. He died of heart failure in Yunnan during his very successful seventh expedition, planned as his last, in 1932.

Some cherry species—such as Prunus sargentii, *shown here—have been bred for blossoms, others for fruit. To the Japanese* sakura, *or cherry blossoms, symbolize the ephemeral life spirit. The word "sakura" is now synonymous with flowering cherry trees around the world.*

Ernest Henry "Chinese" Wilson, born in England's Cotswolds in 1876, came to a position at the Royal Botanic Gardens at Kew with considerable botanical credentials, including hands-on work in botanic gardens and a scholarly background as well. He didn't stop long at Kew, but was snatched up by the famous Veitch nurseries and dispatched as a plant collector in China. Wilson had an eye for horticultural beauty, and he collected new species of astilbe, clematis, and eurya, a white-flowered shrub related

Peanut
Arachis hypogaea

The peanut, also known as the groundnut, is the only nut that is one of the world's leading food crops; only the soybean contains a higher level of protein. Peanuts are native to South America, and the Portuguese carried them from Brazil to Africa, the Far East, and India, now a major world producer. Unlike the chickpea—third highest plant protein provider—peanuts grow underground, making them safe from airborne pests such as locusts. The pollinated flowers are pulled underground as the peanuts develop: The species name means "growing underground."

The seeds of the peanut (opposite) mature underground, thus escaping the boll weevil, which punctures and lays its eggs in ripening seedpods. When weevil infestations threatened the economy of the U.S. South in the early 20th century, peanuts proved an answer.

to camellias. He took great risks to get up close, document, and collect rhododendrons in rocky and subalpine to alpine settings. The Arnold Arboretum at Harvard sent him to western Sichuan in 1910, specifically to collect conifer seeds. Wilson, however, had other ideas and pursued his personal quest of collecting specimens of the glorious regal lily *(Lilium regale),* a Chinese symbol of harmony and unity, glimpsed on a previous expedition. To get to them he gingerly descended the dangerous Min River gorge—and was rewarded with some 6,000 bulbs.

For his troubles Wilson ended up with a right leg one inch shorter than his left. On the way back to Chengdu, the capital of Sichuan Province, his party encountered a rock slide that broke Wilson's leg in several places. Using a camera tripod as a splint, his companions tended to his broken limb and carried Wilson to Chengdu, where he nearly lost the leg to infection. A French army surgeon managed to save it, however, and Wilson returned to Boston. The lily bulbs, carefully packed to travel in clay and charcoal, made it to the United States as well in fine shape, and in a season or two they thrilled all who had the privilege to see their magnificent blooms at the Arnold Arboretum.

Joseph Rock's childhood in imperial Vienna was an unhappy one, and so he ran away, eventually arriving in New York in 1905 at the age of 20. A diagnosis of tuberculosis sent him to a more favorable climate in Hawaii, where he quickly became an expert in island flora, to the point that he is now regarded as the father of Hawaiian botany. This expertise led to an assignment from the U.S. Department of Agriculture to collect seeds from the chaulmoogra tree *(Hydnocarpus kurzii)* of Burma (today's Myanmar), which provided the first successful treatment for Hansen's disease, or leprosy.

Rock then spent most of the next three decades in China, introducing an astounding 493 rhododendron species to the West. The National Geographic Society sponsored many of his expeditions and shared his adventures with the world in its magazine. Photographs he took in China and Tibet now provide baseline images used to study glacial retreat through the last century. National Geographic's man in China ended his days where his botanical career began: in Hawaii, where he continued to botanize—noting the loss of species in the decades since his first researches—and taught Oriental studies at the University of Hawaii until his death in 1962.

OLD VERSUS NEW: THE SCIENCE OF BOTANY

BOTANICAL RESEARCH IN THE EARLY 20TH CENTURY RECEIVED A MAJOR BOOST FROM THE work of German-Austrian priest Gregor Mendel, whose painstaking experiments mainly on pea plants laid the foundation for the field of genetics. Though quietly published in 1866, Mendel's writings were not circulated in scientific circles until 1900 and after. At the same time, an African-American botanist at the Tuskegee Institute in Alabama was beginning experiments on alternating crops to ameliorate the effects of cotton monoculture in the South, so that poor African-American farmers could successfully grow crops

Papilionaceae
(Arachideae)

W. Fitch, del et lith.

Vincent Brooks Day & Son Imp.

BAMBOO

Subfamily Bambusoideae

With so many seeking environmentally friendly lifestyles, bamboo's reputation is growing. Indigenous woody bamboos exist almost everywhere, except in regions of extreme cold—literally hundreds of species and varieties of these tall, treelike grasses. Bamboos are primitive grasses dating back perhaps a million years, with 1,200 species known today.

The earliest evidence for bamboo use dates back 7,500 years, in China, but actual use most likely goes back even further. Bamboo has long been used by East Asians for food, medicine, and lumber and as a material for essentials from baskets to water wheels, musical instruments to arrows.

Alexander the Great wrote to Aristotle about bamboo in the 4th century B.C., and Spanish and Portuguese explorers brought it to Europe in the 16th century. Amazonian bamboo may have been the first to actually reach Europe, however, a giant thorny variety of the genus *Guadua* that can grow ten feet tall. Evidence of bamboo use in the New World includes structural frames and musical instruments found at sites in Ecuador and Peru and dating back more than 5,500 years. As the American continent opened to exploration, natural historians

Dozens of bamboo species exist, including the ruby-flowered Bambusa striata *(opposite). Bamboo harvests far predate recorded history in Japan (above).*

wrote of great canebrakes of *Arundinaria gigantea,* which spread through forests and floodplains of the southeastern United States. These bamboo stands provided food and shelter for birds and mammals, big and small. Even bison, bear, deer, and later the introduced European black boar moved through these bamboo habitats.

When settlers cleared land and those bamboo stands disappeared, so did the Carolina parakeet, passenger pigeon, and Bachman's warbler—all residents of the canebrakes. *Arundinaria* still exists across the southeastern United States north to the Ohio River, but not as broadly as it once did.

In recent years bamboo has gained the most attention for its role in construction. Stronger weight for weight than steel, it is a popular substitute for hardwood, particularly for flooring. Bamboo has also found a place in the fashion world. Its stalks are pulverized to separate the natural fibers, which are then woven into a material that looks like cotton but has important advantages. Considerably softer than other plant fibers, bamboo makes a natural fabric that wicks moisture. An ancient plant that has come into its own, bamboo holds an important place in the environmental movement of today—and tomorrow. ∎

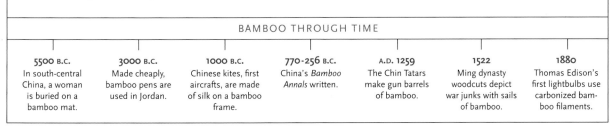

BAMBOO THROUGH TIME

5500 B.C.
In south-central China, a woman is buried on a bamboo mat.

3000 B.C.
Made cheaply, bamboo pens are used in Jordan.

1000 B.C.
Chinese kites, first aircrafts, are made of silk on a bamboo frame.

770–256 B.C.
China's *Bamboo Annals* written.

A.D. 1259
The Chin Tatars make gun barrels of bamboo.

1522
Ming dynasty woodcuts depict war junks with sails of bamboo.

1880
Thomas Edison's first lightbulbs use carbonized bamboo filaments.

America's favorite Christmas plant first came to the United States in 1825, introduced by Joel Poinsett, first U.S. ambassador to Mexico, for whom the plant is now named: poinsettia (Euphorbia pulcherrima).

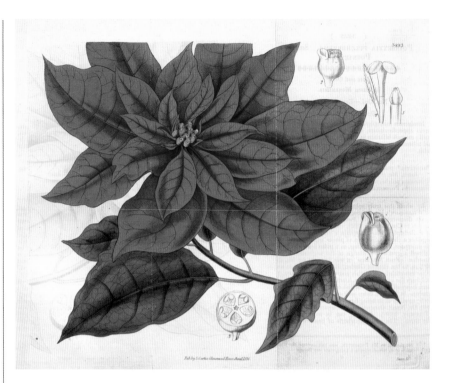

"Many indigenous groups around the world—the Indians of the Amazonian regions, for example—are literally masters of their ambient vegetation as a result of inherited knowledge. . . . The loss of this knowledge, and of the natives themselves, will be a grave hindrance to progress."

— RICHARD EVANS SCHULTES, "THE IMPORTANCE OF ETHNOBOTANY IN ENVIRONMENTAL CONSERVATION," *THE AMERICAN JOURNAL OF ECONOMICS AND SOCIOLOGY,* 1994

in depleted soil. George Washington Carver found the peanut and the sweet potato to be particularly suitable for these purposes and spent decades promoting the concept of crop rotation and developing hundreds of products from these unassuming plants. In the early decades of the 20th century, the identification of the previously unknown category of nutrients called vitamins fueled a whole new field of botanical research to identify and isolate those derived from plants.

The discovery of the structure of DNA in the 1950s cast a new light on traditional methods in natural history and biology, including botany, favoring molecular studies instead. Some prominent museums even started to divest themselves of their natural history collections. But the trend reversed in the 1980s when it was recognized that the problems of habitat and species loss required an ecological approach and could not be resolved from a molecular vantage point only. One of the most outspoken advocates of this natural orientation has been Harvard biologist Edward O. Wilson, who gave a name to what was at stake if attention were not paid to the critical situation: biodiversity.

Wilson's *Diversity of Life* (1992) articulated a wake-up call to preserve the world's flora and fauna in the face of human population pressures and habitat destruction. In harmony with these ideas many museums, including botanical gardens, added conservation research and conservation education to their agendas. Often these initiatives have included establishing a permanent presence in strategic conservation areas such as the tropics.

The Missouri Botanical Garden, for example, operates in more than 30 countries, with a large presence in Madagascar and Latin America. Such an on-site base attracts interested local individuals to the field of botany and conservation, provides training that otherwise would not be available, and forges a stronger community of support for conservation work. But molecular studies also have their place in the field of botanical conservation. Even specimens in seemingly lifeless herbaria have yielded up DNA, Jurassic Park–style, that can shed light on evolutionary connections and ecological adaptations, and help distinguish between seemingly similar species.

THE BIRTH OF ETHNOBOTANY

WITHIN HARVARD'S EXTENSIVE BOTANICAL COLLECTIONS LIE SOME WITHERED SPECIMENS OF *Panaeolus campanulatus*, a fungus collected in 1938 by a young graduate student. He was hoping to shed some light on the use of hallucinogenic mushrooms in the religious ceremonies of the Mazatec Indians of southern Mexico. Richard Evans Schultes sought a link from the present day to the mushroom used by the Aztec and known as *teonanácatl,* flesh of the gods. Though Schultes never used the term, *Panaeolus campanulatus* and its ilk have become known as magic mushrooms, thanks to the publicity following a 1957 article in *Life* magazine written by an investment banker who had gotten hold of one of Schultes's scholarly articles and made his own plant-seeking pilgrimage to Mexico.

Red-fruited partridgeberry, an American native, was named squaw vine for its use as a medicinal by Indian women during pregnancy and childbirth.

CASTANEA Vesca.
American Chesnut.

Beosa del. *J.N. Joly sculp.*

"Unless concerted action is taken by the States, in conjunction with the Department of Agriculture, arboriculturists say that within a very few years the chestnut tree will be extinct in this country. A strange disease has attacked the trees."

— *NEW YORK TIMES,* APRIL 16, 1911

Up to the 20th century, the mighty American chestnut (Castanea dentata) dominated forests from Maine to Mississippi. These giants fell rapidly to the chestnut blight, accidentally imported on Asian chestnuts, which are immune to the fungus.

Soon scores of the curious headed to Mexico in search of mind-altering experiences. Schultes himself wrote a volume on hallucinogenic plants in the very mainstream Golden Guides series in 1976; controversial from the start, it was pulled after four printings. This kind of publicity created an impression for many that the field of ethnobotany is synonymous with psychoactive plants, when, in fact, they form only one dimension of the ethnobotanical pharmacopoeia of some, but certainly not all, cultures. Schultes did much to advance the notion that traditional medical uses of indigenous plants have important implications in westernized health care. The plant that produces curare, for example—the substance used to poison dart tips in the Amazon—also yields a muscle relaxant used in modern surgery.

Schultes spent his entire academic career, as student and as professor, at Harvard. A former student, the ethnobotanist and National Geographic Society Explorer-in-Residence Wade Davis, described him as "the last of the great plant explorers in the Victorian tradition," not only for his garb but also for his thoroughness and dogged perseverance. For practical reasons Schultes wore a pith helmet in the field, but at Harvard he was a traditional, almost geeky scientist in a white lab coat and Harvard crimson tie. His lab featured samplings of his travel artifacts, and it didn't take much coaxing to get him to demonstrate his Amazonian blowpipe.

But Schultes was a highly regarded scientist who in 1992 received the Linnean Society of London's gold medal, botany's highest honor. In appreciation of his work in Colombia, its government designated 2.2 million acres of rain forest as Sector Schultes, a protected area—a fitting legacy for a forward-thinking botanist and conservation pioneer.

BOTANICAL ART: A FLOURISHING FORM

ALTHOUGH THEY ARE NOW MORE LIKELY TO WORK IN MUSEUMS THAN IN the field, botanical illustrators are still relevant more than 180 years after the invention of photography. With total control of light, angle, aspect, clarity, color, detail, and a host of other factors, the artist can present a plant in a manner that often is much more scientifically useful than a photograph. The aesthetic qualities of botanical art versus photography lie in the eye of the beholder, but clearly illustration holds its own against the growing technical wonders of the photographic process. Botanical artists continue to train in botany and the informed depiction of flora in art. Women form a larger proportion of working botanical artists than they did in the days of Maria Sibylla Merian and Elizabeth Blackwell in the 18th century. Australian painter Margaret Stones, for example, now in her late 80s, has produced more than 400 watercolors for *Curtis's Botanical Magazine* as well as botanical monographs of areas as diverse as Tasmania and Louisiana.

Modern botanical artists are also revisiting the forms of their predecessors, such as the herbal and florilegium, and taking advantage of advances in graphics and printing technology to create works that are both beautiful and affordable. Museums and galleries continue to exhibit botanical art and connoisseurs continue to build their collections of botanical illustration, both modern and vintage, often with very high price tags.

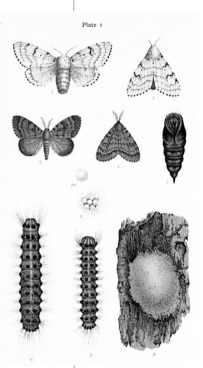

Plate 1

Unknowingly introduced to North America in the 1860s, gypsy moths began munching their way through the foliage of hardwood forests in the U.S. East and Midwest, sometimes denuding entire stands of oak or aspen and threatening their survival.

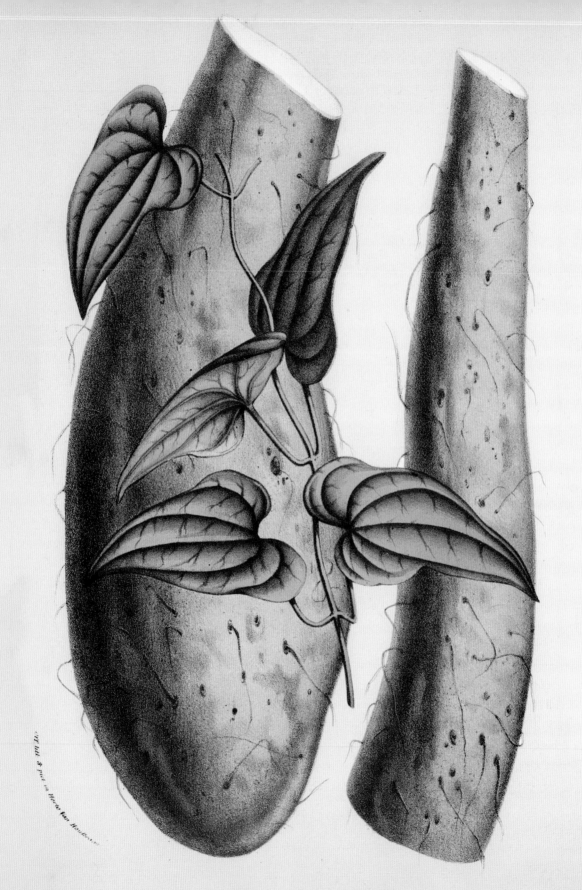

DIOSCOREA BATATAS. Dene.

Igname de Chine. (Rhizòme de grand. nat .)

YAM

Dioscorea spp.

Yams and sweet potatoes: Both are prized as sweet, starchy staples, but in fact they come from different plants. Yam tubers grow up to 120 pounds. There are many different species, but around the world today only 12 or so are cultivated for food and an additional 7 for medicine.

Yams grew during the Jurassic period, when dinosaurs roamed the world and when Earth was made of two massive supercontinents, Laurasia and Gondwana. Yams continued to grow through the millions of years that followed, as the dynamics of plate tectonics shaped the continents as we know them. As landmasses separated, the yam present on each evolved to survive in distinct regions and climates. Asian and African yams crossbred until the Eastern Desert formed, creating a genetic barrier and forcing species on to their own trajectories.

Archaeological evidence suggests that humans have been consuming yams for many thousands of years, but the modern history of these plants is not well recorded. These large tubers appear to have spread around the world during the slave trade, very likely carried as food as well as rooting material. The very word "yam" is said to come from the Senegalese verb meaning "to eat." The story goes that one day European slave traders were watching Africans dig up yams and asked out of curiosity what the plant was called. Thinking that the traders wanted to know what they were for, the Africans replied *nyami*—to eat—and the name stuck.

Root of yam was such an important staple to the Igbo people of Nigeria that they carved ritual effigies depicting its harvest.

Portuguese traders, who visited colonies in Africa and Asia, were responsible for transporting yams around the world. They learned the value of taking yams on long sea voyages, since they are good sources of vitamins A and C, protein, and minerals, and they store relatively well for a long time. When African slaves came to America and encountered the native sweet potatoes there, they used the word that they already knew—hence the confusion that remains to this day. As yams spread around the world, they took a central place in the diets of people in the developing world. Today they are grown in 47 countries, primarily in sub-Saharan Africa.

Yam root has long been used in healing, dating back to ancient China. Believed helpful in treating asthma, digestive or urinary complaints, and rheumatism, *Dioscorea* root preparations appear in modern herbal pharmacopoeia as well. Some hormone treatments and corticosteroids require an essential ingredient from the Mexican wild yam, making this ancient root a modern medicinal. ∎

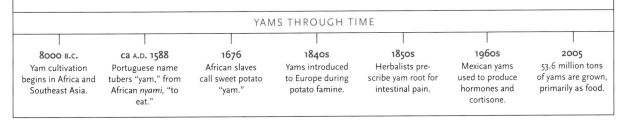

YAMS THROUGH TIME

8000 B.C.
Yam cultivation begins in Africa and Southeast Asia.

ca A.D. 1588
Portuguese name tubers "yam," from African *nyami*, "to eat."

1676
African slaves call sweet potato "yam."

1840s
Yams introduced to Europe during potato famine.

1850s
Herbalists prescribe yam root for intestinal pain.

1960s
Mexican yams used to produce hormones and cortisone.

2005
53.6 million tons of yams are grown, primarily as food.

TOWARD THE LIGHT

STILL, PHOTOGRAPHY SERVES AS A VERY USEFUL TOOL IN THE STUDY OF BOTANY in many ways. Today it would be unheard of not to make a visual record of the ecosystems from which specimens are collected. Photography also can help capture accurate measurements of the numbers and kinds of species in plant communities. Aligned with the magic of the electron microscope, it produces images of complex and fascinating inner worlds. In addition, it has greatly increased our knowledge of the mechanisms of and influences on plant growth.

A banker who left the financial world to pioneer the fledgling field of time-lapse photography in the 1950s, John Nash Ott, Jr., shared his riveting work on the start-to-finish process of flower growth with viewers of the era's *Today* show. He also employed up to 20 cameras to film similar sequences for the Disney documentary *Secrets of Life.* Time-lapse photography can reveal the marked properties of phototropism (growth toward the light) and geotropism (growth influenced by gravity) that many plants display, including cut flowers such as tulips. Time-lapse photography also allows us to see what goes on beneath the soil in the behavior of roots as they work to establish a plant's foundation. In today's world of computer-generated special effects in film, these early advances seem quite modest, but a half century ago they were revolutionary and truly eye-opening.

THE TROPICS OF ANTICANCER

AS EARLY AS THE 1950S, TROPICAL FORESTS WERE IDENTIFIED AS FERTILE GROUNDS IN the search for plant-based anticancer drugs. Cancer investigators zeroed in on a plant known as the Madagascar periwinkle *(Catharanthus roseus),* a species that has figured prominently in the indigenous medical system of Madagascar, where it originated, as well as in all the other places in the tropical world where it freely spead and adapted. Native peoples in Africa, the Caribbean, the Bahamas, and Central and South America have used the plant to treat a myriad of conditions including diabetes, high blood pressure, malaria, asthma, and tuberculosis.

When U.S. researchers began to investigate it, they found the plant to be the source of a number of bitter alkaloids with cytotoxic properties that inhibit the cell division of cancer cells (but affect healthy cells as well). Two of these alkaloids, vincristine and vinblastine, have been used effectively as chemotherapeutic agents in the treatment of various cancers: vincristine for lymphoma, leukemia, and breast and lung cancer, and vinblastine for Hodgkin's lymphoma. They share the prefix "vin-" because the Madagascar periwinkle originally was assigned to the genus *Vinca* with other periwinkle species before botanists learned its true characteristics and assigned it to its own genus, *Catharanthus.* Despite the reassignment, the word "periwinkle" has remained part of the plant's common name.

Tropical and subtropical species, like bromeliads, set down roots indoors as householders came to consider potted plants essential to stylish interior decorating.

These discoveries encouraged the U.S. National Cancer Institute to begin a systematic plant collection and investigation program in 1960, an undertaking often referred to as pharmaceutical bioprospecting. At first the program focused on the temperate regions, which led to the discovery of the anticancer compound paclitaxel in the bark of the Pacific yew *(Taxus brevifolia),* a small, evergreen understory resident of the cool, wet forests of the Pacific Northwest. Paclitaxel, along with compounds extracted from the leaves of both the Pacific yew and the English yew *(Taxus baccata),* has proved extremely effective in the treatment of certain cancers, especially ovarian and breast cancers.

The National Cancer Institute suspended the plant investigation program in 1982 but resurrected it again in 1986, focusing this time on the tropical and subtropical regions. The most promising area is the Amazon rain forest, where an estimated half-million plant species may reside. Unfortunately, the region's 2.7 million square miles have been under constant siege for decades for development and for their many resources, causing habitat degradation and species loss, which greatly reduce the chances for future pharmaceutical breakthroughs.

FROM ONE OLD FOSSIL TO ANOTHER

IN 1994 AN AUSTRALIAN PARKS OFFICER CAME UPON THE SPECIMEN OF AN UNKNOWN TREE in a remote rocky canyon of the Blue Mountains in Wollemi National Park, about 90

Botanical texts from centuries past hold treasures visual and intellectual, rewarding those who explore their pages. Franz Bauer's Illustrations of Orchidaceous Plants, *from the 1830s, depicts flower and seed formation.*

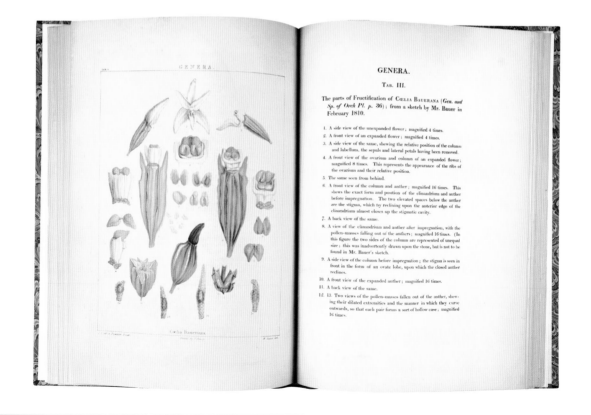

miles northwest of Sydney. The discovery of the conifer astonished the botanical world, as it belonged to a species thought to have been extinct for more than two million years—the Wollemi pine *(Wollemia nobilis)*.

The long-needled plant could be traced back some 200 million years in the fossil record, but its existence as a living plant had remained hidden from all the botanizing teams seeking out Australian flora for more than 200 years. After that first find, a hundred adult trees were counted at Wollemi and efforts began to understand their needs and to propagate them.

The first batch of Wollemi pine saplings designated for public purchase had its own Sotheby's auction in October 2005 in Sydney. The 292 trees on offer sold out, bringing in more than one million Australian dollars, with the proceeds designated for research and conservation efforts. Since then, the Wollemi pine has become a celebrity conifer, a must-have for botanical gardens around the world.

At the Royal Botanic Gardens at Kew, the Wollemi specimen on public display lives behind bars in a specially fashioned metal cage to prevent pilferage. The living fossil has been propagated many times over and has developed a wide following among amateur gardeners, especially in Australia, where it is sometimes gifted to friends and relatives on appropriately senior birthdays.

Even volumes whose information is long outdated—such as The Gardeners Labyrinth, *England's first herbal, published in 1563—tell the story of our age-old fascination with the plant world.*

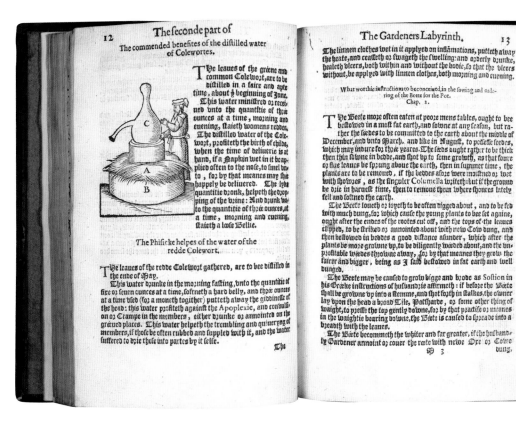

THEOBROMA CACAO.

CACAO

Theobroma cacao

Its botanical name means "food of the gods" in Latin, and there are few indulgences as divinely satisfying to the human palate as chocolate. Today it comes in many forms: a solid bar, a viscous syrup, mixed into ice cream, flavoring a cake—it's a treat that is cheap and easy to find. Originally, however, chocolate was only made into a drink, and a bitter, piquant drink at that. Its lengthy preparation—fermenting the pods, roasting the seeds, then grinding them over heat, to release the fat—made it a treat enjoyed only by the wealthy. Indigenous to Central America, cacao (or cocoa) today grows around the world, with nearly 4.5 million farms growing the beans and manufacturing chocolate products.

The Maya, Toltec, and Aztec are thought to have grown cocoa for the past 3,000 years. According to Mexican mythology, Quetzalcóatl, one of the major deities, left the cocoa tree to humans. Consumed as a beverage called *xocoatl*, bitter water, the drink was often mixed with chili, spices, honey, vanilla, and even maize. The Maya in southern Mexico used cocoa seeds as currency: Ten could buy a rabbit, and a hundred could buy a slave. Chocolate was a favorite beverage of the Aztec emperor Moctezuma, who introduced it to Hernán Cortés upon his arrival in Mexico. In a letter to the Spanish king, Cortés describes it as a "divine drink, which builds up resistance and fights fatigue."

From a sacred drink of the Aztec to a child's treat in Amsterdam, 1899, cocoa has satisfied hungers around the world for centuries.

When people of the Spanish court first tasted chocolate, they found it too bitter and added sugar, keeping the recipe under lock and key for nearly a century. The secret—and the taste for chocolate—reached Italy in 1606, and from there it spread through Europe and eventually to the United States, all the while considered a beverage. America's first chocolate manufacturer—Baker's, in Dorchester, Massachusetts—sold cakes of hardened chocolate, to be shaved into boiling water for drinking. In 1847 the British company Fry & Sons produced the first eating chocolate. It was an instant success, and lower import duties made chocolate more accessible and increased sales.

Swiss entrepreneur Daniel Peter added powdered milk to the mix and created milk chocolate. Soon his homeland came to be known for its chocolate, even though no cocoa trees could ever grow in its Alpine climate. Innovation continues today: Chocolatiers of the 21st century combine the earth-brown ingredient with chili peppers, bacon, mushrooms, or wasabi for ever new interpretations of this age-old sweet. ■

COCOA THROUGH TIME

1502	1519	1660	1778	1853	1940	2005
Christopher Columbus carries cocoa to Spain on his fourth voyage.	The Aztec serve *xocoatl*, a drink, to Spanish conquistadores.	Louis XIV marries Spanish princess, and chocolate gains appeal in France.	Cocoa trees are imported to the Dutch West Indies.	Britain reduces import duties on cocoa beans.	American soldiers in World War II get chocolate bars as rations.	Organic cocoa sales rise from $171 million in 2003 to $304 million.

Echinacea
Echinacea purpurea

Echinacea's use as a medicinal plant began with Native Americans, who used it externally for treating wounds and snakebite and internally for more purposes than any other plant: to treat coughs and digestive upsets and the pain of sore throat and toothache, and even as a cure for rabies. In modern herbal medicine, echinacea is primarily used to reduce the symptoms of colds, flu, and upper respiratory tract infections. It is thought to be an immune system stimulant that promotes healing through its anti-inflammatory, antibiotic, antiviral, and detoxifying effects.

BOTANICAL GARDENS OF EDEN

FORTUNATELY FOR ITS VISITORS, KEW HAS NOT HAD TO RESORT TO CAGES FOR THE VAST majority of its plantings. They are out there for all to see—in garden beds, groves, glades, dells, glasshouses, and conservatories. In the 21st century, botanical gardens are no less significant than they were when first established. If anything, they are more so because they safeguard the planet's floral biodiversity by their extensive public and research collections dispersed as they are in a variety of different climates and conditions throughout the world. Botanical gardens also have assumed a lion's share of the responsibility for public education on matters as pressing as conservation and climate change.

Art also continues to figure into the agendas of botanical gardens. Even if they may not be on botanical garden payrolls, botanical illustrators remain welcome collaborators in their missions and frequently show their work in garden galleries. Other art forms are celebrated as well. More than a million people visited the Missouri Botanical Garden in 2006 to view the installation of garden-themed pieces by American master glass artist Dale Chihuly. And in the summer before its 250th anniversary in 2009, Kew hosted a comprehensive exhibition of the works of abstract sculptor Henry Moore.

With a wealth of rare, expensive, and very specialized materials in their libraries and archives, botanical gardens have taken major steps to make these treasures more widely available to more people. For example, in an ambitious project known as Botanicus (accessible at *www.botanicus.org*), staff at the Missouri Botanical Garden have digitized more than a million pages of rare botanical writings and images that are freely available to the public—yet another form of outreach practiced by the 150-year-old institution.

IT'S A SMALL, SMALL FLORAL WORLD

AS CONSUMERS OF FLOWERS, PEOPLE ALL OVER THE WORLD HAVE GROWN ACCUSTOMED TO being able to obtain nearly any variety they desire—no matter how exotic—at any time of the year, just as they expect to have all their favorite foods available to them year-round. It seems fitting that the country that introduced the frenzy of tulipomania in the 17th century helps make this possible by running the world's largest flower auction.

In what is probably the planet's busiest trade building, up to 20 million stems of flowers and 5 million plants pass each day through the Aalsmeer Flower Auction on the outskirts of Amsterdam. Its nearly one million square meters of floor space hosts 70 percent of the daily international trade in flowers, shepherded by some 12,000 employees. Growers, buyers, sellers, and wholesalers participate in a very fast-paced high-tech auction system that processes a bid on the average of every five seconds.

Cut flowers from places such as Kenya, Ethiopia, Turkey, and the Netherlands itself and potted plants from growers in Germany and Denmark make

Mary E. Eaton

Modern-day herbalists have rediscovered the powers of plants well known to the ancients, such as the root and leaves of echinacea, a North American herb (opposite), and the dried leaves of ginkgo, an Asian tree (left).

Ginkgo
Ginkgo biloba

The only surviving member of the genus *Ginkgo*, the ginkgo tree is considered a living fossil, dating to the Paleozoic period more than 22.5 millions years ago, when dinosaurs were flourishing but mammals had not yet appeared on the scene. Ginkgo leaf extract is now widely prescribed to improve cognitive function and is also thought to improve concentration and mental sharpness in healthy people over the age of 50. Studies have shown that ginkgo's active ingredients also stabilize the structure of brain and nerve cells and protect them from oxidative damage by free radicals.

a brief appearance daily before they are sent off to their final destinations. It usually takes no more than 48 hours for any flower from any source to reach its destination anywhere in the world, many of them via Amsterdam's Schiphol Airport, a short run from the Aalsmeer complex.

WHAT GOES AROUND

AS THE FIRST DECADE OF THE 21ST CENTURY DRAWS TO A CLOSE, WE ARE PROACTIVELY adjusting our relationship with the world's flora. In many respects, we are coming back to practices of the past, when plants could live and adapt in ways that allowed them to continue to evolve.

Botanical art springs eternal: Modern artist Gerald Sibelius created exquisite inked engravings after 18th-century watercolors of Dillenia alata, *a New Guinea tree.* FOLLOWING PAGES: *In his 1851* Flower Garden, *Joseph Paxton included the delicate mouton peony, the Chinese variety from which all garden peonies today derive.*

Our reliance on food crops grown by industrialized monoculture is slowly giving way to the restoration of diverse plantings of locally compatible crops. We are rejecting genetically engineered food plants in favor of ancient cultivars, known as landraces, which grow best under the conditions in which they developed. We collect and preserve the seeds of heirloom varieties—plant lines that have been around at least 50 years and are open-pollinated and never hybridized—and share them with like-minded growers of today and tomorrow, thanks to seed banks created voluntarily.

We visit botanical gardens, which increasingly have become repositories for the world's plant heritage. We join our neighbors in parks on weekends to pull out all traces of invasive introduced plants, such as strangling vines of English ivy and Japanese honeysuckle, which overpower the beautiful and well-adapted plants that would grow naturally in our area, if given the chance.

In our daily lives we use plants in some ways that would seem familiar to medieval herbalists in monasteries. Open the medicine cupboard, and among the array of over-the-counter and prescription remedies—many of them with a plant origin or molecular model derived from plants—we may find, for example, echinacea to ease the symptoms of a head cold, chamomile to promote relaxation, and perhaps an extract of milk thistle, prescribed by the vet for an aging dog with diminished liver function.

We might even have stashed there a dark chocolate bar containing 73 percent cocoa. Consuming a square of it daily is believed to yield a whole host of health benefits, thanks to a group of chemicals it contains called flavonols that help lower blood pressure and promote healthy blood flow through the arteries. This makes for a flavorful new health supplement that for most people is a dose that goes down in a most delightful way.

Our time-honored connections to the plant world on a larger scale, however, are precarious, given the current state of the environment and the consequences of climate change. Though Linnaeus spent nearly a lifetime identifying and cataloging 9,000 plant species, his effort represented only a fraction of the plant life that exists, and so might our current count of some 400,000 known species. Encounters with previously unknown plants happen continually, especially in tropical forests. Yet because of habitat destruction and degradation, species can be lost before we even learn of their existence.

Exactly where we are headed and within what kind of time frame is a great unknown, although multiple scenarios abound. But whatever plants mean or have meant to humankind at any time, and whatever pleasure, not to mention health and sustenance, we derive from them—from their beauty, complexity, or companionability—we must arrive at a global solution that optimizes a healthy and diverse botanical world, the origin of our existence and the hope for our ultimate survival. ✑

Aitken, Richard. *Botanical Riches: Stories of Botanical Exploration.* Aldershot, U.K.: Lund Humphries, 2006.

Attenborough, David. *The Private Life of Plants.* Princeton, N.J.: Princeton University Press, 1995.

———, Susan Owens, Martin Clayton, and Rea Alexandratos. *Amazing Rare Things: The Art of Natural History in the Age of Discovery.* New Haven, Conn.: Yale University Press, 2007.

Barth, Friedrich G. *Insects and Flowers: The Biology of a Partnership,* M. A. Biederman-Thorson, trans. Princeton, N.J.: Princeton University Press, 1991.

Camp, Wendell H., Victor R. Boswell, and John R. Magness. *The World in Your Garden.* Washington, D.C.: National Geographic Society, 1957.

Desmond, Ray. *Great Natural History Books and Their Creators.* London and New Castle, Del.: British Library and Oak Knoll Press, 2003.

Elliott, Brent. *Flora: An Illustrated History of the Garden Flower,* compact ed. Buffalo and Toronto: Firefly Books, 2003.

Fallen, Anne-Catherine. *A Botanic Garden for the Nation: The United States Botanic Garden.* Washington, D.C.: U.S. Government Printing Office, 2007.

Foster, Steven, and Rebecca L. Johnson. *National Geographic Desk Reference to Nature's Medicine.* Washington, D.C.: National Geographic Society, 2006.

Garland, Sarah. *The Herb Garden.* New York: Viking, 1984.

Gollner, Adam Leith. *The Fruit Hunters: A Story of Nature, Adventure, Commerce and Obsession.* New York: Scribner, 2008.

Gribbin, Mary, and John Gribbin. *Flower Hunters.* Oxford: Oxford University Press, 2008.

Grimshaw, John. *The Gardener's Atlas: The Origins, Discovery, and Cultivation of the World's Most Popular Garden Plants.* Buffalo: Firefly Books for National Home Gardening Club, 2005.

Gupton, Oscar W., and Fred C. Swope. *Wildflowers of the Shenandoah Valley and Blue Ridge Mountains.* Charlottesville: University Press of Virginia, 1979.

Hepper, F. Nigel, ed. *Plant Hunting for Kew.* London: Her Majesty's Stationer's Office, 1989.

Hillier, Malcolm. *Flowers.* London: Dorling Kindersley in association with the National Trust, 1991.

Hobhouse, Henry. *Seeds of Change: Five Plants That Transformed Mankind.* New York: Harper and Row, 1986.

Huxley, Robert, ed. *The Great Naturalists.* London: Thames and Hudson, 2007.

Knapp, Sandra. *Plant Discoveries: A Botanist's Voyage Through Plant Exploration.* Buffalo: Firefly Books, 2003.

McTigue, Bernard. *Nature Illustrated: Flowers, Plants, and Trees 1550-1900: From the Collections of The New York Public Library.* New York: Harry N. Abrams, 1989.

Minter, Sue. *The Apothecaries' Garden: A History of the Chelsea Physic Garden.* Gloucestershire, U.K.: Sutton Publishing, 2003.

Missouri Botanical Garden. *Missouri Botanical Garden: Green for 150 Years.* St. Louis: Missouri Botanical Garden, 2009.

Morton, Oliver. *Eating the Sun: How Plants Power the Planet.* New York: HarperCollins, 2008.

Paterson, Allen. *The Gardens at Kew.* London: Frances Lincoln, 2008.

Pavord, Anna. *The Naming of Names: The Search for Order in the World of Plants.* New York: Bloomsbury, 2005.

Pick, Nancy, and Mark Sloan. *The Rarest of the Rare: Stories Behind the Treasures of the Harvard Museum of Natural History.* New York: HarperResource, 2004.

Pollan, Michael. *The Botany of Desire: A Plant's-Eye View of the World.* New York: Random House, 2002.

———. *In Defense of Food: An Eater's Manifesto.* New York: Penguin, 2008.

———. *The Omnivore's Dilemma: A Natural History of Four Meals.* New York: Penguin, 2006.

Prance, Sir Ghillean, and Mark Nesbit, eds. *The Cultural History of Plants.* New York: Routledge, 2005.

Reveal, James L. *Gentle Conquest: The Botanical Discovery of North America with Illustrations from the Library of Congress.* Washington, D.C.: Starwood, 1992.

Rexer, Lyle, and Rachel Klein. *American Museum of Natural History: 125 Years of Expedition and Discovery.* New York: Harry N. Abrams, 1995.

Rice, Tony. *Voyages of Discovery: A Visual Celebration of Ten of the Greatest Natural History Expeditions.* London: Firefly Books, 2008.

Rix, Martyn. *The Art of the Plant World: The Great Botanical Illustrators and Their Work.* Woodstock, N.Y.: Overlook Press, 1981.

Schultes, Richard Evans, Albert Hofmann, and Christian Rätsch. *The Plants of the Gods: Their Sacred, Healing, and Hallucinogenic Powers,* 2nd ed. Rochester, Vt.: Healing Arts Press, 2001.

Swerdlow, Joel L. *Nature's Medicine: Plants That Heal.* Washington, D.C.: National Geographic Society, 2000.

Viola, Herman J., and Caroline Margolis, eds. *Seeds of Change: A Quincentennial Commemoration.* Washington, D.C.: Smithsonian Institution Press, 1991.

About the Missouri Botanical Garden and Its Collections

Thanks to the vision of Henry Shaw and his scientific adviser, botanist and physician George Engelmann, the Missouri Botanical Garden maintains a vigorous scientific research program and the strong collections necessary to conduct research. In 1856 the first books for the library and dried plant specimens for the herbarium were purchased. Today the herbarium contains over six million specimens and the library more than 200,000 volumes, the earliest printed in 1474. These collections are essential to accomplishing our goal to describe, name, and classify the plant diversity growing on Earth.

Despite the dedicated work of thousands of scientists over the past 300 years, a complete list of plants growing on our planet, or even one that we can consider close to complete, does not exist. Unlike mammals or birds, for which finding and describing a new species is a major news headline, plant species new to science are described every day. The issue is one of scale. For example, there are approximately 10,000 species of birds in the world, while the total number of plant species is estimated at more than 380,000. The Missouri Botanical Garden is an active partner in this global effort to identify, describe, and name the plant biodiversity on the planet. We explore the tropical forests for new medicines and other substances yet unknown, racing against the loss of our planet's biodiversity. More than ever we need to learn how best to use, protect, and preserve our valuable plant resources. Our library and herbarium are indispensable tools in this effort, providing a sample of that biodiversity in the form of herbarium specimens and a permanent repository of the accumulated information about plants created by centuries of observation and science.

Although botany is still firmly rooted in science past, today we use the newest technology to make three centuries of research efforts available to a global audience. Herbarium specimens are scanned, their data entered into databases and made available through the Internet. Much of the core literature of botany is also available online for anyone who has a research need or is simply curious. This type of access was unimaginable and impossible until very recently. Leaps in technology and public awareness, made possible by projects like Google Books, have changed the world of botanical exploration and the dissemination of results of that research.

Flora Mirabilis was inspired by and created thanks to the several thousand volumes from our collection that are now available online. Less than five years ago, writers and image researchers would have had to spend months in our library or others, painstakingly working their way through the collections by hand. They can now search, browse, and discover the riches of our collection from the comfort of their own computers, as can the reader of this book. Most, if not all, of the books used in this publication are freely available at the Biodiversity Heritage Library, *www.biodiversitylibrary.org*, with more added each day. The digital books available here are not only those of the Missouri Botanical Garden but of several of the other major natural history libraries in North America and the United Kingdom. This unprecedented effort unites the member libraries in a concerted effort to liberate the world's accumulated knowledge of biodiversity from the library stacks of our museums into the free-flowing world of information on the Internet.

—*Douglas Holland, Librarian*

Contributors

Catherine Herbert Howell is a freelance writer who has authored a number of natural history books for National Geographic, including *Backyard Wilderness, Mountain Life,* and four volumes in the Nature Library series. She also has contributed to dozens of other books, among them National Geographic's *Book of Peoples of the World, Expeditions Atlas,* and *The Curious Naturalist.* She holds a master's degree in anthropology from the University of Virginia and has conducted field research in India as a Fulbright fellow and among Indian immigrants in New York City. An enthusiastic—though very amateur—gardener, she enjoys visiting gardens and arboretums, especially on her frequent visits with family in the British Isles.

Dr. Peter H. Raven, one of the world's leading botanists and advocates of conservation and biodiversity, has served as president of the Missouri Botanical Garden for more than 38 years. *Time* magazine identified him as a Hero for the Planet in 1999. Raven is co-editor of *Flora of China,* an international collaboration destined to fill 50 volumes and describe 31,500 species of plants. He is co-author of *Biology of Plants,* a popular textbook now in its seventh edition, and *Environment,* a leading textbook in environmental science, also now in its seventh edition. He is a Trustee of the National Geographic Society and chairs its Committee for Research and Exploration.

Douglas Holland is director of the Missouri Botanical Garden Library. He has worked at the garden since 1994, serving first in the horticulture department, followed by three years as an assistant in the herbarium and four years as archivist and historian.

FRONT COVER: Jamaica dogwood, plate 41, F. E. Köhler, *Medizinal-Pflanzen in naturgetreuen Abbildungen mit kurz erläuterndem Texte* (Gera-Untermhaus, Germany, 1883-1914).

ENDPAPERS: Chloetru/Dreamstime.com. 2-3: Cylista, plate 92, vol. I, William Roxburgh, *Plants of the coast of Coromandel: selected from drawings and descriptions presented to the hon. court of directors of the East India Company* (London, 1795-1819). 4: Various flower parts, plate XII, *Recueil de plantes coloriées, pour servir a l'intelligence des lettres elementaires sur la botanique* (Paris, 1789). 6-7: Amaryllis, plate 371, vol. 7, P.-J. Redouté, *Les liliacées* (Paris, 1802-1815).

FOREWORD 8: Amaryllis, plate 11, Mrs. Edward Bury, *A Selection of Hexandrian plants belonging to the natural orders Amaryllidae and Liliacae* (London, 1831-34). 9: Brazilian star amaryllis, plate 16, Bury, *A Selection of Hexandrian plants*. 10: Bouquet of anemone, hyacinth, and delphinium, Jacques Bailly, *Nova Recolta . . .* (Rome, 1681). 11: Pears, plate 29, Jaume Saint-Hilaire, *La flore et la pomone françaises* (Paris, 1828-1833).

INTRODUCTION 13: Poppy, plate 13, P.-J. Redouté, *Choix des plus belles fleurs et des plus beaux fruits* (Paris, 1833). 14: Title page, *P. Dioscoridae pharacorum simplicium reiq[ue] medicae libri...* (Strasbourg, Germany, 1529). 15: *Polypodium* fern, plate 86, vol. 2, François-Pierre Chaumeton, *Flore médicale* (Paris, 1828-1832). 16: Gooseberry, botanical illustration by Barbara Alongi. 17: Portraits of the artists, page 897, Leonhard Fuchs, *De historia stirpium* (Basel, 1542). 18: Cartoon, tab. XXI illustration, Jas. (James) Bateman, *The Orchidaceae of Mexico and Guatemala* (London, 1837-1843). 19: *Oncidium* orchid, page 8, Bateman, *The Orchidaceae of Mexico and Guatemala*. 21: Sikkim larch, plate XXI, J. D. Hooker, *Illustrations of Himalayan plants* (London, 1855).

CHAPTER 1: ORIGINS (PREHISTORY-1450) 22-23: Blue Nile lily, plate 70, Redouté, *Choix des plus belles fleurs*. 24: Juniper, page 78, Fuchs, *De historia stirpium*. 26: Distilling flask, Pietro Andrea Mattioli, *Petri Andreae Matthioli Opera quae extant omnia, hoc est, Commentarij in VI. libros Pedacij Dioscoridis Anazarbei De medica materia* (Venice, 1583). 27: (Above) Female mandrake, [page 289], Hamsen Schönsperger, *Gart der Gesundheit,* (Augsburg, Germany, 1487); (below) cyclamen, plate XXVIII, Edward Hamilton, *The flora homoeopathica* (London, 1852-53). 29: Fig, plate LXXIII, Georg Dionysius Ehret, *Plantae selectae quarum imagines ad exemplaria naturalia Londini* (n.p., 1750-1773). 30: Myrrh, vol. 2, plate 185, Köhler, *Medizinal-Pflanzen*. 31: Cardamom, vol. 2, no. 305, Johann Wilhelm Weinmann, *Phytanthoza iconographia, sive, Conspectus aliquot millium* (Regensburg, Germany, 1737-1745). 32: Date palm, tab. I, page 673, Engelbert Kaempfer, *Amoenitatum exoticarum politico-physico-medicarum* (Lemgovia, Germany, 1712). 33: Date palm, NGS Image Collection. 35: *Amanita* mushroom, vol. 1, plate III, Hamilton, *The flora homoeopathica*. 36: Flax, vol. 1, page 60, Robert Wight, *Illustrations of Indian botany* (Madras, 1840-1850). 37: (Left) Madder, vol. 2, plate 326, Elizabeth Blackwell, *A curious herbal* (London, 1737-39); (right) Woad, vol. 1, plate 246, Blackwell, *A curious herbal* 38: Wheat, vol. II, plate 87, Köhler, *Medizinal-Pflanzen*. 39: Book of Hours, Réunion des Musées Nationaux/Art Resource, New York. 40: Peach, plate 28, Redouté, *Choix des plus belles fleurs*. 41: Lily of the valley, vol. 4, plate 227, Redouté, *Les liliacées*. 42: Artichoke, plate 40, Chaumeton, *Flore médicale*. 43: Carrot, plate 98, Chaumeton, *Flore médicale* (Paris, 1828-32). 44: Rice, plate 74, Köhler, *Medizinal-Pflanzen*. 45: Rice paddies, Library of Congress, LC-DIG-jpd-00180. 46: Herbalists, page 11, Schönsperger, *Gart der Gesundheit* 47: Schönsperger, *Gart der Gesundheit*. 48: Caravan, page 167, Kaempfer, *Amoenitatum exoticarum politico-physico-medicarum*. 49: Saffron crocus, plate 129, P. Klincksieck, *Atlas colorié des plantes médicinales indigènes* (Paris, 1900) 50: Olive, plate 99, P. Klincksieck, *Atlas colorié*. 51: Detail, Hans Memling, "Angel Holding an Olive Branch," Réunion des Musées Nationaux/Art Resource, New York. 52: Violet, plate 25, Saint-Hilaire, *La flore et la pomone françaises*. 53: Table of Vertues, John Gerard, *The herball, or, Generall historie of plantes* (London, 1636). 55: Fritillaria, plate 59, Redouté, *Choix des plus belles fleurs*.

CHAPTER 2: DISCOVERY (1450-1650) 56-57: Passionflower, tab. 1, J. E. Smith, *Icones pictae plantarum rariorum descriptionibus et observationibus*

illustratae (London, 1790-93). 58: Banana, tab. XVIII, Ehret, *Plantae selectae*. 60: Dragonfly, plate 133, Weinmann, *Phytanthoza iconographia*. 61: (Above) Fritillaria and tulips, plate 1, Pierre Vallet, *Le jardin du Roy tres chretien, Loys XIII* (Paris, 1623); (below) Nasturtium, vol. 1, plate 23, William Curtis, *The Botanical Magazine* (London, 1790). 62: Mural, photo by Kenneth L. Garrett. 63: Codex Badianus, The Art Archive/National Anthropological Mueum Mexico/Gianni Dagli Orti. 64: Nutmeg, vol. 3, plate 274, Roxburgh, *Plants of the coast of Coromandel*. 65: Sandalwood, plate 43, Köhler, *Medizinal-Pflanzen*. 66: Black pepper, vol. 59 (new series VI), plate 3139, Curtis, *Curtis's Botanical Magazine* (London, 1832). 67: Black pepper, plate 144, Köhler, *Medizinal-Pflänzen*. 68: Hyacinth, vol. 5, plate 157, Curtis, *The Botanical Magazine* (London, 1792). 69: Gibraltar candytuft, vol. 3, plate 122, Curtis, *The Botanical Magazine* (London, 1793). 70: Portrait of Leonhard Fuchs, Fuchs, *De historia stirpium*. 71: Fuchsia, plate 27, Redouté, *Choix des plus belles fleurs*. 72: Sugarcane, plate 169, Köhler, *Medizinal-Pflänzen*. 73: Processing sugar, page 50, Willem Piso, *Historia naturalis Brasiliae* (Leiden, 1648). 74: Botanical Garden of Padua circa 1545, *The Gardener's Chronicle* (London, 1876). 75: Mediterranean fan palm, vol. 47 (new series V), plate 2152, Curtis, *Curtis's Botanical Magazine* (London, 1820). 76: Vanilla orchid, supplement IV, Mark Catesby, *Piscium, serpentum, insectorum, aliorumque nonnullorum animalum nec non plantarum quarundam imagines* (Nürnberg, Germany, 1777). 77: Map of Africa, Geography & Map Division, Library of Congress. 78: Corn, plate 78, Köhler, *Medizinal-Pflänzen*. 79: Corn, page 476, Leonhard Fuchs, *Plantarum effigies* (Lyon, 1549). 81: Cashew, illustration, Berthe Hoola van Nooten, *Fleurs, fruits et feuillages choisis de l'ille de Java* (Brussels, 1880). 82: Sunflower, plate 20, Saint-Hilaire, *La flore et la pomone françaises*. 83: Elizabethan garden, Thomas Hill, *The Gardener's Labyrinth* (London, 1586). 84: Citrus, page 313, Giovanni Battista Ferrari, *Hesperides* (Rome, 1646). 85: Lemon tree, page 380, Hieronymus Bock, *Kreüter Buch* (Strasbourg, 1560). 87: Narcissus, plate 17, Redouté, *Les liliacées*. 88: Pages 518-519, John Parkinson, *Paradisi in sole paradisus terrestris* (London, 1629). 89: Portrait of John Parkinson, frontispiece, Parkinson, *Paradisi in sole paradisus terrestris*. 90: Tulips, n.p., Robert John Thornton, *The Temple of Flora* (London, 1807). 91: Tulip, page 511, Carolus Clusius, *Rariorum alioquot stirpium per Hispanias observatarum historia* (Antwerp, 1576). 92: Yellow lady's slipper, page 19, Redouté, *Les liliacées* (Paris, 1802-15). 93: (Left) Tulip poplar, vol. I, tab. 8, William P. C. Barton, *Vegetable materia medica of the United States* (Philadelphia, 1825); (right) Bloodroot, vol. I, plate 2, Barton, *Vegetable materia medica*. 94: German iris, vol. 6, plate 309, Redouté, *Les liliacées*. 95: Persian iris, vol. 1, plate 1, Curtis, *The Botanical Magazine* (London, 1790).

CHAPTER 3: EXPLORATION (1650-1770) 96-97: Primrose, between tabs. 7 and 8, John Lindley, *Collectanea botanica* (London, 1821-26). 98: Bird-of-paradise, n.p., Thornton, *The Temple of Flora*. 100: (Above) Pineapple, plate 36, M. E. Descourtilz, *Flore médicale des Antilles* (Paris, 1821-29); (below) Armadillo, page 232, Piso, *Historia naturalis Brasiliae*. 101: Butterflies and caterpillars, tab. I, James Edward Smith, *The natural history of the rarer lepidopterous insects of Georgia* (London, 1797). 103: Tab. XII & page 125, Robert Hooke, *Micrographia* (London, 1665). 104: Sweet pea, vol. 1, plate 60, Curtis, *The Botanical Magazine* (London, 1790). 105: (Left) Arum, N. 174, Weinmann, *Phytanthoza iconographia;* (right) African aloe, N. 45, Weinmann, *Phytanthoza iconographia*. 106: Tobacco, folio 34, John Frampton, *Joyfull newes out of the new-found worlde* (London, 1596). 107: Tobacco, plate 146, Blackwell, *A curious herbal*. 109: Cedar of Lebanon, plate LX, Ehret, *Plantae selectae*. 110: Passionflower, plate XXI, Maria Sibylla Merian, *Metamorphosis Insectorum Surinamensium* (Amsterdam, 1705). 112: China tea, plate 136, Köhler, *Medizinal-Pflanzen*. 113: Chinese symbol for tea. 114: Goatsucker, T. 8, Mark Catesby, *The Natural History of Carolina, Florida, and the Bahama Islands* (London, 1754). 115: Frog and pitcher plant, tab. LXX, Mark Catesby, *Piscium, serpentum, insectorum*. 116: Carolus Linnaeus, *Systema naturae* (Stockholm, 1735; facsimile edition, 1907). 117: Portrait of Carolus Linnaeus, n.p., Thornton, *The Temple of Flora*. 118: Arabica coffee, plate 106, Köhler, *Medizinal-Pflanzen*. 119: Coffeehouse, Mary Evans Picture Library/Alamy. 120: American ginseng, vol. 2, plate 45, Barton, *Vegetable materia medica of the United States*. 121: Chilean strawberry, vol. 1, plate 63, Curtis, *The Botanical Magazine* (London, 1790). 122: Grapefruit, page 190, Johann Christoph Volkamer, *Nürbergisches Herperides oder gründliche*

Flora Mirabilis

Catherine Herbert Howell

Published by the National Geographic Society

John M. Fahey, Jr., *President and Chief Executive Officer*

Gilbert M. Grosvenor, *Chairman of the Board*

Tim T. Kelly, *President, Global Media Group*

John Q. Griffin, *Executive Vice President; President, Publishing*

Nina D. Hoffman, *Executive Vice President; President, Book Publishing Group*

Prepared by the Book Division

Barbara Brownell Grogan, *Vice President and Editor in Chief*

Marianne R. Koszorus, *Director of Design*

Carl Mehler, *Director of Maps*

R. Gary Colbert, *Production Director*

Jennifer A. Thornton, *Managing Editor*

Meredith C. Wilcox, *Administrative Director, Illustrations*

Staff for This Book

Susan Tyler Hitchcock, *Editor*

Susan Blair, *Illustrations Editor*

Carol Farrar Norton, *Art Director*

Tiffin Thompson, *Contributing Writer*

Mike Horenstein, *Production Project Manager*

Robert Waymouth, *Illustrations Specialist*

Manufacturing and Quality Management

Christopher A. Liedel, *Chief Financial Officer*

Phillip L. Schlosser, *Vice President*

Chris Brown, *Technical Director*

Nicole Elliott, *Manager*

Rachel Faulise, *Manager*

National Geographic Books gratefully acknowledges the following Missouri Botanical Garden Library staff for their invaluable contributions to this book: Library staff: Michelle Abeln, Andy Colligan, Julie Crawford, Lucy Fisher, Doug Holland, Vicki McMichael, Linda Oestry, Mary Stiffler, and Zoltan Tomory. Imaging staff: Mike Blomberg, Stephanie Keil, Fred Keusenkothen, Linda Rigger, Randy Smith, and Wendy Westmoreland. Press staff: Victoria C. Hollowell and Elizabeth McNulty.

The National Geographic Society is one of the world's largest nonprofit scientific and educational organizations. Founded in 1888 to "increase and diffuse geographic knowledge," the Society works to inspire people to care about the planet. It reaches more than 325 million people worldwide each month through its official journal, *National Geographic,* and other magazines; National Geographic Channel; television documentaries; music; radio; films; books; DVDs; maps; exhibitions; school publishing programs; interactive media; and merchandise. National Geographic has funded more than 9,000 scientific research, conservation and exploration projects and supports an education program combating geographic illiteracy.

For more information, please call 1-800-NGS LINE (647-5463) or write to the following address:

National Geographic Society
1145 17th Street N.W.
Washington, D.C. 20036-4688 U.S.A.

Visit us online at www.nationalgeographic.com

For information about special discounts for bulk purchases, please contact National Geographic Books Special Sales: ngspecsales@ngs.org

For rights or permissions inquiries, please contact National Geographic Books Subsidiary Rights: ngbookrights@ngs.org

Library of Congress Cataloging-in-Publication Data

Howell, Catherine Herbert.
 Flora mirabilis : how plants have shaped world knowledge, health, wealth, and beauty / Catherine Herbert Howell ; foreword by Peter H. Raven.
  p. cm.
 Includes bibliographical references and index.
 ISBN 978-1-4262-0509-5
 1. Botany--History. 2. Plant collecting--History. I. National Geographic Society (U.S.) II. Title.
 QK15.H695 2009
 580.9--dc22
                                    2009019627
ISBN: 978-1-4262-0509-5

Printed in China

09/RRDS/1

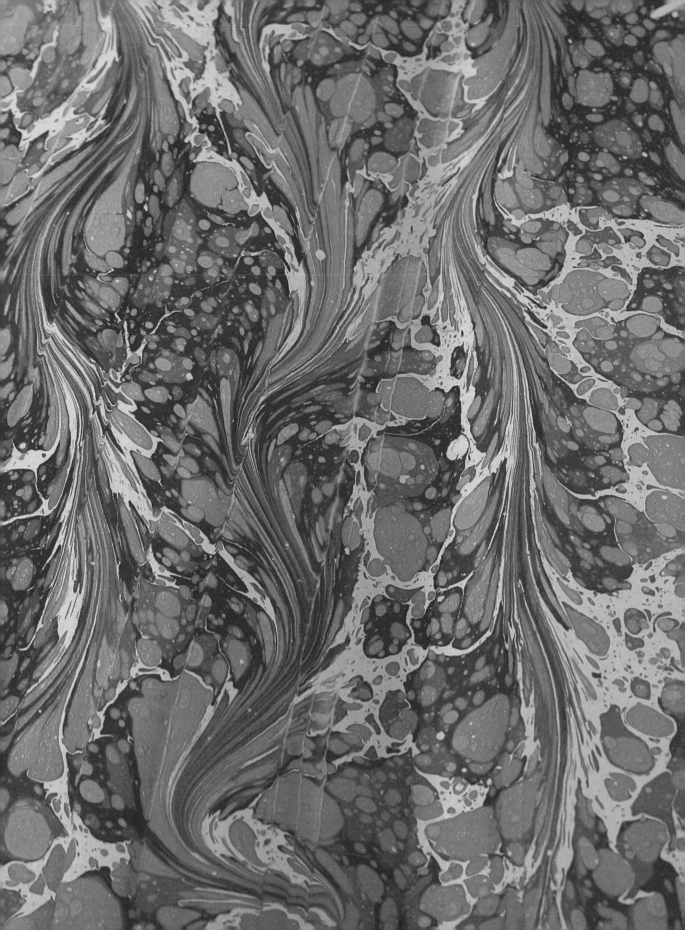